A LIFE
IN JAZZ

by

DANNY BARKER

Edited by Alyn Shipton

NEW YORK
OXFORD UNIVERSITY PRESS
1986

© Danny Barker 1986

First published in 1986 by
The Macmillan Press Ltd
London
England

Published in 1986 in the United States by
Oxford University Press Inc
200 Madison Avenue
New York
NY 10016

ISBN 0-19-520511-1

Printed in Great Britain by
ANCHOR BRENDON LTD
Tiptree, Essex

Typeset by Rowland Phototypesetting Ltd
Bury St Edmunds, Suffolk
in 11/13pt Caledonia

Contents

Preface

Around the year 1942, while playing with Cab Calloway's Orchestra, I was constantly on the road touring the States. As a member of the band I sat by silently so many times listening to discussions about jazz music: who started by playing with whom; who did this; who did that. Constant visitors came round asking questions of the musicians, getting some honest answers and some lies, but there was much discussion of the origins of jazz. There was much ridicule of Mr Jelly Roll, who was having a lip riot with W. C. Handy. Many band members showed sympathy for Mr Handy, mainly because he had control of his music through a publishing company; he was highly respected and successful, and a seemingly nice, sweet, personable old man. But Jelly insisted that he knew where Mr Handy procured many of his great blues songs; Jelly called names of the original composers. To the musicians in New York City Jelly was a liar, a braggart, jealous and envious. About that time *Esquire* magazine came on the scene with special issues of jazz comment—awards, stories, classifications: gold awards and silver awards, honorable mentions. *Esquire* gave jazz a big bright national exposure. Jazz lovers became familiar with the many jazz artists whom they heard on records but rarely saw in person. There was a new importance given to all jazz areas—the evaluation of styles, much history, and biographies of all the honored musicians. I read these *Esquire* issues, and one thing that annoyed me very much was that not one musician respected as an authority in his profession (and whose comments would have been accepted by other musicians) was on one of the judges' panels. The judges were a conglomeration of assorted leeches and self-appointed critics. I had, through the years, seen most of these characters come around bands I had played with. They would sit and stand around annoying musicians during their short intermission asking endless questions, cleverly setting up arguments and debates, while absorbing opinions. Then they would go and write articles the way they decided a musician should be remembered and read about in books and magazines.

In my travels, when I felt the enquirer was sincere about a jazz subject I was thoroughly informed of, I would tell them the facts the way I experienced them. The *Esquire* magazines caused many book publishers to start getting interested in jazz stories and autobiographies. Many books came on the scene together with many falsehoods, lies and cooked-up stories. I read much of this crap and then I was told that I should write some truth, and explanations of many jazz subjects that were not clearly explained. So first I started taking pictures of musicians, and also collecting old rare photos, records, music, and interviews of many old musicians still living, and in a little time I was packing bags, cartons, suitcases with old jazz memorabilia. And then along came the noted jazz writers begging to see the gathered material, and then asking to please let them use a part of this and a part of that. And so in most cases I obliged. Then came many contacts with book publishing editors, many of the big ones on Fifth and Park avenues in New York City. And every time the rejections for some puzzling reason: "It needs editing." But when the stories appeared in books not one word was changed. This presenting to publishers and rejections went on for years. That all started up North, so I came home to the South where I had not the least idea that the material would get some action—and, finally, it happens.

Editor's note and acknowledgments

In January 1984 Trevor Richards, an English drummer who now lives in New Orleans, came to London to discuss the autobiography of Danny Barker. I had known about Danny's writing for some years, as the book he was working on is mentioned in *Hear Me Talkin' to Ya*, and was listed some years ago as a work in progress in the *Mississippi Rag*. I discovered that although he had continued with the book, working and re-working some sections of it, it had been submitted to publishers without success. Parts of the work appeared in various magazines but, it seemed, no-one was prepared to publish the book as a whole.

I arranged to meet Danny in March 1984 at the end of a working visit to the USA, and was amazed by the amount of writing and memorabilia that Danny had amassed. We set to cataloguing and ordering the boxes and files of papers, and out of them more than enough for two books emerged. This, Danny's autobiography, is the first of them. Soon we will start work on *Buddy Bolden and the Last Days of Storyville*, which is based on interviews and correspondence with jazzmen of the generation before Danny's.

During four visits to New Orleans I worked with Danny on the text of this autobiography. A few small sections were filled out by taped interviews, the transcripts of which were then edited with Danny's usual keen attention to the details of his style; but by far the largest part of the book is a text that has evolved over forty years.

I am particularly grateful to Nat Hentoff, Martin Williams and Donald Phelps for allowing us to re-use material that has previously appeared in the *Jazz Review*, *Jazz Panorama* and *For Now*. I must also thank Trevor Richards for his help, encouragement and hospitality, and Caroline Richmond for producing the final typescript. For help on the discography thanks are due to Barry Kernfeld of State College, Pennsylvania, the editor of *The New Grove Dictionary of Jazz*, and I must acknowledge the standard discographical reference works by Brian Rust, Jorgen G. Jepsen, and Walter Bruyninckx. Richard B.

Allen, Curator of Oral History at the William Ransom Hogan Archive of Jazz at Tulane, was also helpful in suggesting areas where interview might supplement the narrative.

Above all my thanks to Danny and Blue Lu Barker, for putting up with my visits and questions and the heaps of paper all over their house. Blue Lu in particular needs to be singled out for her kindness and hospitality, especially as she has not recently enjoyed the best of health.

Chawton
Hampshire
England
November 1985

ONE

The French Quarter and my grandparents

People from all parts of the world came to New Orleans and lived there. The books tell of pirates, adventurers, gamblers, exiles, criminals, Frenchmen, Spaniards, Germans, Englishmen, Irishmen, Africans, Indians, Chinese, Italians, West Indians and others. During the first hundred years following the settlement of the city, which was just one mile square from the banks of the Mississippi, these settlers from all parts of the world lived in this one square mile and did anything they felt like doing.

They fought like cats and dogs.

That first original square mile still exists just as it stood two hundred years ago, except for two fires. The natives call this one mile the French Quarter and that's what it is.

The home of my grandparents was one square away from the French Market and the Mississippi River. My grandfather worked on the river as a longshoreman and sometimes, when work was plentiful and he worked double and triple shifts, my grandmother cooked meals for his gang (or group) of co-workers. She would prepare twenty to thirty bucket-pails of food, which she placed in baskets and would bring to the wharves and levees at lunch time. When the whistle blew she would serve the workmen their lunches and they would sit about, on cotton bales, barrels, crates, or whatever they were loading or unloading, as they ate. So I have vivid memories of what was happening on the river and I saw much, for I would roam about the wharves, and was welcome there because most everyone knew my grandparents.

One day they were working on a Japanese ship and I went up the gangplank to watch the almond-eyed yellow men. One of them gave me a present of a little Japanese doll.

One day while my grandmother was serving the longshoremen their buckets of food, I listened as they discussed the *Bald Eagle*, a river packet boat, which had quite a reputation. One of the men asked "Where is it?" and another told him that it was docked right up there at the foot of Ursuline Street, which was only a half block away. The man grabbed me by the hand and said, "Come son, let's go and see the *Eagle*." My grandmother nodded approval and we hurried to see the boat.

When we walked from under the shed and out onto the wharf, there stood the *Bald Eagle*. We walked right up to the boat and the man was very excited as he looked her over. The *Bald Eagle* was a steamboat with the big wheel on the rear. To me it looked like many of the other steamboats I had seen before from a distance and I could not understand the man's excitement. A tall, blond, sleepy looking man leaned against the wall of the boat and looked about the wharf. He noticed us, for the man who held my hand was examining the boat from all angles as if it was something real strange. The blond man looked at us and said, "Come on board."

"Thank you, suh," said the longshoreman. "I've heard so much talk about the *Eagle* and here it is."

We walked on board and the tall, blond man said, "Look her over but don't wake up the rouster" (roustabout). The longshoreman gleefully thanked him again and we continued to walk slowly around the bottom of the boat looking at everything.

It was a bright day on the wharf but inside the boat it was sort of dark. There was but one small window on each side. The boat was rather empty. All about there were men lying on the floor asleep. When we walked to the rear of the boat there were some men playing cards. They were seated around a large barrel and turned to look at us, for they heard us approach. They smiled at me and one said, "Ah, looks the little rouster—you looking for a job, boy?"

"No sir," I replied. The men laughed at this and went on playing cards.

There were about seven men sitting around the barrel. They wore no shirts and were all huge men and looked like giants. They all needed the barber—hair all over their chests and arms. Our walk continued. We circled the boat, again passed some sleeping men, and then were back to where the tall blond man still stood, in the same position we had found him in. "How you like the *Eagle*?" he asked, looking at us and smiling.

The longshoreman said, "She's a fine boat. When you all leave?"

"In a couple of days," was the reply.

"Have a nice trip," said the longshoreman, "and thanks for letting me come on the boat."

We left the boat and walked back to my grandmother and the gang of workmen. They asked if we had seen the *Eagle*. "We were on her," said the longshoreman. "She's some boat!"

My grandmother asked, "Did you go on her, son?"

I said, "Yes, ma'am," and I told her the man had offered me a job.

The longshoreman said, "They wanted to hire Son as a roustabout." Everyone laughed, and talk of the *Eagle* continued until the whistle blew, which meant they had to start work again.

The *Bald Eagle* was the last of the famous river packets. The men who sailed the boat were the last of river roughnecks and bad men. The *Eagle* was one of the fastest boats on the river.

I was talking with Gene Sedric, the St Louis clarinetist, who had played music on most of the big excursion boats around St Louis. Gene laughed when I mentioned the *Bald Eagle*. He told me it was considered the fastest steamboat on the river and that it would be seen all over the Mississippi River basin. It would be seen on the Missouri, Ohio, Arkansas, Red rivers—everywhere. He also told me that the owners of the big pleasure boats hated the *Eagle*, for when the large boats were loaded with merrymakers, people dancing along, suddenly, out of nowhere, from around a bend in the river, or before them or behind them, would appear the *Eagle*, traveling very quickly, with its smokestacks belching cinders and fire, black and evil-smelling smoke. The captain and crew would get in a mad and frantic scramble closing windows and doors, because the *Eagle* was known purposely to speed by and get real close and leave a cloud of smoke, causing those on board to panic. The people would be running in all directions and some would yell, "Here comes the *Bald Eagle*." And here would come the *Bald Eagle*. It was the raggediest boat, all dirty and covered with yellow river mud. The river would be churning up, waves splashing, the whistle blowing and moaning, and you could barely read the name on the side for all that yellow mud. When the *Eagle* did pass, their crew would be standing on deck, laughing like crazy. The captain of the pleasure boat would shout threats and curse the *Eagle*. About ten minutes later the crew of the larger ship would open the doors and windows, for there was so much smoke it seemed as if the boat was on fire.

Regarding the captain's curses and threats: later, we would see the *Eagle* docked, but nothing happened because nobody on the river would challenge the crew of the *Eagle*, who were rough, tough battlers.

If you should visit the French Quarter of New Orleans, go sightseeing in the quarter about 10 p.m., not on the better-known streets,

Bourbon and Royal, near the commercial district where the cabarets, brightly lit stores and restaurants are, but down where the amber street lights are very dim—the 7th, 8th, 9th, 10th, 11th blocks of Chartres, Royal, Bourbon and Dauphin and the side streets as well —St Ann, Dumaine Street, Ursulines, Governor Nicholls and Esplanade Avenue. That is a very weird and spooky neighborhood. Many houses in that section have had some legendary story told and written about them. You will not find many people casually walking about those streets—not even the brave police. When I was very small that section was very active at night. Most of the old families have moved and died out. When you walk through this section (especially Royal, Chartres and Decatur streets) you will see that many entrances and doors and windows are wide and spacious. They were once store fronts.

At one time this section was very thickly populated with Italians. In 1916 when I was a small child it seemed like there were thousands of Italians. During the day and after 3 p.m. the narrow banquette and street were alive with robust, healthy Italian children, laughing and playing. These stores were always very busy and it was no effort to smell the food, wine and other products from the old country. There were large casks which contained all sorts of olives, cheeses, sausages, and the like. The immigrants were arriving in droves.

The center of Italian activities is now very quiet and almost asleep. The children of the immigrants I speak of are now the city's leading politicians, businessmen, lawyers, doctors, and they now dwell in the exclusive residential sections in large and beautiful homes which are surrounded by lovely gardens.

On the northeast corner of Chartres and St Philip stands a three-storied building which, in 1917, was a barroom and gambling joint owned, operated and patronized by Italians. The many tables were always occupied by men; many of them wore black shirts, black suits, black shoes and black hats. The doors were always wide open and the smoke from the long thin black strong cigars which were favored by most of the patrons would drift to the outside. If you passed the joint the strong aroma would damn near choke and suffocate you. I looked about the interior of this place on many occasions because I was fascinated. This was due mainly to the fact that these men looked so very different from the citizens of New Orleans.

They were mostly dark colored. Not real white like the other white people. Most of them were good looking, with pretty silky coal-black hair, and most of them sported long black handlebar mustaches. Mostly their time was spent gambling, never saying very much, or they were engaged in earnest conversation. At night when we passed this place it would still be filled with patrons. There were never any women—only men. I wondered how they could see the cards they played with. I suppose there were candles on the tables.

My grandmother's opinion of this joint and most of the Italians was a very low one. Often she would make remarks to this effect in a disgusted tone of voice. The first time I heard her express these feelings was one night when the smoke from the joint had made her cough and choke as we passed by. When she stopped to catch her breath she said, "That smoking, gambling, whiskey—they goin' dead straight down into hell!"

As time marched on in the French Quarter I saw many things which helped me to understand her attitude and remarks. In the hundreds of tenements in the rear of the front-street buildings there were people of all nationalities, living side by side in these rooms which were surrounded by patios, and there was a whole lot of integrating going on. The poor Italian immigrants, newly arrived from their native land, knew this and did not mind living next to Negroes or people of other races. They were mainly concerned with getting ahead. Soon, however, they learned the southern system of discrimination.

At other times when we passed by the joint my grandmother would glance inside, and then as we walked on to the middle of the block (to 1027 Chartres Street) she would exclaim, "Them Sillians (Sicilians) with them black shirts, black suits, black pants, black hats, black shoes, black mustaches—all that black is death! They ain't up to no good, sitting up in that dive in the darkness, and out here the sun is shining bright in all its glory. Lord, have mercy, Jesus!"

TWO

My mother and stepfather

I lived with my grandparents, the Barkers, as my father, Moses Barker, and my mother were separated. My mother had taken a job and my grandmother Victoria Barker took care of me. When my mother remarried and started housekeeping, the first demand of her mother Josephine and the older members of her family, the Barbarins, was: get your son from the Barkers and raise him, because he is your child and his place is with you, his mother. So I was taken from the Barkers. Next they said, take him out of Medard's private school and send him to public school: it's more modern and old mean Medard is too cruel to children. So I was taken out of Medard's school and sent to Marigny, a public school. At first I grieved for my grandparents, the Barkers, but my two young uncles gladly took me to the French Quarter to see and visit them. Gradually I got accustomed to living with my mother and stepfather.

A whole new free world opened to me. I had been accustomed to playing with the Italian children inside the high walls of the large brick yard at 1027 Chartres Street under the constant eye of the old folks. But at the new home I stepped out of the house and into the street, where colored children played together in groups and white children did likewise, and I had freedom to walk about and explore the sights of the new neighborhood.

I stopped and watched flowers growing in gardens, new neighbors, new faces, new eccentric characters, new customs of doing things —and white people who did not act, speak or dress as the Italians had done on Chartres Street. Here were mobs of colored children playing games I never saw before: playing tops, playing kites, shooting marbles, skating, rolling hoops with a wire guide. I saw boys riding horses, mules, with large goats hitched to small wagons, all kinds of street peddlers, and listened to their calls to housewives, each one different. On Chartres Street I only heard the church bells of the St Mary catholic church, but now I listened to many church bells, all with different notes. There were the groups of boys who did wrong things like hopping street cars and large trucks. I saw people talking normally in conversation. I was used to watching the Italians, so quick to get emotionally upset, shouting and arm-waving as if getting mad enough to burst a blood vessel and fight.

Living with my mother and stepfather our front step was right on the sidewalk, and at night the families most times, especially in the warm summer nights, sat out catching the air if there was any. And the children played games in front of their houses in the streets, the larger boys on the corner under the large street light. At nine o'clock a church bell rang nine times, slowly. Anybody who was not deaf could hear it, and all obedient, disciplined children dashed for home at the sound of the first toll of that bell. It was heard all over the downtown section of New Orleans. All children dashed madly for home. That was called beating the bell. It was a custom handed down: "Look at 'em beating the bell."

This was a comic scene: all the children dashing homeward. You was supposed to make it inside your door before the bell tolled number nine. Parents, most of them, kept the strap, leather belt, slipper, or some object to nail you if you did not beat that bell. You would see children turning the corner, feet flying, trying to make it: some standing outside acting scared to enter the front room, some pleading, some begging, some crying. This scene was a comic show, because the parents had went through the same routine. There would be inquiries by parents of the whereabouts of their tardy children.

These nights there would be many peddlers: the ice-cream man, the snowball man, the crab man, each with a song or some noise to identify them and their wares. And about seven in the morning you heard and saw the day peddlers: the charcoal man, cream-cheese man, vegetable man, stone coal man. And night and day people walking along singing popular jazz songs, sad mournful spirituals. And scores of whistlers: virtuosos whistling jazz songs just like their favorite musicians played their songs.

My relationship with my stepfather, Christopher Colombel, was wonderful. Of course I had known my father and respected him as such, but I never saw much of him—that is to associate with him real close. He was my father, and everybody in the family said I looked just like him before he was taken sick. I went to visit him where he lived on Liberty Street. My cousins or young uncles would take me there until I was old enough to go alone. He and his common-law wife, Mrs Cele (a fine-looking brownskin woman) kept a fairly large rooming house. My cousins and uncles jumped at the chance to take me to my father because he would give them some coins. Sweetie Barker had wasted away, a victim of tuberculosis. it was, the old folks said, lingering consumption. There was another variety called galloping consumption: galloping consumption ate up its victim very quickly, in a few months. The lingering kind just lingered. It was common for people to live a long time, suffering, in and out of bed, up and down, down and up, according to the weather, seasons—winter, fall, summer, spring. Sometimes when I went to see Sweetie he was bed-ridden, other times up. He would be in bed, then suddenly get a coughing spell. Then, gasping for his breath, he would start heaving and spitting up green and yellow phlegm. Cele was very sympathetic and attentive, giving him fresh water, medicine, paper napkins, and putting the chamber pot close where he could heave up the green phlegm.

He had went to Phoenix and Tucson, Arizona, to get relief and maybe the cure, but his case was hopeless. At this house, which was well-furnished, there was generally visitors. Sporting people of the colored underworld: always different attractive women around, dressed in expensive house robes, silks, satins, with much lace and frills, painted, and the air smelling of perfume and powder.

Sweetie always had a plentiful supply of money—green bills. He kept two or three large rolls of money under his large pillows. There were three, I remember. He used these large snow-white pillows to prop himself up when he felt like it. Bill collectors would come to his bedside for the money and watch him, as he slowly raised himself and reached under the pillow for a big roll of bills, slowly peel off the money and hand it to the person. I saw him reach for another roll of bills on occasion. I never went there for nothing—that is for money for clothes, shoes, or something I needed. My grandfather and grandmother the Barkers bought me what I needed; then my mother and stepfather when I went to live with them. When I wanted something from my mother I learned to ask for it in the presence of my stepfather. I remember very well him growling, "Rose, give it to the boy. Yer got him begging like this is some kind of poorhouse." And then I would get what I asked for.

If what I wanted did not make sense, Chris and my mother would explain it to me, why. Chris drank heavy at times. It was the habit of the bakers to stop at their favorite barroom on their way home for a few drinks. Many times they and he drank too much. I always knew which of the barrooms they frequented. When he was late and overdue my mother would say, "Daniel, go get Chris."

I would go to the barroom, see him, walk over and whisper, and while I would be whispering softly the other bakers would start kidding Chris, "Oh, oh! Here the police! The party's over!"

There was also the bar flies around: local neighborhood characters or alcoholics getting their fill of booze, other bakers from other bakery shops. These bakers worked long, hard hours. Chris was what is called an oven man. His job was to put in and take out the bread at the exact right time. Others were bench men, mixers and wrappers. An oven man has to keep watch of that hot oven, watching the temperature on the gauge on the steam boiler, and he is responsible for the finished product. At the precise time he has to put the dough in the oven quickly and in the proper location. Very quickly and at a given time he has to get it out of that hot oven so that the bread is browned evenly. When he opens the door of that oven, that hot air engulfs him. Chris the oven man would throw a clean flour sack around his shoulders, and yell, "Let's go from here." Then he would open the black oven door, take his ladle—a sort of wooden shovel, very flat, with a long handle —and stand aside for a minute to let that vicious heat rush out. Then he would peer inside and quickly start pushing in the ladle and taking out hot brown bread. The bread is laid on a long bench, where the other bakers sort it and the bread-wrapper wraps it and puts it into large crates ready for delivery.

An oven man is the tops in the bakery business. He was in the early days in small bakery shops. And Chris was considered the best in downtown New Orleans. But a man's lungs and eyes cannot buck that constant heat. The intense heat dries the moisture of your lungs and eyes, and that's what happened to Chris: chronic asthma.

With Sweetie Barker it was his lungs.

Now after I would enter those barrooms and talk to Chris, he would insist on me having something: soda, cake, candy. I would always refuse because I knew it meant more money out of his pay check. He would insist and I would persistently refuse. That would generally make the Italian owners angry. They would look at me sternly and I would frown and return their facial expression.

I would hear my mother arguing, saying, "Chris, when you get drunk in them barrooms you don't know how much that Italian is writing down in your credit book." And I believed what she said. If Chris was heavily boozed I would tell him, "Chris, come on home right away! Some thief has done stole your hunting dog (or your new shotgun)," or, "your mother is at the house waiting for you: something done happened."

Hearing this Chris would shout, "Let's go, son! I'll catch that dirty son of a bitch that stole my dog!" (or gun).

He loved and respected his mother and he would stagger as I helped him home. When he arrived home I would say, "Did they find Chris's dog?" or, "Did they find Chris's gun?" or, "Has Chris's mamma gone back home?" Then me and my mother ad-libbed a story as I took Chris's shoes off and we helped him to bed. And Chris mumbled threats until he went to sleep.

Chris was great to me. We went fishing, hunting. And he liked music. Chris was raised in the lower swamp section of Louisiana in Plaquemine Parish. He knew all about the woods: hunting, fishing, trapping—all about wildlife. He was at home in the woods and around lakes, bayous, rivers. He knew all about fishes, sea food, and the small wild animals which he hunted: rabbits, squirrels, coons. He called me in the woods, "Come here quick!"

I would say, "What is it?"

He would point, saying, "There's snakes over there." Sure enough, there would be one in the foliage which I could not see.

He would look at tracks in the soil and say, "There's turtles or alligators here!" And sure enough he would fashion a trap out of wire clothes hangers we always took along, and catch a large swamp turtle or a small alligator hidden under the sand, under logs, or under something nearby. Chris knew the woods and swamps and was a fine fisherman. For a while he stopped baking and fished for a living: catching crabs, by the bushels full, sorting them in crates, submerging the crates in lake water, covering them. This process caused the crabs to shed their hard shells and become soft-shell crabs, which quadruples their sale value. For a couple of years he bought a horse and wagon and peddled charcoal about the streets of New Orleans. I worked on the wagon with him during school summer vacations; I was then at the age of fourteen or fifteen.

Chris's parents had eight children: four boys and four girls. His family were from Plaquemine Parish, a location thirty miles or so below New Orleans. His mother would visit us occasionally and, during World War I, while he served in the US Army, my mother and I visited his mother regularly on Sundays. While there I got to know and played with the children of that branch of the family and got acquainted with Chris's brothers and sisters.

THREE

Animule Hall

This small hall was located in the eighth ward on Marigny Street between Johnson and Galvez streets. Marigny Street is one block below Elysian Fields Avenue, which is very wide. The L & N Railroad tracks were in the center: about eight tracks were laid there. The famous little engine and coaches of the Pontchartrain Railroad excursion train rolled on one of the tracks, from Canal Street to Milneberg, the famed resort. The little train was called "Smoky Mary," because this ancient little engine with its huge, funnel-shaped smoke stack used coal and pinewood in its furnaces, and the black smoke, cinders and soot dirtied the clothing that the housewives hung on their lines. Elysian Fields Avenue and the track divided the seventh and the eighth wards. People from the seventh ward spoke of the eighth ward as "back of the tracks."

As each ward and section of the city had its halls, the eighth ward had its Animal Hall (I don't know its legitimate name). I recall returning home from a fish-fry with my mother one Saturday night at about midnight. We passed the Animal Hall and saw the patrol wagon in front of the place, and we watched a group of police pushing men and women up into the wagon. We walked on. My mother said, indifferently, "The law is raiding the Animule Hall." In front of the hall there was a small electric light bulb, above the door. As we walked on the paddy wagon passed us, and it was loaded with cursing men and women. Later I heard the story of the Animule Hall while I was standing on the corner and listening to a group of men who were kidding a man who had his arm in a sling and his head bandaged up. The bandaged-up man was laughing as they kidded him. He had escorted a woman from the eighth ward to a dance at the Animule Hall, and that was a great act of bravery for a man from the seventh ward.

The Animule Hall was a notorious joint. It was nicknamed the Animule because the patrons behaved like animals of the jungle once they entered. They would be real tame on the outside, but once they entered and began to dance and drink the bad, cheap booze sold there,

they became very antagonistic, belligerent, nasty, vulgar and provoca-
tive. The hall was operated by a very rough man called Joe Baggers,
who was the floorwalker and bouncer. He always kept an iron pipe in
his hand or under his arm, and when the battles got out of hand he
whipped both men and women alike with this pipe. (Baseball bats
would crack and split on those hard heads, and were too expensive, so
he used a two-inch thick pipe.)

The star attraction at the hall was Long Head Bob's Social Orchestra.
The patrons loved Bob's music; in fact, no band would play there but
Bob's orchestra. Bob's repertoire consisted of the blues, and only the
blues: fast blues, medium blues, slow blues, and the slow, slow drag.
The evening's program began at eight and was scheduled to stop at
3 a.m., but the attraction was never known to have lasted that long.
This was because of the hall's casualties, which were a great nuisance to
the police of the fifth precinct and the doctors and nurses at the Charity
Hospital. The men and women who patronized the hall were very
hard-working people: stevedores, woodsmen, fishermen, field hands
and steel-driving men, and the women were factory workers, washer-
women, etc. All were very strong and physically fit.

Nobody went to the hall until he or she felt that they were grown and
capable of protecting themselves, for when you walked into the
Animule Hall you were expected to be a grown adult and afraid of no
one. In this element of people the general attitude was, "I work hard,
make an honest living. You all look down on me and I am looking down
on you all. Everybody thinks they are more than me: white folks and
yellow and colored folks. You all don't want to associate with me when
you all go for a good time, so I have my good time at the Animule Hall,
and you gotta be a real good strong brave man or woman to go there."

It was a test of bravery when you entered the Animule Hall. If a
young man or woman had a warm feeling for someone they wanted,
they were told, "Meet me at," or, "Take me to the Animule Hall
Saturday night," or, "Come to the Animule Hall and I'll dance with you
when Long Head Bob plays the slow drag." That meant if you wanted
the man or woman, you kept the appointment and waited until Bob
played the slow, slow drag. Everyone in the hall and on the outside
knew the importance and significance of the dance.

So when the slow drag commenced it was a great act of bravery and
defiance if you danced with someone's lover, and everybody watched
to see who was belly-rubbing with whom. This was primitive animal
jungle tactics—survival of the fittest. You were taking you a man, or he
a woman, and that's what started the humbugs, because the news

would spread that so-and-so danced the slow, slow, slow drag with so-and-so's property, and then everyone wanted to see who was "chicken."

Joe Baggers was well known, and familiar with everybody in the seventh, eighth and ninth wards. When some upstart boy or girl entered the Animule Hall and Joe Baggers felt they were too young, he kicked them in the behind and chased or dragged them to the street, yelling, "Get out of here. You're still pissing in your drawers." That was very embarrassing, because everyone stopped dancing and laughed at you, even your relatives. But if Joe Baggers thought you were ready and able to protect yourself and he let you stay in the hall, somebody was sure to challenge you before the hall closed that night, by stepping on your foot, by elbowing or by pushing your hat off (the men never removed their hats).

When an argument or fight started the crowd made a ring around the combatants and cheered them on. Men battled like bears and women like wildcats. No weapons were allowed, just bare fists. The loser, all out of breath, was dragged out by Joe Baggers, then kicked in the behind. Joe Baggers would stand there and call you a coward or bastard or bitch (and other nasty names), and the large crowd on the outside would kid the hell out of you. It made no difference who lost a battle—a man or a woman. While the battle was in progress Joe Baggers always rushed to the center of the fracas and saw to it that the contestants fought man to man, or woman to woman. He kept the wild crowd a safe distance with his menacing iron pipe and he would yell to the frantic crowd, "Stand back! Let 'em fight! Don't crowd 'em! Give 'em air! Give 'em a fair chance! Don't nobody get in this humbug!" He would allow the fight to continue until one fell, badly beaten or exhausted. Then he decided who was the winner, and he would grab the loser and plant his long, pointed-toed shoe on the loser's rear end. That was the process of departure. The crowd inside and outside knew what was coming.

Most times the women fought until they were naked on the floor. Then some man would cover the naked woman with a coat after she was kicked out of the front door. The naked winner was taken into the rear kitchen and covered with a checked tablecloth, while a friend or relative went to the winner's home and returned with a fresh gingham dress (which most of them wore). She would also get a pair of drawers or a chemise.

There was always a large crowd of neighborhood characters outside the hall, listening to the music (if it was not raining) and anxiously waiting to see Joe Baggers kick someone through the front door. These outside characters were mostly young folks who intended to some day walk inside the Animule Hall (when they felt they were mature enough).

Mr Joe Baggers wore extra special long-toed shoes, the tips of which were as sharp as an ice pick. When Joe Baggers kicked somebody through the door the crowd outside would laugh and yell hysterically. The unanimous comment was, "That kick done give him (or her) the piles!" When a young man or woman of the neighborhood made their debut at the Animule Ball it was like a coming-out party—like being presented to society. It would be rumored in the neighborhood with great concern that so-and-so is going to the Animule Ball Saturday night. The candidate would dress in his "Sunday go to meeting" (newly bought) clothes, and the immediate friends, brothers and sisters would escort them to the door in a sort of honored procession. As the candidate walked up the stairs and paid the admission the friends stood on the outside, looking on with great intent for about ten or twenty minutes. That was ample time to give the candidate a chance to be viewed by Mr Joe Baggers. After about twenty minutes had passed there was a general feeling of relief if the candidate was not kicked out. The friends outside would then relax and say, "They made it!" and, "Joe Baggers must have seen 'em by now." It was these friends on the outside who escorted a beaten battler home when he was kicked out. When a candidate was accepted and not chased by Joe Baggers it was considered an honor; you were a neighborhood celebrity for quite a while and respected. You had reached maturity.

The program of activities at the Animule Hall was accepted by the guests as being well supervised by Joe Baggers, and what went on there was all part of a good time. No weapons were allowed, for if Joe Baggers caught somebody with a knife, razor blade, ice pick or gun he would beat this person unmercifully with his iron pipe and then have the person arrested by the police who were detailed there. The same policeman, Kennedy, was always stationed at Joe Baggers's affairs. He didn't have to ever lift a hand, because Joe Baggers was the boss and ruled with his iron pipe. The policeman just sat off in the kitchen or near the stand, watching the festivities while eating and drinking.

At about 2 a.m. the bad booze and Long Head Bob's lowdown blues would affect the crowd so that they were at the edge of an explosion. When Bob played his slow, slow, slow drag, sometime between 1 a.m. and 2 a.m., everyone would search out his or her lover—that is if you were supposed to love them. When Bob started the blues there was great searching around the hall for the one you loved, and you were expected to dance with your lover only and no one else. So it was a nasty insult to be shaking and belly-rolling with someone else's lover. Joe Baggers always told Bob when to play those blues. When Bob got the OK Joe stood upon a high box, and Officer Kennedy would casually sneak over to the telephone. Joe Baggers would nervously stand upon the box and look over the hip-shaking dancers, so that he could locate the first argument and the fight which was sure to follow. Officer Kennedy would put a nickel in the phone and call the fifth precinct, speak to the desk sergeant, and leave the line open as he watched the crowd dancing those slow, slow, slow, sexy, body-twisting blues. There were always three or more arguments going on: then the fights would start. Joe Baggers could not be all over the Animule Hall at the same time, and when he jumped off that box and rushed into the midst of a fracas Kennedy would scream into the phone to the fifth precinct, "Send the wagon. The fracas has begun."

No matter how furious the fighting became Long Head Bob's band continued to play the slow blues as if nothing was happening, because many of the dancers were in tight embrace with the ones they loved with all their hearts, and fights just don't matter when you are holding and kissing and squeezing the one you love. That booze and those blues and holding the one you love make you feel that the world can end right now.

Then, very quickly and quietly, the patrol wagon arrives, carrying two officers. The wagon stops in front of the hall and the policemen rush up the steps, open the door and blow their whistles. Many of the dancers are still wiggling as Bob continues playing; they are in another world. If the fights are still in progress the police just stab the fighters in their bellies with night sticks—real hard. That knocks the wind out of them.

The older patrons are wise to Kennedy's phone calls, and when they hear Bob start his slow blues and see Joe Baggers mount the box they leave the hall if they are not too drunk. At times someone would yell, "Kennedy's calling the wagon." Then there would be a stampede out of the hall, and in three minutes the place is empty. When the crowd stampedes out of the hall the people gathered outside run off in all directions to their homes. When the wagon arrives many couples still in hypnotic ecstasy are dancing to Bob's blues. Their usual comment when awakened to the fact that the wagon is going to take them to jail is, "Jail ain't made for dogs. I've been to jail before and I'll go again." Going to jail was a weekly routine to most of Joe Baggers's clientele. The wagon made only two round trips to the hall and to jail. When the folks were lined up the older patrons always went to the rear of the line, because after two wagon-loads had left the rest of the people were released with a warning from Officer Kennedy. Joe Baggers traveled with the second load and paid their fines: one dollar a head for disturbing the public peace.

During all the time that the wagon is being loaded Long Head Bob still continues to play the slow, slow blues, and the couples in line stand real close to one another, shaking their bodies and talking, "I've been to jail before and I'll go again." The police don't stop the blues; they like the blues. When the car returns the second time and is again loaded Joe Baggers waves to Bob to stop, "It's all over, Bob." Then he walks out and steps into the patrol wagon to go to the precinct and bail out his many patrons.

The Animule Hall crowd differed from the folks of the district. These were hard-working folks, and the action and excitement at the Animule Hall and Joe Baggers's tactics entertained them. Very few of these folks dressed in expensive clothes or sported diamonds or had plenty money. The men wore box-back suits, high, broad-rimmed Stetson hats, yellow shoes (called yellow yams), and the women mostly wore common gingham dresses, starched and ironed stiff. Most of these people had nicknames (they were rarely called by their proper names): Scuzzum, La La, Dibbles, Poom Poom, Rough Joe Rucker, Nick Nack, Tick Tack, and the four bad brothers Poot, Fot, Shit and Crapper. If you got into a humbug (as a fracas was called) you had to whip and fight all four of these brothers and two dozen other near relatives in the street. Joe Baggers tolerated them because they never would miss a dance, and bought and drank plenty booze.

These four brothers were very bull-headed, obstinate and ignorant. When one got into a humbug the other three brothers, also their sisters and dozens of relatives, became insanely furious. No matter where they were in Animule Hall, just the mention that Poot or one of the other brothers or sisters were in an argument made them push through and rush to the scene to add their insults to the combatants'. No one could get any sense into their heads. Then their clique would join in the scuffle: Apey, Juggum, Josh, Siccum, Scuddum, Sprat, Mud, Rilla, Mule, Horse, Ass, Goat—these were all live young men and women, and all were healthy, full of wild primitive strength. Just the thought that one of their bunch was involved in a fracas exaggerated their viciousness.

It would take about an hour for Joe Baggers to bail out his patrons, and then they were released with a warning. They would leave the fifth precinct in a mean group of about twenty persons. On their homeward route, if they passed a grocery store, the men would break open the bread and milk boxes which were outside of these groceries, and they would continue their walk while eating hot doughnuts, rolls and bread and drinking cold fresh milk. Of course the grocers complained to the police.

The Animule Hall came to an end. The police received so very many complaints from the reserved people of that neighborhood (about the street fights which occurred after the hall closed, and the morning brawls, loud curses, running, chasing, and all sorts of noises), that they finally gave orders to Joe Baggers to close the hall, which he did. Joe did not make plenty money with the hall, for most of the money went for bailing out his patrons. Joe Baggers set up business at another small hall with a tin roof which was located in the seventh ward. He called it "Joe Baggers's Respectable Hall." But the clientele there was much tamer in the seventh ward.

A well-known minister, known as Elder Lockett, bought the Animule Hall, erected a steeple above the front, painted it white, cleaned it out, and blessed it. Then he called it the First African Baptist Church. It still stands today.

The favorite, and the one and only drink that Mr Joe Baggers concocted and carefully bottled was called "Cherry Bounce." This was composed of one hundred and ten proof pure alcohol, if the price was not too steep. If it was, he sold sherry wine with cheap alcohol. He mixed the very strong alcohol with water and then tested the mixture to be sure it burned the mouth and singed the tongue. Then he would color and sweeten this mixture with a cherry-flavored syrup. Joe Baggers served the drink in fairly large whiskey glasses for fifteen cents a drink. If you drank half a dozen glassfuls and still stood on your feet you deserved a medal of some kind.

After each trip to the makeshift bar the patrons would boast to one another of how many drinks they had consumed, "Ah just had mah fifth swallow of Cherry Bounce and ah'm still all right." When you consumed more than three drinks of Cherry Bounce and it flowed down your throat and into your stomach your mentality became impaired and your nervous system became disrupted. Your stomach became a bottled-up volcano—that is, on fire. The Cherry Bounce twisted your brain to such an extent that you lost all sense and reasoning power. You began to think and feel that the whole world was against you; folks did not like you, they brushed against you or stepped on your foot purposely. Nobody in your family loved you, not even your mother or father or sisters or brothers. The Cherry Bounce forced all sorts of ugly memories into your brain. It made you feel as if you could and should whip the world, the devil and a cage of lions. Joe Baggers kept an eye on the bar. If he saw someone on the verge of getting the horrors he would say, "That's all for you," which meant no more Cherry Bounce. Then he would command a friend or relative to carry you home, and they did as he said.

Officer Kennedy just looked on straight-faced and sort of unconcerned, because all the patrons feared and respected Mr Joe Baggers. Kennedy was just detailed at the hall, but never arrested anyone. He was known for just the act of phoning for the wagon. The patrons had no hatred or anger towards him, for he never showed any authority or acted like the other New Orleans police officers. He always coolly and carefully avoided any arguments; just walked off to a safe distance and looked on, straight-faced.

At the police station, when the battlers arrived, Officer Kennedy was known to speak softly to the desk sergeant and walk to the rear. Then he would change his uniform for street clothes and walk past Joe Baggers and the arrested crowd and then out the door. He never once condemned or spoke or pointed out any of the arrested group as trouble makers. He left all the explaining and transactions to Joe Baggers. So at the Animule Hall Officer Kennedy was considered a completely harmless individual. The scene at the hall at no time seemed to excite him in the least. He would shake his head while he looked at the twisted faces of many of the patrons who, full of Cherry Bounce, would start to cry. They were in a deep state of melancholy and self-pity. Some would be dancing, some were lonely wallflowers, and they would all listen to Long Head Bob's band playing the sad blues songs: *Careless Love*; *I got a brand new lover, don't want you no mo'*; *Easy Rider*; *Mamie Desdune Blues*; *Buddy Bolden Blues*; *Up in Mattie's bunk*; *I'm through dealing in coal*; *Blacker the berry, sweeter the juice*; *There's a new mule kicking in your stall*; *Das all—you all*.

Some of the patrons would get so carried away by these blues that their crying and wailing could be heard above the band. This would greatly annoy Joe Baggers, and he would search out the criers in the hall, yelling at them loudly, "Cut out the goddamn crying! Git your simple ass outer heah and go on home." The criers would leave, their sobbing louder as they slowly walked through the jam-packed crowd and out through the door. The other dancers never laughed or paid any special attention to the departing mourners because it was a common occurrence, and they all understood the deep inner feeling—the Blues.

Joe Baggers always followed these mourners, and as they walked down the steps into the midst of the large crowd which always gathered outside the hall he would bid them a sarcastic adieu, "Git out and stay out of heah, you soft chicken-hearted sons of bitches." And this would be loud enough so the inside and outside crowd could hear him. Then he would slam the large wooden door so hard it would shake the building. From a distance Officer Kennedy would stretch his neck and look towards the front door with his expressionless face, and as the door slammed he would relax and rub his chin, light a cigarette, and lean against the wall near a window as he breathed the cool air, and his smoke would flow through the open window.

At family affairs and other social functions I often saw men and women get real juiced up and suddenly start crying hysterically. No amount of consoling could stop the laments which went on and on. The older folks would say indifferently, "Aw, they got the horis." Yes, that's the way the folks pronounced the weeping person's condition. I went to clubs and saw folks take off on the crying jag and said to myself, "They got the horis."

But at a very ultra-social affair on Park Avenue in New York City an aristocratic cultured lady started the crying jag. Everybody got excited and she was given smelling salts, ice bags and stimulants. Finally they sent for a doctor. The doctor very coolly gave her some pills and left. Another high-class lady consoled the crying woman saying, "Poor thing, she has the horrors." I watched the scene and said to myself, "The horis." I was sober, and when I heard her precise pronunciation of the word I compared the two words: horrors and horis. That rang a bell. Horrors is the word as spelled and spoken in the correct English custom of describing the condition, but in New Orleans the natives really mutilate the English language.

When someone who attends a social affair goes into the tantrums of the horrors their actions generally turn a happy scene into one of silence and sadness. There is this crying, and the heavy flow of tears which looks like a waterfall. It is remarkable how much water can come from a person's eyes. Then the wails of self pity, "Nobody loves me in this world."

"I'm in this world by myself."

"I love everybody but nobody cares for me."

"I shouldn't have been born."

"Everybody takes advantage of me."

"I wish I was dead."

On arrival in New York City—Harlem—I soon started checking on all the many clubs. I heard one musician tell another, "I'm playing at Joe Baggers's Club." I recalled Joe Baggers in New Orleans's eighth ward, and later I went by and checked on the basement club under the Alhambra Theater, 126th Street on Seventh Avenue. I looked at this Harlem Joe Baggers and he was not the New Orleans Joe Baggers, but in the same cabaret business.

FOUR

Barbarin house and my first funeral

While living with my grandparents the Barkers in the French Quarter, and being a small child, I saw none of the social action: the weekend good times, parties, and excitement that happened around my other grandparents the Barbarins, who lived in the seventh ward a mile or so away.

At the Barbarin home the main topic of daily conversation was music. My grandfather, Isidore, played with the mighty Onward Brass Band, and much of what happened within this very busy band was discussed in this home. Being small, I did not understand much of the music talk, but my grandmother Josephine loved music and encouraged her four sons to play an instrument. I associated with the two younger sons, Willie and Lucien. I saw the older two, Louis and Paul, but they being older—that is young men—I did not know very much about their interests. But I did see them practicing drums.

In New Orleans it was never any problem to get a band together to provide music for a wedding, birthday party, christening, funeral, or other social function or celebration. This was because many of the musicians were related to each other. It was merely necessary to send word that a celebration was anticipated, and the many related musicians would gather with their friends.

The following list will give you an idea of the close relationship which exists amongst the New Orleans musicians connected with my grandfather's house:

Isidore John Barbarin	Alto horn
and Louis Arthidore	Clarinet
Isidore Barbarin married Louis	
Arthidore's sister	
Paul Barbarin	Drums
and Jimmy Noone	Clarinet
married two sisters	

Paul's wife's brother, T. J. Thomas	Saxophone
Louis Barbarin's wife's brother, Billy Phillips	Drums
Louis Barbarin's daughter married son of Louis Nelson	Trombone
Louis Barbarin's son, Louis, Jr	Trombone
William Barbarin's son, William, Jr	Drums
Isidore's grandson, Danny Barker	Banjo
Danny Barker married Louisa Dupont (Blue Lu Barker)	Blues singer
Blue Lu's Nephew, August Dupont	Saxophone
Blue Lu's cousin, Joseph Thomas (Brother Cornbread)	Clarinet
Blue Lu's cousin, Bibbs Lazard	Drums
Dan and Blue Lu's daughter, Sylvia Brunner	Monologuist, actress, poet, preacher
Isidore's cousin, Esther Bigeou	Blues singer
Octave Clements, Isidore's cousin (Big Belly Fob)	Trombone
Isidore's cousin, Lionel Tapo	Banjo
Lionel Tapo's brother, Charlie Tapo	Guitar
Lionel Tapo's brother-in-law, Howard Mandolf	Piano

A little further research will surely uncover more cousins who were connected through New Orleans music.

Isidore Barbarin's home was located on St Claude Street near St Anthony. On that corner stood Dileo's grocery store, which included at the side a barroom and a gambling room. Dileo's sin den was called the St Claude Social Club. Three and more men's marching clubs centered their activities there. Their parades and advertising started and finished there. All these groups gave periodical social affairs. I remember they were called Vegetable Packers, the Four Thousand Good Livers, the Seventh Ward Sports, and of course the St Claude Social Club.

During the spring and summer months placards would appear on street posts announcing the coming affairs. These would list the club's name, all the officers, the hall and, in large letters, the name of the band that would play for the affair. Last, "There will be a gala advertisement or street parade." Reading and studying these fairly large placards made you familiar with the names of all the local characters and the different jazz and brass bands. There were a dozen or more halls and clubhouses in the sixth and seventh wards, which bordered on each other. The youngsters all knew where these places were located.

When the club or society members got together on the Sunday of the street parades large crowds gathered in their hundreds to see the excitement of the colorful parade or advertisement. The first advertisements were in buggies—funeral buggies. Then, when automobiles became plentiful and a common sight, cars were decorated with colorful ribbons and flags. All the club or society members dressed in new flashy sports outfits: fancy expensive silk shirts, new pants, hats, ties, socks—everything new and costly.

The jazz bands I saw and followed in about 1917 or 1918 were Joe Petit's Camelia Band; Walter Blue's band; Long Head Bob's band; Manuel Perez's Imperial Band; the Tuxedo Band; the Maple Leaf Band; King Oliver's band (he was called "Bad-eye Joe" then); and Buddy Petit's band. I saw these bands leave from Dileo's corner, but before leaving they would all play a few pieces for the large crowds which always gathered. I saw how these musicians were greeted, applauded, the reception they were given. I saw how the crowd gathered closely, listening happily, tingling all over. I heard the comments, the acclaim. I noticed the vibration the jazz created. I felt it. I watched how the musicians' names were yelled and screamed out.

"Play man."

"Blow your horn."

I watched the hysteria and emotion this jazz music created inside all these people, each and everybody moving in rhythm. When the buggies and the furniture wagon carrying the band left, we boys would follow, because the procession moved slow. But when they started using automobiles and a long furniture truck carried the jazz band, they moved fast, and the second line could not keep up the pace.

The first time I saw Joe Oliver he was blowing with the Onward Brass Band. There was a funeral of a prominent preacher in the Barbarin neighborhood, so naturally I went to the funeral second line with my two young uncles. This was a large funeral. Many dignitaries were there at the church. There was much preaching, and eulogies of the deceased. The outside became restless. Finally the church bell tolled and the mourners started coming out of the church. During the long wait we stood around the band members, watching them like they were gods or saints. This was the Onward Brass Band, the greatest in the city, and highly respected. There was Manuel Perez, Andrew Kimball, Joe Oliver, Lorenzo Tio, Ernest Trappanier, and my grandfather Isidore. They were standing in position at the right side of the entrance of the front door of the church. The great band struck up to the boom of Trappanier's big bass drum and long tall Eddie Jackson's huge bass horn. It was like lightning struck the huge crowd. Hats were snatched off and all talking stopped.

I watched as a long double-file line of men slowly walked out of the church. It was the masons. I saw the aprons they were wearing. I have to laugh sometimes now when I recall this scene. I said to myself, looking at the snow-white aprons, "Oh, they must be waiters and dishwashers. They must be gonna serve food at the cemetery." After them, out stepped the Knights Templar with the ostrich-plumed admiral hats. "Oh, they must be chicken cleaners; oh yeah, with all the feathers on top of their hats." I didn't say nothing to my uncles as we followed the funeral out of the sight of Isidore in the brass band.

They marched to the St Rock Cemetery, which is in the eighth ward, about a mile from our house. I was so sure that there was gonna be food served at the cemetery, and was disappointed when I did not see the long tables piled with food there. On the way back the brass band wailed, with Manuel Perez, Kimball, Eddie Jackson, Trappanier doing it up. My uncles, excited by the great music, forgot all about my grandfather. We followed right close behind the three great cornet players, my uncles telling each other, "Listen at Joe Oliver." I stumbled along at the side of the tall, heavy-set Joe Oliver, listening.

That was the first funeral I followed.

The march ended at the Perseverance Hall. It was an exciting spectacle. More than a thousand people of all ages dancing to the music until the last note ended in a cloud of sounds.

FIVE

Isidore Barbarin

Isidore was an easygoing, cool-tempered man. He had fathered nine children: five girls and four boys. I guess behind all that child-raising it was a natural attitude for a man to be callous to just about anything, especially excitement. His children were all very respectful and disciplined in his presence, even the grown and married girls. He was "Pop" with an emphasis. They only engaged him in conversation if the matter was of interest and serious. No nonsense or foolishness. He ate his fine meals alone at a table, where sometimes my grandmother joined him. There was another large table for the children and relatives. He ate slowly, correctly, and always there was the full bottle of claret or burgundy wine. At lunch time, if he was having his meal and we youngsters ran playfully through the alley, my grandmother gave out a shout and we panicked in our tracks, as if lightning had struck.

I saw Isidore many times at funerals in the neighborhood, sitting atop that shiny black hearse with the well-fitting high hat on, looking straight ahead. No matter how much a bereaved family of people were carrying on, crying, screaming, moaning, fainting, in a hysterical pandemonium, Isidore never moved a muscle. He sat as if his mind and thought were miles away. Yet some of these funerals were so highly dramatic they would make strangers looking on cry. I guess Isidore had seen so many funerals he was immune to tears and grief. I had been real close to my other grandfather, Mr Barker, who had none of Isidore's stiffness.

I shocked the Barbarin family early when I moved back with my mother. One day at lunch time, which was every day between twelve and one, my grandmother served my uncles and myself at the large table. As soon as I received my plate I picked it up and went over and sat with my grandfather Isidore, blessed my food (which my uncles never did), and started a conversation about music and then horses. He spoke and answered my questions and did some explaining. All was very quiet and I looked around at my young uncles and my grand-mother, who was standing with her hands on her hips looking at me in utter surprise. My uncles were laughing silently at my nerve—"sitting at the king's table." My grandmother said in French, "Now I've seen everything." I kept up the serious questioning until the meal was over. Then my grandfather said to my grandmother in French, "That boy's got plenty sense." I felt proud inside myself, but I never sat at the table with him again until I was a grown man.

Isidore was a light-colored man about six feet tall, always neat and well-groomed. He wore dark suits tailored to his exact measurements, and soft black shoes. He had extra-large brown eyes which were very piercing, and always looked everyone in conversation in direct focus. His large eyes were remindful of a water spaniel dog. He was not a regular church-going man, I guess because he was constantly about churches, religious services of many denominations, and knew the inner workings of churches, preachers, priests, hospitals, death, cemeteries: everything concerning a mortal's last hours on earth. He was a member of the great Onward Brass Band in which I had heard Joe Oliver play. Manuel Perez (a good friend) was the leader. To many critical musicians Perez was the greatest cornetist in the city and the jazz world.

Manuel Perez was a powerful built man. He looked like a Mexican or Spaniard, and was the idol of the downtown Creole colored people. To them nobody could master the cornet like Mr Perez. When this brass band played a march, dirge or hymn it was played to perfection—no blunders. The personnel of the Onward stayed intact as a highly polished musical organization for many years, and that was also the case with the great Excelsior Brass Band. Many of these marching musicians only played in brass bands, never in dance or jazz bands.

My grandfather's very close friend was Adolph Alexander, Sr, a baritone horn player. He had a large family. In fact his children somewhat resembled Isidore's children; four or five of the boys also played music professionally. To the youngsters Isidore and Adolph were fondly called Mr Barbarin and Mr Taton (Adolph's nickname).

I saw Mr Taton often. He was a short brownskin man, very French in manner. He always seemed in a state of deep inner unrest and, like the Italian men, he went into many facial expressions and hand motions when talking. It seemed like he was always explaining some misunderstanding. Isidore just looked at him sadly with his large wide-opened brown eyes. It seemed, for example, that if the Excelsior or another brass band played for some affair and the Onward missed out, it would hurt Mr Taton very deeply. I heard them on the front steps discussing music and musicians very critically. The alto and baritone horns walked in front of the three cornet players in the brass band, and they would hear very closely and clearly who was and was not playing to perfection. That was when one of the regular members sent in a replacement for the job, for naturally there would be a difference in the sound of the band. But not enough for most baritone and alto players to get so upset. But these two did, and Mr Taton's actions showed it. Musicians who replaced regular members of both of the great brass bands knew beforehand that when they were handed the music parts to be played that all the ears in the bands were listening sharply at what they were playing, whether right or wrong. My grandfather Isidore and Mr Taton were subject to much contemptible talk, "Them two old so-and-sos."

Now in later years they both almost went insane over the action of Oscar "Papa" Celestin. After Manuel Perez stopped leading the Onward (for what reason I don't know, I believe his health), Papa Celestin took over the leadership. His dance band was very popular and called the Tuxedo Orchestra. Being the leader, most of the Onward's work was contracted by him, so naturally he was the power—the boss. Well, he announced suddenly before an affair that he was changing the name of the Onward to the Tuxedo Brass Band. The old band members went into shock, panic. All hell broke loose. "Is he crazy?"

"Who the hell does he think he is?"

The Onward name was famous, stood for class, the greatest.

Papa Celestin stood fast and announced, "From this day on the band will be called the Tuxedo Brass Band, and who does not like the change can quit."

The whole band quit. But in a couple of months most were back playing with Papa Celestin's brass band.

Isidore referred to musicians who played jazz music in the many six-piece jazz bands about the city as "routine" musicians. It was a slur. To him, "routine" meant playing by ear, with no music, in the now "classic" jazz pattern: melody, then variations on a theme. All hot jazz bands were now using this set-up, and playing free. If you couldn't read well you could still master this pattern of playing, jazzing a melody: noodling around the theme, doing many things on your instrument with taste and within reason. Once you learned the pattern and played the routine it was OK. The better you mastered the style the greater you became. This style of playing music had become popular, and so many were now playing it. Who cared if you read music? You were free: free to take liberties, free to express yourself from deep inside. The public was clamoring for it. Routine? Sure. But everybody could not master this pattern. Many tried but never could get it just right and master jazz so that they could play with other masters of jazz.

I heard Isidore once say of Bolden, "Sure, I heard him. I knew him. He was famous with the ratty people." I soon learned what ratty people, ratty joints and dives meant: it meant good-time people, earthy people, who frequent anywhere there's a good time, regardless of the location or the element of social class distinction or position. So, ratty music is bluesy, folksy music that moves you and exhilarates you, makes you dance.

One thing I learned very early from listening and watching the actions of my grandfather Mr Barbarin and his friend Mr Adolph "Taton" Alexander, and also my two older uncles who were just getting started in music, and that was, "Never be sure of a music job until you're playing it." The music business is so uncertain and unpredictable. There are so many happenings that can cancel out entertainment. In my years of playing music, the eight-year period as a member of Cab Calloway's Cotton Club Orchestra was the only time I could relax in complete faith that his band bookings were for real, and I cannot recall one cancellation.

The New Orleans brass band and jazz band business was a very serious one. At the Barbarin house I heard discussions, snatches of complaints about music jobs that did not go well or that did not come off as scheduled. My uncles Louis and Paul were having their problems, and old Mr Taton, whom I never saw smile once and who was serious and touchy, would wrinkle up his face as if in agony if another brass band contracted a job or funeral that he and the Onward had expected to play. He would relate in detail how the other musicians got the job, what was the connection, who lied, who connived. He would have a deep grief inside, and at the ending of the calamity Isidore would console him very comfortingly, saying, "Taton, there will be others. The job just was not for us." And almost tearful, Taton would reply, "I guess you are right, Bar-bar-rin."

My uncles came home telling of their problems, telling of different musicians, calling their names. I did not know these many musicians, but was familiar with their names, their reputations. I heard the names of so many places they played, or would play. Being a small boy and not having seen all of New Orleans, I wondered if it was possible to have so many halls and amusement places, but as I grew I began to see all these many places of pleasure. So many musicians stopped playing, died, left town—I heard of them but never saw them in person. And many halls were demolished for newer buildings.

SIX

Barbarin boys and Walter Blue's
death

All Isidore's four sons, Paul, Louis, Lucien and William, were playing and starting to get on the jazz whirl. So naturally I was entangled in this scene. I couldn't escape: all they did was talk, play, dream, eat, sleep, argue, follow music—jazz that is. They knew and discussed everything that was happening about jazz. During the period 1916 to 1920 there was a big demand for jazz musicians. If there was to be a jazz affair in the immediate neighborhood I followed my younger uncles Willie and Lucien to the scene, and watched and listened as they commented on who was playing (good, great, bad or lousy). And they knew jazz. Then I began to hear of the great musicians. They talked of who was away, up North or East, doing great. Who was going away. Who came back.

Sidney Bechet was the topic of much discussion. He would write his family who lived near, a couple of blocks away. They knew when he was in New York City, Chicago, Paris, London, Russia, Germany. I heard tales of how he created so much excitement, admiration and fame for his playing. Nobody at that time was spoken of with the same level of sensation as Sidney Bechet. Listening of Bechet's travels and the great demand for New Orleans musicians who could play well caused me to decide to become a musician.

With Willie and Lucien I began to follow around the neighborhood. I began to absorb what was happening. They were nice to me, their little nephew, who was so naive and curious. I asked question on top of question and got answers on top of answers: the smart and right answers. Don't do this; stay away from there; that's bad; that was good; watch and keep your guard and defence up; that's our friend; they are no good; they look for trouble; if they hit you, tell us, we'll get 'em later.

The first day I went to public school, which was a supposedly rough school in the eighth ward (I lived in the seventh ward), my two uncles played hookey from their school, came by and got in a friendly huddle with the tough bunch at my school. I was introduced to the leaders, who said they would look out for me, which they did from the third grade to the eighth grade. When I graduated I was one of the boys. I was very popular in school, particularly because the larger boys and those who loved music knew that I was related to so many musicians, and they saw me at many social affairs.

When there were music arguments and discussions about who was the greatest they would call me to settle the argument. Many of the school children had relations who played music. When I came to school playing the ukulele I was instantly a celebrity. I started jazz sessions which would get out of hand: swinging, hand-clapping, happy scenes at twelve o'clock, until the stern, serious Miss Fannie Williams, the principal, called me to her office and put a stop to that. She told me not to bring the ukulele to school again.

My uncle Lucien, my mother's brother, was a smart, clever, nerveless youngster, who was active as a bumble bee. He would try anything, would get into things and talk his way out. He was the commander of us three: me and Willie. He would say, "Let's make kites!"

"Let's go to work!"

"Let's go junking!"

"Let's go look for money!"

"Let's go to the bayou!"

"Let's go to the lake!"

"Let's go in the woods!"

"Let's go get blackberries!"

"Let's go by Mrs Barker and get some biscuits!"

"Let's go to the French Market and get some spec's!"

"Let's go watch Jeff Holloway!"

"Let's go hop a freight train!"

And off we would go following Lucien.

Willie and Lucien were forever whistling, imitating the different cornet and clarinet players of that time. They both had good memories of the playing styles of many popular musicians. They would challenge each other: "Whistle like Buddy Petit."

"Whistle like Big Eye Louis."

"Whistle like Manuel Perez."

"Whistle like Walter Blue."

If Lucien said, "Let's go to work," it meant that he had passed some place and saw that some chore or light work was needed: like a pile of bricks out on the sidewalk, a load of sand, some light lumber—things that boys could move. When this happened Lucien did the business and paid us off equally. It was not because we were hungry or poor—no. He liked to have some money, always.

My stepfather and uncles' bakers' wagon would drop off hot fresh French bread every day without fail. All branches of the family believed in eating, and eating enough. The pots on all the family stoves were full or half-full of something good to eat. No jive cooks for this family and its relatives. All the children just had to mention about being hungry and they were promptly fixed a large sandwich, and their young friend also received one. It was sacrilege to have hungry children with empty stomachs around.

Now if we went junking, we each got burlap or flour sacks which were always around, and we walked the neighborhood streets picking up bottles, rags, metals—zinc, brass, copper, lead—anything that could be used second-hand. We would see articles and things of all sorts in people's yards. We would knock on the door and ask for the objects: old beds, old chairs. We made wagons with large, heavy wheelbarrow wheels and hauled the things to a junk-shop, where Lucien bargained (generally successfully), and then there was the equal split-up of money.

If he said, "Let's go look for money!" OK. We three walked a street. Lucien walked the right side scanning the gutter, street and sidewalk; Willie walked the left side, slowly, doing likewise; and I walked the center. Our six sharp, keen eyes missed no area, and we found money almost every time.

We often went to the large French Market to get spec's, as overripe fruits and vegetables were humorously called. The large French Market is about four blocks long. We went to the wholesale section, where the produce was bought, sold, sorted and delivered. There were always the tables where the overripe and spoiled stuff was put. My uncles would somehow always ask the right man for some spec's and almost immediately with their pocket knives would start cutting off the bruised or spoiled part and eating the different fruits as if they were famished, and I would join them. We would eat until we got stuffed and short-winded and then slowly walk home. That was fun for me, but I wondered, sort of scared, what would happen if any of the Barkers had seen me doing this savage devouring of this supposedly rotten fruit. We would eat peaches, pears, plums, bananas, oranges, pineapples, mangoes, grapes, all varieties of summer fruits.

My grandfather Mr Barker liked fruit, but only bought the choicest, the best, from the first-class stands in the market, and there was always a large bowl of sweet-smelling fruit near his kitchen—no spec's. He bought giant ripe sweet watermelons and cantaloups that we feasted on. He knew about melons, which ones to pick from a large pile. So while I gorged myself with spec's with my young uncles I looked about at the people cautiously, so that I could duck or hide or quickly turn away my face and head in case a Barker or someone who knew them should see me eating spec's like an orphan or piccaninny, as colored youngsters who did such things were called.

Lucien was a great persuader. He could talk his way out of rumbles with other youngsters. But not Willie—he had a quick, violent temper. When we met up with young roughnecks and it looked like trouble, while Lucien argued, compromised, appeased and conned the enemy, Willie and I looked about for weapons. Willie picked up anything that he could lift that would wound, maim, kill, cripple. Then he went furiously into battle. Be it a stave, brick, bottle, bucket, large plank, board, iron pipe—anything lethal he would see quickly at hand. He was accused of having a quick temper by the family and most of the youngsters in the neighborhood. He seriously believed, "Fight first, fuss after." When his anger built up inside until he started crying and the blood vessels bulged, he was almost physically uncontrollable. Grown folks—men—had to take hold of him. He was ready to die in combat if he thought that you were taking advantage of him or someone close to him.

There were few paved streets then, and on the mud streets there lay small cobblestones, oyster shells of varied sizes, broken bricks of many sizes, pieces of broken bottles (the bottoms that did not crush easily). When Willie was walking in the street looking down for money he practiced throwing these missiles at targets, and was a sharpshooter or marksman. Many times we would gather in open lots playing marbles or tops. Willie was champ at these skilled games. We would also stand up empty bottles like pins in a bowling alley and use baseball-sized stones for balls, pitching at the bottles from a distance about fifty feet away. Willie was the champ at crashing the group of bottles in all directions.

Then some days Lucien would say, "Let's go to Mrs Barker and get some hot biscuits!" OK. We walked to 1027 Chartres Street, through the long alley into the large yard, up the long steep stairs to my grandmother's kitchen. There we were greeted like long-lost wayfaring prodigal sons. The Barkers, being from the country and not influenced by anything French, never served store-bought bread, that is French or white bread. The family ate homemade bread, biscuits, cornbread, corn muffins, which my grandmother cooked. She used Ballard flour, which was the best biscuit flour at that time. Now her cooking was different from my other grandmother's cooking. Lucien and Willie's mother cooked in the French fashion, my other grandmother cooked country-style. This country cooking was new to my two uncles and they much loved it. Mrs Barker knew what we wanted and would oblige with her food, which was always plentiful. First she would hurriedly make a large pan of wonderful fluffy biscuits. And then there was the dessert: jars of preserves like watermelon rinds, peaches, apples. Then the large jar of molasses for the biscuits: hot biscuits and butter—the best. We at until every biscuit had disappeared. I would naturally get uneasy or restless, but Lucien the promoter used to smile and say, "Thank you ma'am, Mrs Barker, for the nice dinner," and I would kiss everybody. We would walk lazily back to the Barbarin residence, and there my uncles would relate in details about the great feast, especially the big pan of biscuits.

At that time I was too small to hang in the company of Louis and Paul Barbarin, the two older boys, who were young men. The larger brothers by then had decided to become musicians—drummers. They were going through the frustrating musician's apprenticeship, which was especially tough in New Orleans. This strict period was trying on a young musician who was just beginning, because there were so many youngsters grabbing up musical instruments. One of the bitter experiences you had to tolerate in silence was that the old veterans saw to it that a youngster did not get a big head, or that his reputation did not exceed his ability. No matter how well you mastered your instrument in the presence of these veteran pros, the comment was always the same, "Some day that boy is going to make a good musician." This "some day" business would be very unnerving, especially after you had sat in one of the many jazz bands, played well, maybe sensationally, and shook up the listening public. Then you would hear this "some day" statement, said with apparently indifferent expression. But if you looked at the older band members' faces, you could see expressions of contempt, jealousy and fear—of a potential rival.

There was one musician, Sidney Bechet, who as a youngster would come into one of the many dance halls unexpectedly, with empty hands, but with his clarinet apart and three separate bits each in a separate pocket. The usual crowd standing looking and listening at the band and its soloists would applaud, whistle and implore the young Bechet to play. He usually did. Slowly he took the parts of the clarinet and joined them together. His keen musical ear gave him as close a tuning as possible. Then he waited politely until the leader of the band signaled, "Take it!" Then Bechet proceeded to play his own great jazz improvisations to the amazement of the audiences.

On one occasion I was there, second lining, beside the Perseverance Benevolent Mutual Aid Association. It was a Sunday morning at about 11 a.m., and this well-organized society of men were having their annual street parade celebrating one of many past anniversaries. There were two brass bands, the Onward and another, I don't recall the name. My young uncles (who knew all the musicians like boys know baseball stars and teams) mentioned that Walter Blue was in the other brass band. I planned to second line for a few blocks out of sight of my grandfather, who was in the Onward band and forbade all of his boys to second line because it was dangerous on occasions. Police on horseback would sometimes chase the large second line to keep them under control and out of the path of the parade, as their presence was annoying the society members.

I followed my uncles through the crowd of hundreds of spectators, right by the side of the other band and Walter Blue. The band struck up and the parade started. We followed, bouncing along to the great-sounding music and watching the playing and sound of Walter Blue. Then I remember two members of the band taking hold of Walter Blue and helping him to a stoop on the sidewalk. He was laid down and the crowd closed in around the stoop. I tried to get through to see what was happening. Then I heard a familiar commanding voice, "Daniel, git out of that crowd and go home. I'm gonna tell your grandfather!" It was my father's brother. I split for home. I looked back and the parade had turned a corner in the distance, but a crowd was still around Mr Walter Blue.

Later that day the news spread that Walter Blue died while playing the parade. He had eaten in the corner barroom three pickled eggs and some whiskey. After starting to blow his horn, the pickled eggs and whiskey came up and choked him to death. The people who assisted him to the porch should not have laid him down on his back—they should have sat him upright. Walter Blue was a great blues player. He never was given his proper acclaim.

SEVEN

The Boozan Kings

On the sawdust-covered floors of the many New Orleans barrooms, strolling musicians and entertainers were never refused permission to put on their act, as long as they were sober and known. All that was necessary was to walk in and ask the bartender or owner for permission to perform. While shining shoes in the commercial section, which borders on the District, I would see small boys dancing and cutting the fool for tourists, who would throw them coins. I would pass through the District on my way to Canal Street to shine shoes. I saw these small boys open the swinging doors of these honky tonks and say sweetly, "Mister, can we come in and dance?"

And they would enter and start a small camp meeting. After a while they would come out and start arguing over the money. They would be arguing about large coins and paper money. A performance in one tonk earned them more money than I earned with the shoe shine in a whole day. I got to thinking, and a bright idea was born. I would organize a spasm band. There were many spasm bands in the city. They played all sorts of gadgets that produced sounds: musical saws, washboards, spoons, bells, pipes, sandpaper, xylophones, sets of bottles (each with a different amount of water), harmonicas, jews harps, one-string fiddles, guitars, small bass fiddles, tub basses, kazoos, ram horns, steer horns, bugles, tin flutes, trombones, and many others I just can't recall. These performers and musicians were welcomed by the patrons in the joint, although the first time was mainly out of curiosity. "Let's see what this fool's gonna do." If the fool was an artist and performed well, he was always welcome to walk through the swinging doors and perform. Sometimes these performers were hired to keep the joint jumping.

I was then studying the clarinet, taking a few lessons with Barney Bigard until he left for Chicago and the King Oliver band. The ukulele craze was rampant then, and my aunt had a banjo ukulele. She got a corn on her finger and gave it to me. I started practicing day and night for about a month, to the annoyance of my mother and all the neighbors.

Then, like the War Department in a hurry, I drafted five of my friends. I sat them down and related what I had seen happening in the barroom: all the money these boys in the district were earning playing on makeshift instruments. My friends were interested in the money and so I organized a spasm band. I named it the Boozan Kings. The word "boozan" is Creole. The folks spoke of parties as boozans. Someone might say, "So-and-so is having a boozan at her house." The band members were Joe Francis on kazoo, Russel on drums, Herman Henderson on ukulele, Charles Blaine on suitcase, I played banjo ukulele, Clarence Smith played the harp and watched for the police.

The first Saturday evening we made our debut in a barroom in our own neighborhood. While we were playing to an excited audience and going over big, Herman Henderson's father pushed through the crowd, smacked Herman Jr, viciously grabbed him by the back of the neck, and thrashed him all the way home. So we lost one member. Herman's folks were well-to-do; his mother and grandmother were midwives, his aunts were teachers, his father was a mailman. The patrons laughed at the tragic exit of our star musician. We made a killing that night touring the joint—about five dollars apiece. The band members counted all them dimes, quarters, half dollars, nickels, pennies, and a few counterfeit coins we thought (foreign coins, I guess, from colored seamen). After all that loot and the confidential lecture I gave them of our future fortunes to be made, my band unanimously gave me one thousand percent cooperation and respected my wise counsel and leadership.

When I arrived home that Sunday morning, about 2 a.m., my mother was silently waiting up for me. When I walked into the kitchen, where she was sitting drinking coffee like at a wake and with the serious expression of a widow at her husband's bier, she said sharply, "Boy, where you been this time of the night?" I hurriedly emptied my pocket of the coins and spread them on the kitchen table, saying, "Ah been playing music and I made all this money!"

She looked at the many coins and said, "What hall you played at?"

I said, "I didn't play in no hall, I played in different barrooms."

She said, "You got me worried. If you have made up your mind to play music, well, it's alright with me." And she went to bed.

The next day the news had spread in the neighborhood about our success. The band members were celebrities, and every weekend we made the rounds, always welcome, and we came home pockets jingling and shoes full of sawdust.

The members of the band were all excellent shoeshine boys, but the big-money entertaining and the notoriety and the celebrity of musicians made us forget the bootblack scene. We were all wise to the goings-on in the city. We heard all the news on the street corners, listening to the men and larger boys telling of the gossip. We knew how to act in all situations—a sort of jungle instinct—when to speak, when to talk, how to speak, when to leave, when to stay, when to run, when to walk fast or slow, and the classic southern negro proverb, "Keep your eyes and ears open around them white folks, 'cause you never know when they'll change on you. They laugh with you one minute and getcha killed the next minute."

Each Saturday evening we went our rounds we ventured closer to the District. Men would tell us to go to joints where we would make lots of money, and we would go there. Some would take us to dives. Sometimes we would give a concert in front of joints and be invited inside. I was very nervy. I would take the band where small combos were playing. They would watch us perform, glad for the recess. In the negro joints we played relaxed, at home; but in the white joints we were all eyes and ears, and anything could happen. In the colored joints the smiles were pleasant, but in the white joints you saw all kinds of expression.

The southern white supremos would enjoy our music; they got a big kick out of us kids. But every time, without fail, there were descriptive slurs. We were used to hearing them as far back as we could remember. The comments bounced off our ears in torrents, especially when our white audience was boozed up. The common saying amongst our elders was, "Let them poor white bastards call you what they want. Make that money!" As we smiled and entertained the drunks, both men and women reared back and yelled this epithet, "Dem coons sho' can play." And if it wasn't that it was niggers, darkies, Zulus, piccaninnies, Africans, monkeys, gorillas, Ubangies (I learned years later what a Ubangi was—the African tribe that wears a disc in the lips), Ethiopians, tar babies, ink spots. When spoken to individually there was these sharp crisp comments, "You boy/blackie/Sam/Rufus/Rastus/nigguh/monkey/coon/bozo," and so on.

On one occasion a man kept yelling, "Hey blackie! Hey blackie!" I kept on playing, because these remarks slipped off me like water off a duck's back. Then one of the men nudged me and said, "That feller over there is calling you." I looked at the man he pointed to, I guess with an unconcerned expression, and our eyes met. He raised his eyebrows and laughed, saying, "Oh, I'm sorry. You're brown, you ain't black." I kept on playing and he yelled a request, which we played.

Then he looked at each of us. I think he said to himself, "Them niggers is all colors" (we were all tints). Clarence Smith, our hat-passer and police lookout, did have a primitive African physical appearance. He was very dark, had small beady eyes of grey or blue, scarlet-red thick lips, peanut head, large snow-white teeth. He was short, with long arms and short axe-handle legs (legs that bend in the front). He could say, "Thank you sir, thank you ma'm," real sincere and sweet. Those words were covered with molasses when he said them.

One night, as he passed the hat around, he said, "Thank you all nice folks for helping the poor." One of the men laughed and mimicked Clarence, saying very piously, "And the helpless." The crowd laughed while Clarence continued passing the hat. Everybody in the crowd started saying phrases of the needy with southern drawls as they put money in Clarence's hat. "Thank you Lord for helping the homeless/cripples/lame/blind/legless/wretched/orphans/widows/dying/starving." This went on for about ten minutes. The place was in an uproar. Clarence circled the crowd about five times. When the laughing stopped some of the crowd were in tears and going to the toilet. Clarence's hat was loaded with coins. We kept that bit in the act. I took out money and bought Clarence a tambourine and added that to the band. The tambourine helped the income, because people threw money in the tambourine to hear the jingles ring.

Clarence learned to do all kinds of tricks with it. One night we were playing on a street corner and a large group of white tourists were watching us. We were playing *Didn't he ramble*. A tall colored preacher came out of nowhere, grabbed the tambourine from Clarence, and started singing with us. He sang on and on, and then preached a little about how sinful the District was. Then he passed the tambourine around and picked up quite a few coins. He emptied the coins in his hand and started giving us a tongue-lashing about using the Lord's name in vain and singing *Ramble* jazzed up. We listened respectfully with bowed heads and wounded hearts, shamefully. We did not look up. When we did, the Reverend, the tambourine and coins had disappeared in the night air. We came to our senses and looked at one another. Clarence said, "Ain't that a bitch. He took my instrument."

Clarence was quite a comedian. Our best number was a song called *A Chinaman and Mabel*. It was a show-stopper, especially in negro joints. Joe Francis learned it and taught it to the band. I would announce it like this: "For you all fine, nice, kind folk, we will now render that famous song about the Chinaman." Whenever I said

"Chinaman" loud and the joint was not too boisterous, the joint generally became quiet as an undertaking parlor. Everybody would listen attentively. All the old-timers would get serious as we started the song. With my soprano voice I would sing the song very dramatically and sincere. Everybody wanted to hear about this Chinaman and Mabel.

> A Chinaman and Mabel
> Sat down at a table
> Down in a cabaret.
> He wined her and dined her,
> He couldn't be finer,
> But this is what I heard him say:
> "Good night, little girl, good night,
> I hope you git home by the light.
> Your kisses were fine
> With each drink of wine.
> You're pretty, my honey,
> But you can't ever be mine.
> Good night, little girl, good night,
> Keeping you out this late isn't right,
> Because that ring on your finger
> Tells me not to linger.
> Good night, little girl, good night."

The men loved to hear this song, and many times I was asked to repeat the song by the applause. The band became very popular in the joints we played. When we entered, the first request was always, "Sing that song about that Chinaman." I'd hear these comments. "Listen at that kid sing about that Chinaman."

"Dey got a hell of a song they sing about a Chinaman."

"Sing that song 'bout the Chinaman and that whore Mabel."

"The Chinaman spent his money on the bitch, saw she had a ring on her finger, and he wasn't going to spend anymore."

We would pause for a few minutes while Clarence passed the hat, and then many conversations started about the Chinese people. I'd hear good and bad talk about the Chinese. How they minded their business, kept to themselves, and so on.

At that time—1923—Pearl White and Warner Oland were big movie stars. The local theaters featured serial pictures: "To be continued next week . . ." Many of these movies showed Chinese people, who were always villains. There was one Chinese villain called Hong

Kong Harry. He was always stabbing a victim in the back. A very sinister, sneaky character. He had a joint with all sorts of trapdoors, dungeons, falling floors, walls, roofs. He would trick a white victim, drop him through a trick door into a dungeon or cave, and then let a flow of water rush in until it reached the victim's neck.

Continued next week . . .

The white victim would fall in a cave with a huge crocodile or snake, or a lion or other ferocious beast. Harry's accomplices wore pigtails, black oriental costumes, pill-box caps. You would see them smoking long pipes, moving their eyes very mysteriously. One white man would whip dozens of Chinese. The Chinese were forever plotting destruction, splitting heads open with axes, meat cleavers, and all sorts of knives.

We kids would sit on the edges of our seats at the Ivy Theater when the Chinese were handing out all this brutality. They were never shown favorably, and we were all anti-Chinese. We would leave the theater praying that next week the white star would kill all the Chinese in China—especially a female Chinese actress who was real nasty (the older colored folks leaving the Ivy Theater called her Tomato Nose), and the women all wished and prayed that they would love to get their hands on Tomato Nose. "Hong Kong Harry and Tomato Nose, they gonna git it nex' week in the next chapter."

The Boozan Kings became famous and were often playing in the Creole section of the city. We could imitate the songs featured by many of the city's jazz bands. Joe Francis blowing his kazoo could imitate Chris Kelly's solo on *Careless Love*; Kid Rena's *I wonder what became of Joe*; Sam Morgan's *Sammy's back in town*; Papa Celestin's *My Josephine*; Wooden Joe Nicholas's *Make me a pallet on the floor*.

Until the time I picked up the ukulele, stroked the strings and listened to the sound, I had not looked upon jazz music playing seriously. In school I was constantly scratching on the tablets etchings of human heads and bodies, animal heads and bodies, landscapes, and studying the objects and distances in proportion that made up land-scapes. I had learned by practice, challenged myself with watercolors to mix just about any color. I read the labels on paint cans, the ingredients in different paints. Then there were brushes—all sizes. I carefully examined them, did some crude sign painting, helped with painting done by relatives, carefully watched house painters and annoyed them with many questions. I liked the smell of paints, and soon felt that I would do painting for a living. I had decided when the time came to go to work, I would get a job with one of the many painting contractors as an apprentice, learn the trade, and be a painter. I thought of using the roll-on process back then, and wasn't surprised when the rollers were introduced by the paint manufacturers. I was still going to school when the ukulele craze shook up the country. After buying the banjo ukulele from my aunt I annoyed a very smart boy in my neighborhood, Ashton Murray, who studied and played the piano, and also could tune and play the ukulele well. I played and studied that ukulele night and day—took it to school, to bed, everywhere. It was never out of my reach or my sight.

The Boozan Kings became real popular, because the music we created sounded fine, especially the rhythms. Our girls organized a fan club, and called themselves the Boozan Queens. Then the popularity of the Boozan Kings and Queens spread all over the sixth, seventh, eighth wards. Every weekend there were house parties and social functions. Then Wilhemina Bart, a prominent jazz pianist, a lady much respected in the downtown Creole French (colored) section of New Orleans, contacted me and suggested since my Boozan Kings were so popular, would we play a concert at the Frans Amis Hall. I went for that and the band agreed to perform. Now the Frans Amis Hall was New Orleans's most stuffy, exclusive, discriminating social-gathering location in town. This Frans Amis Hall was the meeting house of the real hard-core class of colored people who were mostly mulattos and considered themselves superior to darker-colored people. The attitude of these people had a strong influence in confusing youngsters. Besides the Jim Crow practices of Whites you had these colored people to contend with—their aloof attitudes when you were in their presence, their children playing amongst themselves.

Mrs Wilhemina Bart Deroun was a popular pianist and gave parties, soirees, concerts for the pleasure of her associates. She promoted these affairs at the Frans Amis Hall, which still stands today; it is a spiritual church. Playing for this concert for Mrs Bart and at the exclusive Frans Amis was quite an achievement for the novelty band. We were billed, "The Famous Boozan Kings will perform, etc." The big hall was jammed packed with people. We were acclaimed with much applause and a standing ovation. Mrs Bart paid us, thanked us and said she would give another ball.

But I soon joined the professional ranks.

EIGHT

My graduation as a professional

When I started playing music my knowledge of jazz was mostly of the New Orleans area—what I saw, what I heard, what I came in contact with and participated in. Of course there was plenty of action: dozens of bands, hundreds of musicians, and what I heard on records and what I read in the one music journal. Now of course there was much talk of Chicago, because so many musicians went there seeking fame and fortune. And my greatest inspiration was the regular flow of Armstrong records on Okeh, each to me and the other young musicians a masterpiece in jazz playing. All the alert jazz musicians and local music lovers waited anxiously for each of Louis Armstrong's latest releases, as there was much to learn from these classics. I went to Dave Karnosky's South Rampart Street record store and listened to records and checked on when Louis's next great record would be released and arrive in New Orleans. I was impressed by Johnny St Cyr's great banjo playing on many of Louis's recordings, especially *The Heebie Jeebies*.

I heard many young musicians. I saw them with their instruments going to lessons, going to and coming from jobs. Don Albert, who brought New Orleans style jazz to Texas in 1927 and for many years had the finest orchestra in Texas and the Southwest, was my neighbor, lived across the street opposite my house. We were boyhood friends. We used to talk nothing but music as boys. There were two younger boys nearby who I saw and heard practicing daily, and who later became fine musicians: Rene Hall, the great banjo guitarist and arranger, and Cyril August, a highly respected clarinet and saxophone player. Rene started studying on the violin early and seriously. First becoming a competent reading musician, having learned the correct fingering technique of the violin, he immediately mastered the banjo, surpassing all banjo players with his fast, correct finger technique. In my opinion he was at one time in the thirties just about the greatest banjo player anywhere. The New Orleans jazz fans and citizens marveled at his speed, inventiveness, harmonics. He was just plain sensational, so they nicknamed him "Plectrum." Later he picked up the guitar and mastered that instrument. During his stay in New Orleans he was the "Boss." He went to the Southwest and played with the Ernie Fields Orchestra of Oklahoma City. Had he come to New York City in the thirties I am sure he would have created a stir with his artistry. I heard him in New York in the forties and he sounded similar to Charlie Christian. I never asked him about that, but I still wonder who was playing like who—whether he sat by and listened at Charlie, or Charlie Christian stood by listening at him.

It was a well-disciplined practice by the older musicians in New Orleans to never over-praise or heap compliments on younger musicians, no matter how well they mastered their chosen instrument, lest they get the big head, become pompous, overly proud of themselves. They generally complimented you, saying straight-faced, "Son, you are coming along fine on your instrument, keep up the good work." But then I noticed some deep inside envy, jealousy. But they would praise you to high heavens if you were not on the scene to hear it.

Sidney Bechet was the subject of all kinds of acclaim, because he challenged everybody (all horn men), not directly, but just a little foxily, pointing his horn in the big stars' direction, saying nothing, but asserting, "Blow! Blow! I'm gonna follow you, blowing more, better, greater jazz than you!" Sidney was one of the truly great jazz giants, born and reared in the downtown Creole section of New Orleans. At an early age he became fascinated by the jazz sounds he heard played in the many great jazz bands that paraded and played for the many social functions in the city. At around twelve years of age Sidney got himself a cheap tin flute—priced then for ten cents—and promptly began playing the solos of the great jazz stylists who were idolized in those early days. He became a virtuoso, a wizard on that tin flute. His older brother listened amazed at the virtuosity of Sidney, and bought him a clarinet. With a few lessons from the Tio brothers he was on his way. That clarinet never left his hands, and at the early age of fourteen he was the talk of the downtown section of the city. His exciting playing and complete mastery of the clarinet amazed all the great jazz men.

Around the year 1917 there were many other young exceptionally talented musicians around. And so Bechet and six of these other youngsters organized a jazz band and named it the Young Olympia Jazz Band—Olympia being the name of Freddie Keppard's band, which at that period was considered the best band in the city, the world. Sidney and the other musicians in the Young Olympia Band—Buddy Petit (cornet), Ernest Kelly (trombone), Simon Marrero (string bass), John Marrero (banjo), Mack Lacey (drums)—this young band promptly began a war on all other jazz bands. In street battles on corners, they came, conquered, and departed victors. And as the old-timers recalled this young Olympia Jazz Band, people like Lee Collins, it was stated without a shade of doubt that it had been the raggediest aggregation of urchins the world has ever seen. If they were all undressed and the tattered garments were offered to a junk man, it is doubtful if he would offer five cents for the bundle of rags.

This band did not stay together long, because they were all great stars and all joined the other first-rate jazz bands who played more often, being well-organized and having regular bookings. Sidney went into the red-light district, playing the cabarets, honky-tonks and dives, and soon he was the idol of the underworld, the pet of the celebrated, notorious characters, gamblers, madams, fast girls.

Sidney left New Orleans and went on tour with a road show, with a band led by Clarence Williams, who later became a very successful songwriter and publisher in New York. Sidney then went to Chicago and New York, where he repeated his triumphs. He then journeyed to Europe: London, Paris. He eventually settled in France, where he ruled the roost until he passed on. The French people embraced him as their own "Sidney"; their love for him was so deep and sincere that they named a street after him. They gave him all kinds of high honors. Here was this man who was at home amongst the French people. He spoke French with southern drawl—patois, Creole—introducing many new words and meanings to the French language. The Frenchmen were greatly amused when he spoke.

Youngsters, as they came long, improving on their instruments, heard praise from other youngsters. "Man, I heard Mr So-and-so tell some musician that you are a bitch on your horn." Generally that's how you received encouragement. So that kept you constantly watching all players on your instrument, then comparing their jazz playing with yours. Around the years 1925 to 1930 there were scores of young musicians and many bands all over the city. There were relation bands, friendship bands, close-organized bands that rarely changed personnel. No matter how well you mastered your instrument you would never join these bands—or only in the case of death. Kid Rena used only one drummer during all his playing days: his brother Joe Rena. Joe was with him for a period of about 24 years, until he became a Jehovah's Witness. And that was the case in many other bands: relations and close inter-relations through marriage. That is the main reason why so many musicians left the city when they became great on their instrument. There was no chance of advancement on the local New Orleans scene.

A youngster knew and felt that he was an amateur until he advanced by joining one of the name bands, or being called to replace or substitute for a big-name musician on his instrument. It was rough, because you were constantly watching and waiting for an opening. Musicians in New Orleans eat, sleep, and talk music, gossiping and relaying news, scandal, anything that happens. You could bet in twelve hours everybody in hearing distance would hear the news, generally amplified out of proportion, good or bad. If a youngster was seen playing with a star-name band, everybody soon knew, and anything that happened on the bandstand.

There was on the scene a large group of musicians whom you saw playing about the city, some in small organized bands, many who played part-time and worked at other professions and trades. These musicians never seemed to improve on their instruments; they were indifferent, simple-minded, never tried to get any better, or tried to impress. They played limited repertories: simple songs, nothing complicated or exciting.

I have watched these groups of musicians (referred to as "ham fats" because they were careless and indifferent) enter the place of entertainment, walk to the bandstand, seat themselves, adjust their instrument, see if they are in working condition. Then they sit at attention, barely speaking to each other, waiting silently as the minutes, then seconds count down to starting time. As usual the leader stomps the band off and the band starts playing, with none of them concerned about getting the tune-up note from the pianist. It is just as well, because the beat-up pianos are generally out of tune.

In New York City the bandleaders who were musicians would, from respect for their music, ask for the pianist to hit an A, especially if the gig was a one-nighter. But in New Orleans there is still that same old attitude in jazz—complete freedom: "You play your horn, and I'll play mine; I play what I play and you play what you play. That's that." There is this touchy personal attitude because a jazz band is composed of six or seven musicians, each playing a different instrument, and there is the deep inside feeling that, "My ear knowledge of jazz is as fine as yours," or, "Ah knows when I'm in tune." So to keep peace and harmony each jazz musician generally just plays the job and clams up about the band's sound—unless a member is a very close friend or relative. In an orchestra sections always tune up because of the four sections of instruments: saxes, trumpets, trombones, rhythm. If a member of one of these sections is careless or ignorant of the importance of being in tune he soon knows it.

You saw and heard these musicians. They were relations; they were friends. During this period, say the years 1920 to 1930, I could differentiate talent and no talent. You listened to this very poorly inspired jazz, and inside to yourself grunted, "Ham fat jazz." All New Orleans musicians were, and today are still critical of this jazz element: "Ham fat jazz—and played by ham fat musicians!"

After a period of time as a playing musician you will soon find out what your status rating in the jazz fraternity is. Now these musicians after a period of time found out exactly how they were respected. Jelly Roll has a song he composed called *Big Fat Ham*. It meant you were an extremely poor musician, and most times when you worked it was on your own job, a playing job that you engaged. And it is true, I can recall that many very successful bandleaders have been just ordinary jazz men—nothing special—but very talented in attending to the business dealings in music. I left New Orleans and lived in New York City thirty-five years, which is some time. I came back home to New Orleans, and here there was still a large active group of these same ham fat musicians, playing this very poor, careless jazz. But I guess the saying is true, "Once a pancake, always a pancake."

I talked to a European boy who is now in New Orleans hooked on the old jazz kick. He plays trumpet and his idol is one of these old jazz trumpeters who plays very tame trumpet, but who has made a half-dozen trips to Europe and the Orient. I see this boy tagging behind this old trumpet player. Curiously I asked him why he is so dedicated to the trumpet man. He answered, "I like him because he is such a nice person." I have experienced in my career that most old tame musicians are "nice sweet people." This boy tells me that he digs old jazz music, the old-time jazz, so I suggested he collect and listen to Louis Armstrong's music, Sidney Bechet's music. In my opinion they are the greatest New Orleans jazz soloists. He said he did not think Louis and Bechet were the true exponents of New Orleans jazz, and I saw he was preparing to argue till hell froze over, that Bunk Johnson's band that started the revival in the forties were the all-time greatest band ever to play New Orleans music. I call this a calamity—this cult of international jazz cranks who now worship "the Bunk fallacy."

I still at times find myself in puzzlement as to why and how young aspiring musicians cannot differentiate between genius, greatness, sensationalism, mastery of musical instrument, true pure artistry; how they cannot compare recordings of masters of jazz playing and hacks. Much of the greatest New Orleans jazz of the past is well recorded and documented, and the proof and evidence is on records that are at hand

and easily available for close analysis. I discussed this annoying situation with Louis Cottrell, a fine clarinetist who was very fair in his judgements and views. I said I believed this false-god worship of these current international jazz gods is because they are easy to imitate, and one does not have to really learn the fine points of an instrument to get started in jazz playing. Cottrell laughed and said, "You know, I've been thinking the same thing."

To play like Armstrong, Bechet, Bix, Trumbauer, Miff Mole, Ory, Jelly Roll, Hines, Buster Bailey, Jimmy Harrison, Red Allen, Baby and Johnny Dodds, St Cyr, Noone, Simeon—to play in the patterns set by these great musicians you definitely must study, and do a whole lot of woodshedding.

NINE

Jazz funerals and brass bands

Natives of New Orleans generally stop and watch in wonderment at the physical behavior of tourists and their reaction on witnessing the city's famous jazz funerals. Tourists behave in many strange ways on seeing their first funeral. First, it's the sound of the brass bands, the booming sounds of the big bass horn and the big bass drum. The sad wailing notes of the horns always hit you deep inside. If that soul music don't get to you, something's wrong with you. Then there is always the large crowd of many hundreds of ordinary people who follow the funeral procession from start to finish, because after the deceased brother has been taken to the cemetery and interred pandemonium breaks loose —from silent, respectful, slow marching to the cemetery in a sudden burst of approval, "A job well done," "He was put away nicely," "He's in God's hands." And as the Bible states, "Cry when you enter the world and rejoice when you leave trials, troubles, tribulations behind." Black folks in New Orleans have been practicing this social custom many, many years. Old writers relate of such funerals way back in the slave days.

On the way back from the cemetery some funerals have as many as three bands—according to the popularity of the deceased. Outside the cemetery the bands walk a half block and strike up one of the familiar popular jazz songs, and all hell breaks loose. Surprised tourists will witness this large group of black folks dancing, many under multi-colored umbrellas. People of all sizes and ages, and each dancing his or her thing as the exciting parade marches on. No inhibition: everybody lets his self go out to his full physical extent. The old folks doing their old-time dance steps—cakewalk, turkey trot, shimmy, the wobble, Georgia grind, the peacock strut—and the youngsters doing the monkey, the twist, the dog: these are the same dance steps, but under different names for different periods.

The tourist will see all these black people, and many Whites who are beginning to understand black soul action, following the funerals from beginning to the end. And when the brass bands play the last notes and the huge crowds disperse and disappear and all is quiet again, these questions are asked and answered. "Who was this dead person who had all these people attend his funeral?" Generally, most of the crowd don't know the man; but if he has music at his funeral, he must have loved it and was a swinger. "How long has this been going on—jazz funerals?" "Jazz funerals"—that phrase is new, only a few years old. Tourists who repeat trips to New Orleans always ask jazzmen when, or if there is a jazz funeral scheduled. Then there is the jazzman's comic reply, "No, there's no funeral that we know or hear of today or tomorrow; but if you have enough money we can arrange one—get some cat killed." That always gets laughs.

One old writer relates that with the founding of New Orleans by the brothers Bienville and Iberville there was a body of soldiers with the explorers, and that a trumpet player with the military band died and was buried in the military fashion with music in funeral procession and at the grave site. That occasion happened in the 1600s.

Before the arrival of the big insurance companies New Orleans had organizations called Benevolent Societies; some small, some large. Members banded together in these societies as protection and pre-caution in time of sickness, trouble, death. Tourists visiting New Orleans's dozen or more very old cemeteries can see hundreds of tombs, grave sites, mausoleums bearing the name of the societies, and the sextons have old books and records in many languages—French, Italian, German, Spanish and English. Yet, quite a few of the old societies are still active, especially amongst black folk. The black societies were mostly small operations, and today it is mostly owing to custom and tradition and personal love that they are in operation. In the old days membership dues were very reasonable on the pocket-book—25 cents monthly, rarely more. Nowadays the money in the treasury barely pays the electric light bill, but the remaining members want to exit in style—New Orleans style: the big brass band, three thousand people.

These old societies bear the names (most with a significant title): The Young Men Olympia, The Venus Star, The Young Men Liberty, The Young Men Charity, The Young Men Perseverance, The Young Men Vidalia; and there are the old tombs of many other fraternal societies: Masons, Elks, Knights of Phythias, Oddfellows. Years back they all buried their members with brass band music. In the twenties just about every day a brother was buried in blazing glory. Currently, most jazz musicians are taken down for the last time in style. Jazz funerals and the social club parades keep the brass bands functioning: the Jolly

Boys Caldonia Club, Ruth's Cozy Corner Club and the Olympia Benevolent Society parades are exciting and beautiful to behold. Tourists have a field day, especially if they have cameras. Camera bugs are seen running, jumping, climbing, focusing the lens on obliging paraders emblazoned in colorful expensive clothes.

The club members bedeck themselves with silk- and satin-ribboned streamers, badges, umbrellas, fans, small baskets covered with flowers and ribbons of every color of the rainbow. It is a fantastic sight to behold, and people are all ages, everybody dancing, doing their thing. This sight is real—no put on—and there's no music as exciting as New Orleans jazz brass band music. This scene shakes up all the neighborhood pets, dogs and cats. Dogs get excited, scamper and bark and create commotion at the action; you've never seen dogs act up as like at these funerals and parades. I have seen many jazz dogs get into the act just like their owners—really dance and jump about.

There were many brass bands down through the years: the Excelsior, the Onward, the Pacific, the Eureka, the Tuxedo, which was the old Onward. Henry Allen's Pacific Brass Band, whose home base was Algiers, the westside suburb across the Mississippi River, was a great marching band, on a par with the Onward and Excelsior. The Pacific played for all of the many benevolent societies in the many small towns and villages on the westside of New Orleans. When the larger clubs, societies and union organizations paraded on holidays, like Labor Day, it was a toss-up as to which of these four bands would lead the line of march directly behind the high officials and the grand marshal. When the Oddfellows, Knights of Pythias, Masons, stevedores paraded, the large line of marchers hired all four bands. The bands at the front part of these parades played dignified, heavy, serious marches for the very dignified marching of the officials. The dignity diminished as each band and the marching members passed in view. The large second line generally crowded and did their frantic dances around and about the last band. Many times the members marching to the second and third band would get annoyed at the strict serious music and tell the leader to play some barrelhouse or gutbucket music, and then the battle would be on. The bands would usually be a city block apart and the music would not conflict, so when the fourth band finished a song, the second line would hear the wailing third band and rush to dance to that band. Then the second band would be heard and they would rush up to that band, until the police on horseback would chase everybody back by galloping the horses right in the midst of the second line. Then there would be pandemonium.

These brass bands were highly competitive. The lineups would have, in the first band, Manuel Perez, Andrew Kimball, Ricard Alexis on cornet. The second band would have George "Patat" Moret, Joe Oliver, Freddie Keppard, Third band: Bunk Johnson, Buddy Petit, Mutt Carey. Fourth band: Joe Johnson, Chris Kelly, Tig Chambers. In later years a cornet section would have Kid Rena, Papa Celestin, Red Allen; or Lee Collins, Guy Kelly, Herb Morand; or Kid Howard, Kid Punch, Kid Thomas. It was the custom for each of these great jazz horn men's followers and fans to second line within close hearing distance, interested in only their playing. So there would be clusters of groups following their idol, who could be Bechet, Baquet, Tio, Johnny Dodds, Jimmie Noone if a fan liked a clarinet. Each instrumentalist had his followers, who would boast for months, years, of how their idol blowed on such-and-such an occasion. But everybody acknowledged the fact that the king could be heard all day from ten in the morning until the parade disbanded, screaming in the upper register of his cornet—Mr Manuel Perez.

As the observer recalls, the most exciting form of musical entertainment was not the jazz bands, but the brass bands. The bass beat on the bass drum, beautifully executed by Black Benny Williams, Ernest Trappanier, or Albert Jiles would suddenly silence a crowd of seven or eight thousand loud and boisterous pleasure seekers, all ears perked maybe a minute, anxiously waiting for the lead trumpet to blow the three double eight notes, ta ta ta ta ta ta, signaling the band members who were scattered nearby, having wandered among the crowd. Characters like Bunk, Buddy Petit, Chris Kelly, Red Happy would be in the nearest barroom jiving some sporting woman, drinking to everybody's health, and ruining their own. The bandmen who didn't indulge would be corraled by groups of admirers, answering questions on the merit and playing ability of the stars. It was the greatest thrill to a kid to get to hold the instrument of a musician whom he idolized. The most miserable feeling a youngster in New Orleans can experience is to be in the classroom studying when he hears a brass band approaching, swinging like crazy past the school and then fading off into the distance. You will witness a lot of sad expressions in that room. Now if it happens to be lunch-hour recess—12 to 1—when the bell rings at 1 p.m. a lot of seats will be vacant, that is in schools in the bus-out sections of New Orleans. That's an honest fact, as this observer was guilty three or four times. The music would excite and move you to such an extent, that when you would realize it, you had second lined maybe ten or twenty blocks from school.

My maternal grandfather, Isidore Barbarin, was one of the top brass band musicians, originally a cornetist who changed to alto horn and mellophone on the advice of doctors. They told him the cornet was too strenuous. I guess they were right, as he was still very much alive at the age of ninety. Isidore worked for undertakers as a carriage driver, most of the time for Emile Labat and Laudumiey, the Creole section's most successful burial establishments. Emile Labat owned two famous horses, the most beautiful in New Orleans. They always pulled the hearse, which was driven by a very old, dark, solemn man who never smiled. His name was Joe "Never-Smile." On occasions when the widow was sincere in the sorrow, the undertaker would suggest that the horses be draped with a beautiful lace covering. If the deceased was grown, the covering was black; if a child, white. The fee for that was $15 to $20 extra. It gave the funeral procession a very solemn look—in fact, the spectators felt extra sad: "They's sure putting so-and-so away in fine style."

Now, getting back to Joe Never-Smile and the two horses: it was known throughout New Orleans and vicinity that these two horses cried on certain occasions, that is, if the deceased person was going upward and not below. It was a mystery to everybody. On one of my trips to New Orleans I casually asked grandfather what the gimmick was. He said Joe Never-Smile was a very slick character. Joe always kept a bottle of onion juice. In his spare moments Joe would buy some onions and squeeze the juice into the bottle. Just before leaving for a funeral he would pour the juice on a cloth and wipe the horses' eyes so the tears would flow. He did this while no-one was around, as Emile Labat would have raised hell. Labat was a humanitarian and kind to his animals.

Since Isidore worked for Labat and Laudumiey, he had advance information on all Negro deaths and the condition of the sick and what societies they were members of. It is a very interesting and very clever tie-up. The doctor, undertaker, commissary of the society (who visited the sick and officiated as grand marshal at the funeral) and the brass band leader were all in cahoots. All sorts of espionage was employed when a sick brother was at death's door. The Onward and, later, the Tuxedo Brass Band played most of the funerals and parades due to Isidore and Taton Alexander. But there was keen rivalry from another great brass band, the Excelsior, which had a tie-up with other undertakers. Uptown it was the Eureka, led by Willie Cornish on trombone, an original member of Buddy Bolden's band, a very rough, nasty talking gentleman, who quit the union and invited the officials to kiss the back of his lap. All through the years they were called a bunch of scabs, but they were always on the scene when there were two or more bands in the large parades, like the Balls Club parade, San Jacinto Club parade, Carnival parade, Labor Day parade and large picnics at the fairgrounds and other amusement areas. Later on Percy Humphrey took over the leadership of the Eureka, and it became acknowledged as one of the best New Orleans brass bands playing strict to the tradition.

Today there are five or more brass bands that can be engaged on a moment's notice for a funeral or parade: the Onward Brass Band, Harold Dejan's Olympia Brass Band, the Young Tuxedo Brass Band, the Majestic Brass Band or Doc Paulin's Brass Band. And when the tourists see these brass bands, it's more likely that most of the players are carrying on the heritage and tradition that only lives on in New Orleans.

I heard a tourist couple ask a grand marshal at a funeral, "This dead man must have been quite a big figure to rate a big funeral like this, huh?" The answer was the usual one, "Oh no, he was just an ordinary fellow, an old porter who worked at a bank for forty-five years. He was a paid-up member in the old society, and that's what the society does—turn out with music for all the members who wants it. If you was a member of the society, we would turn out for you. In fact, it's the brass band music that draws all the people. Now, when people hear the band music, they grab up an umbrella for the sun or rain and come on out and get with it—a whole lot of free action and fun."

The tourist asked again, "All these umbrellas these people are dancing with—does the umbrella have some meaning?" The answer again was, "Yes, it shades the sun and shields the rain, and you can do tricks with the umbrella. Also Chinese and African people have umbrellas at funerals for some sacred reason; I saw that when I was a seaman." The tourist asked again, "I guess the umbrella goes way back in history?" The grand marshal shook his head, annoyed at the conversation, and said as he walked off, "When Noah built the ark and it rained forty days and forty nights, do you think Noah could get all them animals on the ark bareheaded, without some kind of umbrella?" He walked off, not looking back to the line of society members and the brass band. He blew his police whistle, then the bass drum hit, the band struck up *Closer Walk* on the solemn march from the church to the cemetery.

I thought, "These tourist people have never witnessed something like this before—the New Orleans Jazz Funeral, only in New Orleans."

Tourists, if they care, are always made extra welcome by the ushers as soon as they enter any of the many small Protestant churches. It is generally an experience of natural folk drama that will touch you deep down in your insides. When the funeral cortege leaves the undertaking parlor or the home and arrives at the church for the service (if the deceased has a church service; some don't—the body is blessed sometimes in the funeral parlor); when the jazz funeral arrives at the church, most of the second liners, the huge crowd of people who follow the music, rarely enter the church to see and hear the service. Most of them always make a hasty dash for the nearest barrooms, and there is the mad dash for cold drinks to cool off, as the sun is most times hot and the air is humid. The crowd has a carnival atmosphere. The organ music and the gospel music and the dynamic preaching of death, sin, repentance, and serious warning of Bible prophecy and the sad laments of the relatives will really shake a sinner up. It is the practice of the preacher to direct his gospel message looking the notorious characters dead straight deep in the eyes, so it's usually just the immediate relatives and close friends who sit in the front-row pews.

To most of the second liners who take part in these jazz funerals, dancing and frolicking about, grief for the deceased does not move or affect them deeply. They see the whole slow drama of the funeral carried or acted out; it's not new, or the first time. They know that the efficient funeral directors perform that duty to the letter with dignity. They have all heard the preaching of, "Dust to dust we must return." And again the corpse is a box of clay, no longer a life. Everything humanly possible must have been done to prolong the life. It was God's will—his time to go—all the lamenting and outward grief can't bring him back. Everybody must go through the last act. There's the one classic comment, "They sho' laid him out nice," and the common remarks, "Just like he's sleeping"; "He looks bad in that coffin"; "He must have suffered"; "Lost a lot of weight"; "That don't look like him."

What tourists will witness is the last public appearance of the dead man—his last curtain call on the stage of life. I have gone inside churches and witnessed quite a few of these jazz funeral sermons. I dig them because you don't forget them very easily. There was the sermon for a well-known notorious fellow, Manuel Jimmy "Sweetie Pie" Green. Sweetie Pie was a real swinger, a high liner—big timer. He owned two taverns and partnership in a few others. He traveled about day and night always in a new shiny cadillac car—the big models. He wore the best of fashions, latest styles. Everything he wore looked always new. Sweetie Pie was just an ordinary black man, nothing handsome or special physically, but the clothes and the cadillacs and the big thick wad of green money he always carried and peeled off made people take notice. His taverns did good, steady business, because Sweetie Pie was well liked and popular. None of his steady clientele ever sat around thirsty if he knew it, or saw a long-standing empty glass. The rumors were that he did not like to sleep long, did not get enough rest, and he died in his sleep; his heart just stopped.

The minister looked from the pulpit down into the huge engraved bronze casket, shook his head sadly. "Friends, we're gathered here for a very sad occasion. Here lies the remains of our dear friend, Jimmy Green. He was not a church-going man, but each and every day he did many good deeds that were so Christian-like. He helped the poor, fed the hungry, sheltered the homeless, aided the sick, comforted the dying, and never refused charity. I asked him countless times to come to church services and give Almighty God one or two hours on Sundays. He would say, 'Reverend, I'll try and come next Sunday, I promise.' He never did, but would dig in his pocket and hand me twenty, thirty dollars and say, 'Put this in the basket Sunday.' A few years ago an old church organ went bad. Somebody told Jimmy. He saw me and called me, saying, 'Reverend, I heard that you need a new organ. Is that right?' I answered, 'That's right, son.' He said, 'Would you object if I got you a new organ? I know the money I make is sinful money, but you see, money is money; it passes from Christian hands to sinner's hands. If you feel it's OK, I will buy you the organ. Here's five hundred dollars. Have your organist pick out the model you want for your church. And I'll try to come to service Sunday.'

"Now, that beautiful organ that's sitting down at the side of this pulpit cost three thousand dollars, and Jimmy paid for the organ cash. I can go on telling of the Christian deeds that Jimmy did for hours. Jimmy once told me, 'Reverend, I am on one corner selling alcohol to sinners, and you are on the next corner fighting sin and saving souls. When I look at your church I get upset inside—sick.' I told Jimmy, 'Son, relax yourself and count your blessings. You are a good man, and remember, Satan will give you this whole world for your soul, but keeps you running.'

"Now Satan the evil one never sleeps; he is constantly on the prowl for working up his iniquities. He will shower you, if you let him, with an abundance of worldly materialistic wealth: with fast money, fast beautiful women who dash to your beck and call, and false friends who will seek you out. And like the sinning folks talk, Satan puts you in the trick bag. He gets you into all sorts of devilment: wild parties, wild people, sin dens, gambling joints, jailhouses and penitentiaries. All that fast living, all day and all night, it's too much for the human body; dressed up in all these expensive clothes you get so you only think about your body and completely forget your soul, and bye and bye your body weakens and your heart gives up.

"I've prayed for and with so many dying sinners. It's so sad and pitiful to hear them pray, 'Oh Lord, please have mercy on my soul.' Now here lies the mortal remains of very popular Mr Green. He was not an old man, but just in the prime of life. You see, he had a sort of magic touch: everything he seemed to touch turned to gold. Now, will the choir sing for Jimmy, and may his soul go on to glory and rest in peace. Please sing sweetly *Precious Lord take my hand* as I read from James, iv: 14–15:

> Whereas ye know not what shall be on the morrow. For what is your life? It is even a vapor, that appeareth for a little time, and then vanisheth away. For that ye ought to say, if the Lord will, we shall live, and do this, or that."

The musicians who most times join the crowd of second liners at the bars will start back to the church. After a length of time they seem to feel the funeral services are coming to an end. The crowd always follows the musicians back to the church. As the pallbearers carry the casket slowly and carefully out of the church the band strikes up softly and slowly *What a friend we have in Jesus*, as one of the great gospel hymns. All hats and caps are removed.

This is the last exit for Jimmy or any other of the late brothers. Now there's the slow march to the cemetery if it is in the city. If not, or if the burial place is way out on the outskirts, there is the custom of turning the body loose. Turning the body loose, the society members, band and second liners open up and silently let the funeral cars pass through as the hearse passes. All who are near tenderly pat the hearse, saying sadly, "Goodbye, Jimmy"; or "Goodbye, Sam," etc. Then the cars sort of speed off. In a few minutes the big bass drum strikes three extra loud booms and the band starts swinging *The Saints*, or *Didn't he ramble*, or *Bourbon Street Parade*, and the wild, mad, frantic dancing starts, and the hundreds of all-colored umbrellas are seen bouncing high above heads to the rhythm of the great crowd of second liners—tourists who can feel the spirit. All traffic stops on the way back to some popular bar in the near neighborhood. It's the greatest real-live free show on earth.

TEN

Feudin' and a-fussin'

There were so many musicians, and everybody had idols and rivals. They were from uptown, downtown, front o'town, back o'town, and the outskirts of town. Everybody watched everybody, and they silently listened to one another. The idols were listened to enviously and they were worshiped. The youngsters would patiently wait for the opportunity to catch a star off-guard or in poor shape before a crowd, and cut him down when the occasion presented itself. A star could easily lose his reputation and his following as a result of a poor performance at an affair. When these contests would occur the news spread and the battle was discussed all over town for months and years. "So-and-so made so-and-so look and sound bad."

"It was a hell of a battle."

"I felt so sorry for so-and-so."

While playing with Lee Collins and David Jones's Astoria Stompers we met Kid Rena's band at the corner of Conti and Roman, one of the famous street corners which is noted for many band battles. This neighborhood is a thickly populated Negro neighborhood. A huge crowd gathered. Kid Rena lived in a house which was near the corner. Three squares away, on Robertson Street, was the red-light district, and as the two bands battled, the music drew dozens of whores in their uncouth dresses to the scene. Kid Rena was the king trumpet player, and his six-piece band was acknowledged the best in town. On this Sunday afternoon he stood up in the truck and blew his best, but Lee Collins played a half-dozen tunes which were currently popular on records by Louis Armstrong. These trumpet solos were considered phenomenal at the time. Lee stood up in the truck and angrily blew in the direction of Kid Rena *Cornet Chop Suey, When you're smilin', Savoy Blues*—he blew his solos exactly as on the records. The crowd screamed and applauded. Kid retaliated with the old traditional hits, *Panama Rag, High Society, Careless Love, The bucket's got a hole in it.*

As the battle progressed the applause became louder for Lee and softer for Rena. Finally all the applause was for Lee. Rena's followers did not want to appear ridiculous by applauding for the beaten Rena so they applauded for neither; they just stood and frowned at the sight of their idol, beaten. Lee closed the battle with *When you're smilin'*, and the promoter, Prof. Sherman Cook, told the truck driver to drive off, which he did.

The crowd screamed and whistled as our truck slowly moved through the large crowd of about two thousand people who had gathered. The truck went in the direction of the red-light district, followed by the loudly dressed notorious whores, who had been dancing their vulgar dances all through the battle, and hundreds of boys and men who could enter the forbidden district (it was not frequented by decent women and girls). We finished playing the advertisement, followed by hundreds of women and men of the district, as the truck slowly moved from corner to corner, and Prof. Cook sat on the tailgate of the truck with a large megaphone and preached to a crowd of how great the dance would be. He also told of the great battle of music which had just taken place and told that Lee Collins had won over Kid Rena. "Lee Collins has blown Kid Rena away!"

I asked Lee why he had been so angry at Kid Rena, for I knew that they were childhood friends, and had seen them together many times at barrooms having friendly chats while drinking together. Lee said, "I've been waiting for that chance for six years—waiting for the opportunity to cut Rena."

I said, "Why, ain't you all friends, and he's from downtown?"

Lee said, "One time Rena caught me in a truck on a corner with a pick-up band. He knew then that I could not play as good as him, but you think he would pull off and not embarrass me like most great leaders would do when they saw the other band was mediocre? No, he insisted that the trucks stay and battle, which humiliated me and the youngsters in my truck. The crowd only applauded for Rena. He acted as if he did not know or recognize me. He saw me stand up and do my best, and he knew that I was no match for him, but he just took advantage of me. So that's why I tried to blow him in the Mississippi River today."

Later I asked one of the musicians who had been in Kid Rena's truck that day why Kid Rena had not played any of Armstrong's songs that were on record and so very popular, for every other trumpet player (especially the younger ones) were copying Louis's style and featuring his sensational solos. I was told that Rena had said he would copy nobody, and asked why he should copy Louis Armstrong when Armstrong used to ask him questions when they were both in the Jones band at the Waif's Home for Boys. He said Louis was trying to play a peck horn when Rena was playing cornet in that band. "And because Louis was up North making records and running up and down like he's crazy don't mean that he's that great. He is not playing cornet on that horn; he is imitating a clarinet. He is showing off and he's gonna bust a vein in his neck screaming on that horn." (Rena's remarks were in the true New Orleans attitude towards competition.)

There has always been rivalry and keen competition between the musicians and performers of each section of New Orleans. There were countless places of enjoyment that employed musicians, not including private affairs. There were balls, soirees, banquets, weddings, deaths, christenings, Catholic communions and confirmations, and picnics at the lake front and out in the country. There were hayrides, advertisements of business concerns, carnival season (Mardi Gras). Any little insignificant affair was sure to have some kind of music and each section engaged their neighborhood favorites: Joe Oliver, the cornet player around the corner, or Cheeky Sherman and somebody's piano, or Sandpaper George whose pockets were always loaded with different grades of sandpaper and who said, "Good music must have variety; different music, different grade of sandpaper." Hudson on toilet pipe (now called the bazooka), George Picou on kazoo (a kazoo inserted into an old E flat clarinet which he fingered as he blew). This Picou was the brother of Alphonse Picou. He was a member of the Roody Doody Band, which was a spasm band. The headquarters of this band was a notorious barrelhouse called the Roody Doody. When you entered the Roody Doody the strong scent of stale wine soaked in the sawdust on the floor greeted you—you became intoxicated. The band entertained there on weekends. Slow Drag Pavageau played a small homemade bass fiddle in this band.

I have compiled a fairly good account of some of the many musicians who once played around New Orleans. It would be near impossible to attempt to list them all. I would just start asking about clarinet, cornet or piano players when with a group of musicians, and that would start a heated debate, somewhat like a tobacco auction. These musicians would recall dozens of forgotten musicians whom they regarded as great, and they would argue at great length over their talents. Here's an example: they claim that Penn, a banjo player whom I never knew or saw, was the greatest they had ever heard, fast and jazzy as lightning, able to play classics and to read anything on sight. He blossomed forth during the Depression, 1930 to 1935, and was the leading soloist and star of the W. P. A. Concert Band. I was told to ask any member of that band of two hundred of New Orleans's finest musicians. I asked about him, and everybody verified his greatness.

Another was Joe Johnson, a cornetist. It is claimed that he was in a class with Joe Oliver, Armstrong, Petit, Bunk, Keppard, and was highly respected by all.

There was Jimmy Williams, a clarinetist, who on more than one occasion extended Sidney Bechet to the point of busting a blood vessel.

There was Blind Freddie, who was a great clarinetist, highly respected, but his blindness hampered him. He also played great harmonica. A great boaster, like Jelly Roll.

There was Lil Dad, a great banjoist.

There was Mack Lacey, the best of the young, second generation of drummers, after Vigne, McMurray, etc.

There was Eddie Walker, a great drummer, who sailed from New Orleans during World War I on a ship loaded with mules for the US Army. The ship was sunk at sea by German submarines, and he and the mules went down to the bottom of the ocean.

There was Cleo Babe, another great bass player. He wanted an expensive bass fiddle, so he joined the Merchant Marines during World War II. The oil tanker he sailed off on was sunk in the Gulf of Mexico one hundred miles from New Orleans by submarines. The ship can be seen on occasion in the clear, shallow water. He was a real happy and jolly fellow.

The truly great forgotten man is David Jones (clarinet and saxophone). He was last living on the West Coast. Armstrong spoke of his great talent and showmanship. What a story he could tell. I worked with the Collins–Jones band in 1928, and he was a sensation everywhere we played. Jones went from St Louis to New York City with the Missourians. He created much excitement with smooth variations all over the tenor saxophone. This caused musicians to stop slap-tonguing on the tenor—and cease that "plap-plap" novelty noise that some saxophone players used to make. With his New Orleans style variations, running changes up and down the horn, he introduced something new to New Yorkers: harmonic explorations.

As a youngster I went all over New Orleans, and still did not get to know personally all the many musicians. I would see bands, six-piece bands, playing on trucks during my era there, and never see their faces again. It was a very confusing scene. These bands would be playing good jazz. I would remember them, but not their faces or anything real personal about them. This I saw many times. I am not nearsighted or farsighted and wasn't drinking and can remember faces, but damn if I would see them again. I would watch these bands on the trucks or wagons play on a corner before a large crowd to advertise some affair. The crowd would look on, enjoying the music. When they finished playing they drove off and the crowd dispersed. Nobody commented on any member of the band; they just walked off. I am sure other musicians will tell you the same thing.

Chris Kelly was a master. He played more blues than anybody I ever knew. In those days there was a caste system in New Orleans. It's died out now. Mulattos, Quadroons, Octaroons, all those different people in New Orleans had different halls. You went to them according to your family standing or your background, or where you felt welcome—or you didn't go there. That's how it was. They had those speakeasy peekholes at the dance hall. You would go to the hall, to dance, and presented your invitation. The man was watching and if you didn't belong, you didn't get in. He didn't care who you came to see there, if you weren't in that groove, you couldn't come into the hall. Each one of those caste systems had its own trumpet player. Chris Kelly played for those blues-loving, real primitive cane-cutting people; people who worked in the fields, who worked real hard, and who wore those box-backed suits, hats with two-colored bands on them, and shoes with two-dollar gold pieces in the toe (when the sun was shining it would light them up). Chris Kelly played for those people. They would give a ball at the New Hall, which was the Young Men of Charity Hall. Chris always had three or four stooges with him. He would never have to carry his horn or anything, because they idolized him.

Sam Morgan used to have a band that would go from New Orleans to Mobile. If you went on the road with Morgan you would play Bay St Louis, Pensacola and Mobile. You would stay in Mobile and play Friday, Saturday and Sunday. You would do the same thing when you came back, when you would go around through Bogalosa. I made a couple of trips like that with Sam. Now Mobile had a great musical influence. Cootie Williams, Ed Hall, Dick Fullbright and others came from there in Ross's band. That band came as far as New York where, like so many bands, it fell apart. Chris Kelly used to go and play in Mobile, where they had the same caste system as in New Orleans. He played a dicty dance in Mobile one night and played nothing but barrelhouse, with the plunger. He was the first one I saw play with the plunger. New Orleans never featured it, but Chris could play with the plunger and he played church music, especially *Swing low, sweet chariot.* He really moved the people. He should have been a preacher. But he preached so melodiously with his horn that it was like somebody singing a song. And he would go into the blues from there. When he went to Mobile and played like that, Sam Morgan and others lost their popularity. The people there only wanted Kelly.

Chris would come on the job with a tuxedo on, a red striped shirt, a black tie, a brown derby, and a tan shoe and a black shoe; whatever he picked up in the house before he left, that's what he wore. Nobody said anything to him because they wanted to see him. He would work all the little towns, like Chalmette, Louisiana. He worked quite regularly and always made the job. He talked a real broken patois, African almost. The Creoles couldn't understand him. They didn't like him and his music, because he played for what was supposed to be the bad element. When he would play a street parade all the kitchen mechanics would come out on the street corners, shaking. The Creoles would hate to see that. I used to hang around him and try to sit in his band, but he would look at me with a straight face; he knew my uncle was Paul Barbarin and he knew my grandfather. Everywhere he played they had to fry fish and have gumbo especially for him. He wouldn't eat just anything, because he was suspicious. He would bring red beans and rice or chicken in his bucket. King Oliver was suspicious too. They wouldn't eat anybody's food, but they had to feed their band. That was in the contract: for four- or five-hour jobs, musicians blowing hard could get real hungry.

When my grandfather Isidore Barbarin heard the name Black Benny, his face would light up in a happy smile. Ernest Trappanier, who was considered the all-time great brass band bass drummer, would send Benny to play in his place in the band. Ernest Trappanier was an exceptionally handsome man and was usually kept busy with many other chores, mainly lonesome ladies. The polite Creole members of the Onward Brass Band were constantly annoyed by the belligerent, sarcastic second liners, who would get carried away by the music and dance in the path and in and about the musicians. The musicians were cautious about talking up to the thug second liners, because when the band would stop at some corner bar while the society members went about the business of the occasion, the thugs would look surly and threatening at the band members. Naturally, the bass drummer and his rhythms would attract the second line like bees around honey. Trappanier would have to watch his stuff and maneuver around the cluster of frantic, screaming, leaping whirling dervishes. This scene is the most vibrant, extrovert show on earth. My grandfather laughed because the second liners had their match with Benny, who was once a second liner. His beater was extra heavy, a blackjack, and when the cluster of thugs danced and pranced in Black Benny's path, he would beat heads as well as drums, and there would be dozens of second liners on the ground holding their heads, backs, shoulders, arms, backsides, not knowing what had struck them. When there was a challenge somebody would take Benny's drum as the band marched on, and Benny would join in a brutal fracas.

Black Benny, on being arrested for one of his many infractions of the southern police department laws, would tell the rookie cop, "Don't worry about it, I'll be down to the police station later. Just tell Captain Jackson or Captain Podean, I'll be down there," and he would walk off hurriedly, to the embarrassment of the young rookie policeman. Benny's offenses were usually minor, as they were involved with Negroes, i.e., beating a gambler, smacking a hustler, pummeling a streetwalker, half-strangling a girlfriend, stomping a bartender, threatening an owner of a honky-tonk, half-killing a neighborhood bad man, commanding a couple of kid punks to kneel down and pray loudly Our Father's prayer as long as he cared to stand over them while a large crowd looked on. If a trollop was sick, he would get medicine from the drugstore, food from the grocer, fuel from a peddler, clothes from a second-hand store, and just walk off with the merchandise while the merchant screamed after him. If the shouts were too curt and nasty, Benny would suddenly turn back and make a ferocious stampede for the screamer, six foot six inches, 200 pounds of primitive African prime manhood, and there would be silence as he turned and went on his way.

There were two brothers who lived across the Mississippi in the weird and exciting little town of Algiers, Louisiana. They were Buddy Johnson and his younger, happy brother Yank Johnson. Both of these men were highly respected as first-rate " 'bone blowers." Mr Buddy Johnson was a member of the Onward Brass Band when I first laid eyes on him. He was highly respected by all the members of the great Onward Brass Band and by all jazz musicians and second liners. When I first met Mr Buddy in 1920 he was an elderly man, I'd say about fifty years of age. Mr Buddy was always smiling and seemed perpetually happy playing in the Onward Brass Band. His happy behavior was a great lift to me in my daily puzzlement at the New Orleans Jim Crow social scene. Here was a great man laughing and playing his horn, and not fretting about nothing; old, healthy, short, real dark, and respected by the Creoles in the great Onward Brass Band. My grandfather would smile when Mr Buddy Johnson's name was mentioned; he would smile proudly with a sort of deep, inner secrecy. "Buddy is the greatest parade and reading trombone player who ever placed a 'bone to his mouth."

The acknowledged king of the trombone, as accepted by serious New Orleans jazz lovers, was Kid Ory. But here's the word. When Kid Ory arrived in New Orleans the real, true masters of that particular style of slippery, sliding, smearing and animating, a sort of comical playing on the 'bone, were a dozen of 'bone players who were in competition with flashy drummers, screaming clarinets, monkeyshine banjo players, bowing and slapping bass players. Such masters of burlesque on the 'bone were Ambrose, Jack Carey, Joe Petit, George Fields, Willie Cornish. Frankie Dusen, Nory (Honore Dutrey, nicknamed Nory—it rhymes with Ory). Ory was sharp-witted and clever. He grabbed all the gimmicks on the 'bone, and cunningly flabbergasted the patrons in New Orleans and Chicago so masterfully with the 'bone tricks, that the folks screamed, "Oh, Mr Ory!"

Mr William Marrero, respectfully called Billy Morand, was acknowledged by all the musicians and bass players as the greatest bass violinist. The happy and ever-smiling "Mr Billy," as everybody called him, was the leader and manager of the Superior Jazz Band, considered by many the best jazz band in New Orleans around 1910. He taught Pops Foster, Wellman Braud, Al Morgan and most of the best bassists. He was a rhythm section in himself, a show. People crowded about him six deep to watch him and his syncopation. The Superior Band consisted of Bunk Johnson, Walter Bundy (drums), Buddy Johnson (trombone), "Big Eye" Louis Nelson (clarinet), Peter Bocage (violin), Richard Payne (guitar). There were many battles between the Superior and Imperial bands. Mr Billy's four sons, Simon (bass), John (banjo), Lawrence (banjo), and Eddie (bass), were considered the best on their instruments. Simon came to New York City in 1930 and worked at the Nest Club with the small band of Harry White, who once played with Duke Ellington and Cab Calloway. Harry used to marvel at Simon's playing. Simon did not like Harlem and returned to New Orleans. McKinney of the Detroit Cotton Pickers begged Simon to join the Cotton Pickers, because Duke had Braud and Calloway had Al Morgan sparking their stiff rhythm sections. Simon left, saying, "I don't like New York City because I get nervous, 'cause all these big tall buildings look like hospitals." The Nest was packed nightly with New York bass tuba players watching Simon pick the fiddle. The vibration would shake the bandstand.

Danny's uncle Lucien Barbarin, drummer and entertainer

Louis Arthidore, the early clarinet virtuoso, whose sister married Danny's grandfather Isidore Barbarin

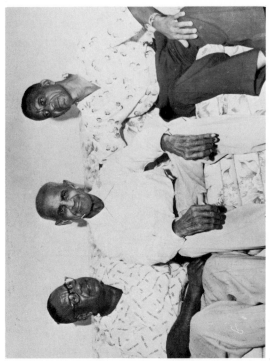

Above: Isidore Barbarin (centre) with his sons Paul (left) and Louis (right)

Left: Danny flanked by his grandfather Minor Barker, and mother, Rose Barbarin Barker, in the late 1930s; Louis Barbarin, rear, right

Courtesy Louis Barbarin

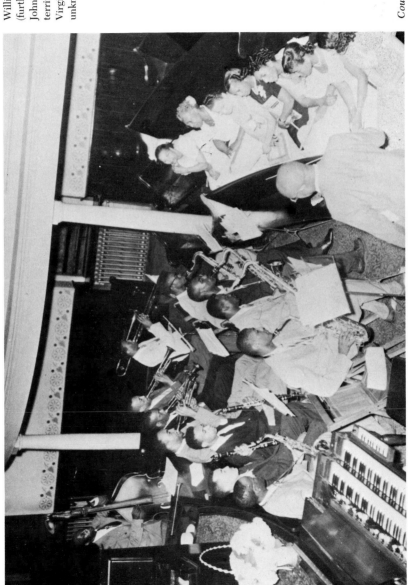

William Barbarin, Sr, on trumpet (furthest from camera) with Johnson's Happy Pals, a noted territory band of Richmond, Virginia; other musicians unknown

Courtesy Louis Barbarin

Danny with Orville Brown's band in New York: Sam Utterbach (trumpet), unknown (drums), Carl Frye (alto saxophone), unknown (tenor saxophone)

Jelly Roll Morton outside the Rhythm Club in New York, mid-1930s

Lucky Millinder and the Mills Blue Rhythm Orchestra in the Roseland Ballroom, New York, 1938: Billy Kyle (piano), Johnny Williams (double bass), Trevor Bacon (vocals), Danny Barker (guitar), Walter Johnson (drums), Charlie Shavers, Sweets Edison, Andy Gibson, Carl Warwick (trumpets), Tab Smith, Benny Williams (alto saxophones), Harold Arnold (tenor saxophone), Fernando Arbello, ? Rocks, Eli Robinson (trombones)

Danny with Cab Calloway's Orchestra in the Strand Theater, New York, 1943: personnel includes Shad Collins, Jonah Jones, Paul Webster (trumpets), Keg Johnson, Tyree Glenn, Fred Robinson (trombones), Dave Rivera (piano), J. C. Heard (drums), Milt Hinton (double bass), Al Gibson, Hilton Jefferson, Rudy Powell, Bob Dorsey, Ike Quebec (saxophones)

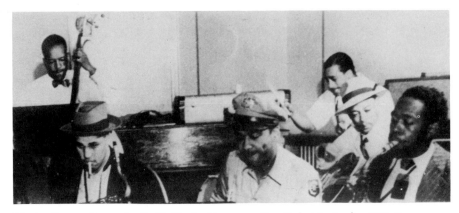

The Apollo recording session for Sir Charles Thompson, New York, 4 September 1945: Jimmy Butts (double bass), Dexter Gordon (tenor saxophone), Buck Clayton (trumpet), J. C. Heard (drums), Danny Barker (guitar), Charlie Parker (alto saxophone)

The Cab Jivers, Chicago, 1945: Milt Hinton (double bass), Danny Barker (guitar), Al Gibson (clarinet), Buford Oliver (drums), Tyree Glenn (vibraphone), Jonah Jones (trumpet), Ike Quebec (tenor saxophone)

I will give you a list of the Marreros, Barneses, Fraziers, and Molieres—all cousins:

Billy Marrero	bass	Emile "Mile" Barnes	clarinet
Simon Marrero	bass	Paul Barnes	clarinet
John Marrero	banjo		
Lawrence Marrero	banjo		
Eddie Marrero	bass		
		Frank Moliere	piano
Cie Frazier	drums	Ernest Moliere	clarinet
Mitchell Frazier	piano	Paul Moliere	trumpet
Wilfred Frazier	piano		

There are a half-dozen more relatives I cannot recall now. So if someone in the family needed some music for a celebration, it was no problem. They would all oblige and bring other musicians to play, celebrate and eat and drink.

Mr Buddy Zuzu: when this man's name was mentioned it always brought on laughs. A member of his lodge passed away, so the funeral committee, knowing he was a musician, told him to get a brass band to play for the deceased brother's funeral. Buddy hired ten musicians, which was the standard personnel of a brass band. When the members of the band arrived at the deceased brother's residence they saw Buddy standing outside the home with his bass fiddle. They expected to see him or some other bass player with a big bass horn, so they asked him who was going to play the bass horn, because none of them had ever seen, or could picture, a bass fiddle being played in a brass band, or how that could be done. Buddy smiled and said, "Don't worry, there is a first time for everything." The band members were puzzled. The lodge members were unconcerned and paid no attention. When the march started Buddy held the bass up while a band member tied a clothes-line rope around the middle of the bass, and Buddy and the band played on. Many notes were missed and not heard in the music because the band could not stop laughing. There was a saying around town for a long time when someone did something out of the ordinary, "Man, you got more nerve than a brass-assed monkey."

ELEVEN

The pine-scented sovereign state of Mississippi

In the summer of 1925 there was in the downtown section of New Orleans a very popular gambling house and cabaret called the Alley. The Alley was the headquarters of a lot of illegal doings and rackets, and the doors never closed, day or night, while the gambling tables were always occupied by the most renowned hustlers and gamblers in the city. In the rear of the Alley was the cabaret, which stayed open all night, and the band would play as long as there were customers to listen. To this day the city has never had a curfew.

Most of the younger musicians would come around after work and join in the musical battles and cutting contests. When these occurred, which was frequently, they lasted until broad daylight. The arch rivals at these contests were Henry "Red" Allen and Guy Kelly, a sensational new arrival from Baton Rouge, Louisiana. Red Allen was playing on the steamer *Capitol*, the famous riverboat, in Fate Marable's orchestra. Guy Kelly was at the time playing with Papa Celestin's band, the "best orchestra in the city" (but some folks preferred Sidney Desvignes' Southern Syncopators).

I was considered too young (and under age) to hang around a place of this kind but the manager, Octave Clements, knew my folks, and if I had my banjo he would let me in. When the regular banjo player, Wellington Dowdon, saw me he would call me, give me money, cigarettes and drinks so that I would play in his place as he ran to the gambling table or some other place. There was a very good jazz band playing there: Maurice Dumond on cornet, "Big Eye" Louis Nelson, clarinet, George Henderson, drums, Odette Davis, piano, Wellington Dowdon, banjo, and Nelisca Briscoe sang and entertained. The band was happy when I came around because Dowdon gambled all day and went to sleep on the stand at night. Many a night he would send for me to work in his place.

The Alley was never quiet, dull, or empty. The patrons liked the band and the atmosphere was a happy one. In those times I was working at a grocery store as a delivery boy in the city park section of the city, which was sort of snooty. The store I worked at did not keep a complete stock of delicacies, and when special foods were ordered my boss would send me to Simon's Grocery Store, which sold everything. The vicinity was full of grocery stores and markets, and the owners of these establishments were always having trouble with delivery boys. They were not punctual, or they would run off with the money, or boys would steal groceries while another boy was on a delivery. Weekends were troublesome too, for there were often hold-ups. I had a couple of rumbles when I first went to work out there, for there were a tough, rough bunch who considered that area to be their territory. I had left the bicycle in the street while I delivered an order, and when I returned to the bicycle I saw a couple of boys stealing my orders and letting the air out of the tires. I scared one with a meat cleaver I carried. I was left alone after that—never had any trouble.

When a boy left a job his boss would call my boss and ask if I would get a new delivery boy. I got jobs for about a dozen boys, most of whom were learning music. The lady who owned Simon's would always say hello and smile. In fact, all the bosses would greet me, for I was polite and they knew that the boys I sent to them were neat and honest (somewhat). After a while their delivery problems were over, and they always offered me things—fruit, cigarettes, cake, candy.

There was usually bitter resentment when an unkown boy left another neighborhood to come to work in another section of New Orleans. The city park section of New Orleans is strictly white, and all Negro boys were in a foreign land; but the hazards were not too serious. There were about a dozen Negro boys delivering on bicycles for grocery stores, markets, drugstores and restaurants. We were all out of bands. The city park area was in the control of boys from the fourth and third wards, a tough bunch of cats. They did not like strangers invading their territory and of course the news quickly spread that some new delivery boy was on the scene, so the first couple of days there would be a parade of bicycles to the grocery store to get a look at the new boy. It had happened to me when I started. I saw all of them and looked at them as they looked me over. Not a word was exchanged; they just looked. I smelled trouble in their attitude, so I made plans for self-preservation. I realized that the job I had taken meant that a member of their syndicate was out, so I looked about the shop for some sort of potent weapon. In the back shed of the place I spied an ancient meat cleaver. It was dull and it was rusty, so I pounded some red brick and removed the rust, grime, and sharpened the edge and placed it in the basket which was on the front of the bicycle, first wrapping it in newspaper. I must tell you that I felt real brave with this weapon, because the sight of it scared me. Each day when business was slow I would prepare some brick and add to the weapon's sharpness until you could shave with it.

One day I walked into Simon's store and ran into the young, tall, blond clerk who worked there. He was about eighteen years old and a smart aleck, who resented the fact that his bosses would say hello to me. He gave all of the delivery boys a hard time. Mike was his name. The store was crowded when I entered and he greeted me sarcastically, "Hello monkey." Everybody looked around to see the monkey. I replied calmly, "They got white monkeys, too." Mr Simon laughed, while Mike became furious and turned red. When he handed me my purchase he scowled, saying, "Nigger, I'm gonna get you and run you right into that lake, you black so-and-so." Pointing to the small meat cleaver I carried I said, "And I'll split your head open like a water-melon." Then I left the shop. That evening one of the delivery boys came by to tell me that Mike had announced that on the coming Saturday night (we worked late on Saturdays) he was going to waylay me, him and a gang of friends who lived out that way.

My plan was that after I had scalped and chopped up those cats I would catch a freight train and go North, to Chicago. I went to the Southern tracks which were but a few blocks away, and spoke to a railroad workman about freight train departures, and I even picked a spot where I decided I would hide until I got a train. I had always wondered about Mr Simon laughing when I answered Mike the way I did, for white folks in the South don't be laughing, especially when Negroes talk up to Whites. I'd always dreamed of going North after I began to grow up, and when Mike sent his threat I said to myself, "This is it."

I didn't really want to quit the job, for it was a good job, and I played sometimes with small bands and was making a little reputation. That night I went to the Alley early. The band had not yet arrived. I heard the piano playing in the cabaret, and what I heard excited me because I'd never heard a blues played so slowly, so sad, and so complicated before. I was puzzled because I had thought that I could play all tempos. What I was hearing on the piano that night was a tempo which was precise—on time, in time, but slower than a funeral march. I entered the cabaret in the rear and went up to the piano. The man was playing for his own pleasure and smiling, with his eyes closed. He was singing softly to himself. He played on and on and finally, looking around at me (I guess the expression on my face amused him) he said nicely, "You like these blues?"

"I sho' do," I smiled. "What's the name of them blues?"

He continued to smile and told me, "This is the *Vicksburg Blues*." He played. I listened. After he finished I asked him his name and he said, "Li'l Brother."

I asked him, "You from in town?" for I had heard of hundreds of musicians who I was yet to see and hear.

Li'l Brother said, "No, I'm from Kentwood, Louisiana. I'll be in town until Friday and then I'm going to Miss'sippi for a few weeks and hustle some money, and then I'm coming back here to stay."

"You ain't scared to travel round Miss'sippi?" I asked him.

He said, "No, they like me in Miss'sippi." He smiled as he spoke, but I wondered, remembering the yacht race finish in Mississippi. He asked if I was a musician and I said, "I got a banjo. I'm learning."

"Get it out," he said.

I told him, "I can't play them songs you're playing."

"Why?" he asked.

I said, "I don't understand how you can play them blues so slow and still be in time."

He laughed and told me, "Get your box out." He was smiling all the time. I took out my banjo and tuned up. He said, "Listen. When I play slow you play the first chord on the beat and then tremolo the rest of the bar."

I said, "OK."

He played an introduction and told me the key, and then I played like he had told me to. He smiled, pleased. 'That's it. You catch on quick." We played on and on. I noticed that a crowd from the gambling room had gathered and stood around listening. We both looked around when we heard a trumpet playing real beautiful. It was Guy Kelly, the great trumpet player who came from Baton Rouge and had become a sensation playing the solos of Louis Armstrong. Papa Celestin had sent for Kelly to join his band. He and Red Allen (from Algiers, across the river) were to engage in a series of sensational jazz contests. At that time Red Allen, Guy Kelly and Lee Collins were the talk of the town. Kid Rena and Chris Kelly had bands which were great bands, but in the strict traditional six-piece instrumentation: cornet, clarinet, trombone, banjo, drums, string bass. Most of the bands were now featuring saxes.

While we kept playing Guy walked slowly up till he reached the stand. It was a thrill to me, playing with Guy and Li'l Brother. We continued to play until the band arrived. The drummer and "Big Eye" Louis joined the session. Dowdon was happy, he was free to go to the gambling table. Guy Kelly was off that night and we played all night long. In the morning when we had stopped Li'l Brother said, "Dan, what you doing?"

I told him, "I'm working at a grocery store, but I don't think I'll be there long." And then I told him of Mike's threat and what I was planning to do.

He said, "Boy, you don't want to get in no trouble. Come on with me on this trip to Miss'sippi. You'll make more money in one week than at that job in a year."

"You think I play good enough?" I asked.

"Hell, yeah," he said. "I like the way you play. Come on with me on this trip."

I said I would ask my mother if I could go, and then I asked him how we would travel. He said he had a Ford and told me, "Don't you worry 'bout nothing. We'll just be gone about two weeks and when we get back you'll have plenty of money." He said, "I'll come with you and ask your mother." We stayed at the Alley until seven o'clock and then we got into his little Ford coupe and drove to my house. I introduced him to my mother who looked at me, annoyed, for it was very late to be coming home. She said, "You have been in the Alley."

I told her, "Yes, we've been playing all night."

She looked at Li'l Brother and said, "I thought something had happened, but the way you are smiling I guess everything is alright." My mother knew many musicians, but the name Li'l Brother was new to her. She said, "What you play?"

He told her, "I fool around the piano."

She said, "I never seen you before. What you all up to?"

He said, "Er . . . uh . . . er . . . I . . . came here to er . . . let . . . er . . . uh . . . Dan . . . to ask your permission . . . er . . . uh." My mother looked at him, impatient, and growing angry at his careful slowness and his failure to come to the point. She yelled, "Spit it out. What you rumbling about?"

Li'l Brother looks at me and then he looks at my mother. There is quite a pause. Then he says, smiling, "I came here to ask you to let Dan come and play some dances with me out of town."

My mother asks, "Out of town? Where?"

Li'l Brother pauses, looks her straight in the eye and says, smiling, "In Miss'sippi."

My mother yelled, "Both of you all must be out of your damned minds—Miss-siss-sippi!" She pronounced the long word in precise, clipped syllables, with a bitter emphasis on each.

Li'l Brother bowed his head and said, "Mrs Barker, it ain't that dangerous over there like it used to be. They are getting civilized. I'm goin' to play for colored folks. I been there many times before."

Mississippi. Just the mention of the word Mississippi amongst a group of New Orleans people would cause complete silence and attention. The word was so very powerful that it carried the impact of catastrophies, destruction, death, hell, earthquakes, cyclones, murder, hangings, lynching, all sorts of slaughter. It was the earnest and general feeling that any Negro who left New Orleans and journeyed across the state border and entered the hell-hole called the state of Mississippi for any reason other than to attend the funeral of a very close relative—mother, father, sister, brother, wife, or husband—was well on the way to losing his mentality, or had already lost it. The states of Alabama, Florida, Texas and Georgia were equally fearsome concerning their treatment of Negroes when the least bit of friction with white folks occurred.

The state of Mississippi was so fearsome that any conversation concerning it was one that was hurriedly ended. Chicago was considered to be the safest place near New Orleans; all other places between those two points were looked upon as just visiting points. When it was decided to live somewhere other than New Orleans, Chicago was the place, and the trip there was preferably a direct one, by way of the Illinois Central Railroad. I recall relatives returning to New Orleans telling humorous tales of looking out of the windows of the train at such places as Memphis, Bowling Green, Kankakee, Natchez. They would remark, "Ah just can't figure how cullud folks can live in them places that close to Chicago and not go there."

All stops between "Chi" and "Naw Lin" was out of the question. I had the idea when I was a youngster that getting off a Chicago-bound train (or being put off) before it reached its destination was like a ship's captain, in mid-ocean, putting someone on a small raft to drift without provisions (naturally, thousands of sharks surrounded the craft).

Going to Chicago on a vacation with my young uncle and my grandmother afforded the opportunity to see the city of Bowling Green, Kentucky. I had never seen a place so pretty; everything was so green—pretty flowers too. I must have seen a park and the outskirts. I hear people tell of the wonderful city of Chicago in detail. The end of the telling is always of the porter hollering, "Kankakee and Hammond, Indiana; you are almost there—at the gates of heaven." No more mean white folks. Every stop of the train to Chi was bad territory and to be avoided.

There were other train routes to Chicago, but the one preferred and considered precious was the one of the Illinois Central. It was a common practice among the adventurous young men to suddenly decide to go to Chicago to stay or to just visit relatives. Sometimes a group on a corner would challenge another member of the group to go—that is, hobo their way—and always it was the ICRR, never the Southern or L & N. Why not those railroads? Well, because they passed through Mississippi, Alabama and other terrible places, while the IC track ran virtually straight up north to Chicago—not one slight bend or turn along the whole route.

Back to Li'l Brother and my mother. He told her about my trouble with Mike and what I was planning to do, especially the part about catching the freight train. He asked her to let me make the trip with him. She said, "I'm scared of him going to Miss'sippi, but if you are sure there won't be any trouble he can go, 'cause he wants to be a musician." I was truly happy. I called up the grocery man and told him I was going to Chicago to attend a funeral and I would send him a boy, which I did. My mother had explained again to L'il Brother how she felt, and he assured her as best he could, "Ah avoids and keeps away from them red-neck crackers. I knows how to get around them."

In long syllables my mother again expressed her feelings, "Miss-sus-sippi, uh! uh! uh! If my boy goes with you I won't sleep a wink as long as you all are gone."

My mother prepared my clothes and packed them in a grip. Then she gave me a lecture about watching and staying clear of them mean white folks in Mississippi. The next morning Li'l Brother came and picked me up and we left. We talked as we rode the dust brown gravel roads and passed the small towns and villages. Li'l Brother was a master at traveling through the South. I noticed that he never stopped at any place that was owned or operated by white folks. When he wanted to stop for food or drink he would ask some colored person where there was a colored place. He drove slow and carefully when passing through a community. He watched the road like a hawk, but when we hit the outskirts he would sigh and relax.

At about six that evening we arrived in Crystal Springs, Mississippi, and drove across the railroad tracks down a hill to a settlement of colored people. When we pulled up in front of a cafe the men standing in front of the place looked curiously at the little Ford. When Li'l Brother stepped out they smiled and greeted him. He was well known there. He shook hands with each of them and called me over to introduce me. They were all glad to see him. We entered the cafe and met the owner, after which we sat down to a fine meal of fried chicken and cat heads (biscuits). The owner and Li'l Brother laughed and talked; they planned a juke dance that night to be held in the rear of the cafe. Dances were called "jukes" and "jukers" in Mississippi at that time, and all that was necessary to hold one of these dances in a hurry was to send a couple of men and boys from house to house to inform the populace that some music men were in town and there would be a juker that night.

These people didn't get a chance to hear live music very often, and when such an occasion presented itself they flocked to the dances in droves. The man said, "Li'l Brother, we'll make money tonight. I'll see the sheriff and sell some moonshine. We'll make money."

Li'l Brother told me, "Dan, we'll play here tonight, make this money, sleep over, and go to Brookhaven tomorrow."

That night when we started to play, the large back room was really full of folks who were all wide-eyed and smiling. After a couple of dances the sheriff walked in, followed by two colored men who carried gallon jugs of "smoke" (that's what they called that whiskey). They brought in about twelve gallons of smoke and placed them under a long table. Then the folks started drinking. We played and played, and the place really jumped. The sheriff took a seat at the door and watched us as we played. I kept my eye on him as he took off his two large, ugly looking pistols and placed them on the table. The waiters served him a large platter of fried chicken and cat heads. At about twelve o'clock a pretty, light-colored woman came out of the crowd and asked me my name. When I told her she smiled and said, "I likes the way you play that banjo, and I likes you too." Li'l Brother smiled as he looked at us. I noticed the sheriff eyed us too, and also noticed that the people looked at this woman with glances of contempt. One man looked at me and shook his head warningly and hurried through the crowd. In one minute the owner had called me and I went to him. He told me, "Kid, you ignore that yellow slut bitch; she'll git you killed. These white men will string you up 'bout that whore. She ain't worth the trouble."

I said, "Yes sir, I understand" (which I did). I returned to the stand, and just as I sat down beside Li'l Brother the owner came over, winked at me and said (loud enough for the sheriff to hear), "Kid, you only here for a few minutes; you leaving after the juke is over, so don't pay these women no mind."

I said, "Thank you, sir."

Later I saw him talking to the woman. They argued softly and went to the front of the cafe. When the dance was over we ate, while the owner gave me a lecture about colored women and white men. He gave Li'l Brother a roll of bills, and Li'l Brother peeled off thirty dollars and handed it to me. Next we went to the home of the owner and slept there. The next morning at about ten o'clock we drove off after having breakfast (while the owner gave me another lecture about pretty colored women in Mississippi and white men).

We drove on to Summitt, Mississippi, and there located a piano player named Herman Hill. He and Li'l Brother were very happy to see one another and we went to Herman's house, where his wife treated us like relatives. She washed our soiled clothing and cooked up a lot of fine food. Herman Hill had an old upright piano in his front room and he and Li'l Brother played and talked about dozens of other pianists they knew: how these pianists played, and their songs, and what towns they were in. Li'l Brother and Herman Hill took turns playing all the evening and night. Neighbors and friends came by and stayed to listen and enjoy this music. They played music I had never heard before: all kinds of blues and original piano solos. As they played they discussed the lyrics and the different meanings of moods, and they talked of how other pianists had interpreted these same songs. Li'l Brother and Herman played on and on, and finally I left them at the piano and went to bed.

The next morning Li'l Brother woke me and we ate breakfast. Then he and Herman spent another day at the piano. At about nine that evening we got in the Ford and again rode the brown gravel road. Li'l Brother said, "Dan, we're heading for Pineville, Mississippi. We'll make some money there. My friend Big Jack runs the turpentine farm at Pineville, and if'n I get there early he'll give a juke dance. There's plenty money in that town on Saturday and Sunday."

We rode on as day was breaking, and for miles and miles all I could see along that gravel road was tall pine trees which seemed to reach to the sky. The air smelled of pine—real refreshing. Li'l Brother said, "Dan, we are almost to Pineville." After he had driven about ten more miles I still didn't see any sign of a town, when suddenly I noticed an opening in the tall pine trees and Li'l Brother turned off into a road there. The trees were so tall that the road darkened and the air smelled of turpentine. Li'l Brother turned three or four times to the right and then to the left. Finally we reached a light surrounded by all sorts of bugs—insects flying and buzzing around. Li'l Brother stopped the Ford (in those days Fords made quite a racket when they came to a sudden halt). While he put on the brakes a very dark colored man appeared suddenly. He looked into the car and said quickly, "Are you the sheriff?"

Li'l Brother laughed at this, saying, "No." The man laughed too after seeing our color.

"Who are you?" he questioned.

Li'l Brother answered him, "I'm Li'l Brother Montgomery the piano player. Is Big Jack in? Just tell him Li'l Brother's here."

The man says, "Man, this ain't no time to play no music. There's two dead men laying in the gambling room, and Big Jack is waiting for the sheriff and the authorities and the coroner so he can explain what happened. You all come on in and be quiet, 'cause the boss is raving. His children is fixing him some breakfast. If he knows you, come in; if he don't know you, you all gone on 'bout your business, 'cause the boss ain't for no nonsense today."

Li'l Brother said, "As soon as I park my car I'll come in. He likes my piano playing." He parked the car about fifty feet on the right side of the road turned in the direction we had come from, as this place was a dead end. Then we silently walked into the joint. It was a small cafe, typical of the small southern towns and villages, with the gambling room in the rear.

Mr Big Jack was seated at a large, round table nervously drumming his fingers on a plate. He was huge. A brownskin man in his late fifties. His shoulders were massive and he had huge arms and hands. Also he had a clean-shaven head that glistened under the electric bulb shining overhead. There were three other large young men seated at the table and also two women who looked just like Big Jack. It was very quiet except for those fingers of his drumming on the plate. As we approached the table a woman came out of the kitchen saying to Big Jack, "Mister Jack, is you having yo' usual breakfast?"

"Just bring on the food, girl," he answered. He looked up to find Li'l Brother, whom he recognized at once. He said, "Li'l Brother, boy, you came here when I'm having trouble."

"What happened?" Li'l Brother asked.

He replied that two rogues from Texas came to the place and started running over everybody. "Every payday they won all the money, talking big, running their moufs 'bout. They from Texas. They been here three paydays causing nothing but trouble. I knew they weren't gambling fair, so I got in the game and watched them. I finally caught one switching cards and grabbed him. The other one ups with a pistol and I shot both of 'em." Mr Big Jack looked at Li'l Brother and frowned, saying, "There's more murder on my hands." Then he continued his tale. "These two rogues came here and caused nothing but confusion and trouble. They had no intention of working on the farm. They came here dressed in overalls like they's working men, but I noticed their hands and there ain't a corn or callous nowhere; those hands is soft as a baby's. I sensed trouble as soon as I see'd them. They took off them overalls (and that was to fool the white folks in their travels, but they wasn't fooling me). All the womens got excited 'bout 'em—all, the men got jealous and 'stitious 'bout 'em. They started talking big, loud 'bout Texas, dressing up in tailor-made suits, silk shirts and silk drawers, all that fancy stuff. My youngest daughter Beulah got excited just like a she-cat in heat, and one of them rogues went as far as to fool her and lay up with her. And if I hear that she's pregnant I'm gonna kill her."

Li'l Brother just listened and said nothing. Naturally I did likewise. The cook came out of the kitchen, took off the tablecloth and placed a clean one in its place. Mr Jack said, "Have a seat," and we joined him at the table. The cook started making trips serving food on the table in front of Mr Big Jack. The breakfast consisted of eight fried eggs, twenty biscuits, about a pound of bacon, a pound of country butter, a large pot of grits, a bowl of cracklin, a huge pitcher of buttermilk, a large mason jar of watermelon rinds. Mr Jack devoured the food in large mouthfuls as Li'l Brother hunched me and we silently watched this action. I thought to myself, "What a food bill he must have."

Two sheriffs arrived and Mr Jack went out to them. They asked where the dead men had come from. Mr Jack replied, "From somewhere out of Tex-ass" (that's the way he pronounced Texas).

"Do they have any identification or papers?" one of the white men asked.

Mr Jack said, "I don't know. I ain't searched their pockets. I know they are from Tex-ass 'cause that's all they boasted about."

The white man said, "The niggas is dead and as far as we is concerned that's that, the case is closed. You search the bodies for identification if'n you wants to, and if'n you wants to contact they next to kin that's all up to you. We didn't fetch 'em here and we ain't fetchin' 'em out. It's your job to get rid of the bastards. We leaving it up to you."

I heard footsteps fade away and Mr Jack called loudly, "I'll tend to it." Mr Jack walked back inside and heavily made his way to the gambling room in the rear. There was silence. Then Mr Jack left the gambling room, walked over to Li'l Brother and said, "We can't have no juker tonight, but you all stay around till after I talk to the undertaker. Don't you worry 'bout nothing." Finally he looked at me. "Who is the kid with you?" he asked.

Li'l Brother told him, "He's a music man from New Orleans, plays the banjo."

Mr Big Jack said, "You all stay here till things blow over. Nobody runs over Big Jack." And he returned to the gambling room.

Li'l Brother said, "Come on, let's go back." So I stopped and followed him to his Ford. He got into the car and so did I. Without saying another word he drove off. We drove on to Vicksburg and a half dozen other Mississippi towns playing jukes.

When we were safely back in New Orleans my mother was so happy to see me. She sat us down at the table to eat some wonderful gumbo. "How was the trip?" she asked us. "Did you all have any trouble?"

We both gave her the same reply, "Not a thing happened."

I had nearly one hundred dollars which I showed mother. "Miss'-sippi ain't so bad after all," was her remark.

I didn't see Li'l Brother until about 1944, at which time he was with Lee Collins. I was playing at the Sherman Hotel with Cab Calloway for a four-week engagement, and I spent many nights in the company of Lee Collins and Li'l Brother. One night we started to talk of Mississippi and our trip and those forgotten earthy piano players. Li'l Brother talked slowly, telling me of many pianists, and I wrote down much of what he said in biography form, including a list of the piano players he recalled.

He said Coonie Vaughan was a sensation in the Delta and the greatest pianist he had ever heard until that day (1944), including all of the "wizards." He went on, "Coonie Vaughan was highly respected by all of the great jazz pianists who knew and heard him. The last time I had the pleasure of hearing Coonie was while walking past the home of the Mayor of Hattiesburg. I heard the music and I stopped. Coonie was in rare form. He was playing *Running Wild* up in tempo, and it sounded like two electric pianos. I asked a servant who had left the house who was responsible for the piano playing and he told me, 'Man, can't you tell? That's Coonie Vaughan, and he has been the Mayor's guest all this week.'"

I asked L'il Brother if he classed Coonie with Earl Hines, Eddie Heywood, Sr, Jelly Roll, James P. Li'l Brother indignantly replied, "Hell, yes."

Here is a list of some of these unknown piano players and mention of the territories where they reigned:

Friday	Holly Ridge, Louisiana
No Leg Kenny	Oakdale, Louisiana
Charlie McHorner	Oakdale, Louisiana
Tommy Jackson	St Louis, Missouri
(cousin of Tony Jackson)	
Joe Martin	Arkansas City
	(Mama Titty's Nite Club)
Walter Louis	El Dorado, Arkansas
George Young	New Doria, Arkansas
Black Jake Face	Lake Village, Arkansas
Box Car	Laurel, Mississippi
Mance	Vicksburg, Mississippi
Delco Robert	Wizner, Louisiana
Eddie Heywood, Sr	Butter Beans and Suzie's Show
Skint Head Pete	
Piano Slim	
Milos Davis	Delta, Mississippi
Herman Hill	Summitt, Mississippi
Paul Gayton	Kentwood, Louisiana
Tallie Montgomery	Kentwood, Louisiana
Joe Montgomery	Kentwood, Louisiana
Gunzy Montgomery	Kentwood, Louisiana

The *Vicksburg Blues* as recorded by Li'l Brother is a masterpiece as far as I am concerned. In spite of the poor early mechanics of the sound and reproduction, Li'l Brother's singing in a high-pitched register is secondary and unimportant. What I find so original and wonderful is his piano playing. Most of the early pianists sang on occasion and their audiences were not critical of the voices. What counted was the dramatic interpretation of the story told in the song. So Li'l Brother's composition *Vicksburg Blues* is the only written music in this story. If you like the blues, this is one you'll never get tired of hearing.

Li'l Brother tells that he was born in Kentwood, Louisiana. He said, "My uncle Gunzy Montgomery, who played many instruments, was my teacher. He had a band called The Big Four. I left home at the age of sixteen and started for Ferriday, Louisiana, where I played at Art Henderson's Royal Garden in 1919. My next job was in New Orleans at the Do Do Cabaret; I was fourteen years old then. I went to Vicksburg, Mississippi, played at Zack Lewis's cabaret and doubled at the Princess Theater with Tom Johnson's jazz band. Then to Jackson, Mississippi, at C. C. Coleman's Cafe. I left there with Clarence Desdune's orchestra in 1929 and went to Omaha, Nebraska. Then I came to Chicago and played the King Tut and recorded for Paramount Records. Then back to Jackson, Mississippi, where I organized my own band. It was called Li'l Brother's Southland Troubadors and we played at the Red Castle nightclub. The Army broke up the band. Then it was back to Chicago.

TWELVE

Dixies

Henry Pagaud, a clarinet player, came to my house and knocked on the door. My mother invited him in. He introduced himself and explained to me and my mother that he had an out-of-town job, "three days in Miss'sippi," and wanted me to go on this trip with him. Henry explained that we would play three nights at five dollars a night, for the colored people in the city of Crystal Springs. Mother said, alright, I could go.

I had never met Henry before, but had heard about him. There were a half dozen other Creole musicians named Pagaud, and he was their cousin. He lived uptown with his family. They were barbers and operated one of the finest barbershops in New Orleans, which did excellent business. Henry played clarinet and saxophone and was rated highly. Barbering was his trade; music and its uncertainties was second. He played mostly for kicks and relaxation after the monotonous barbershop routine. He was one of the most handsome men I've ever seen: six feet tall, bronze colored, a full head of silky, jet-black hair, about twenty-five years old, well educated, quiet, immaculate in his clothes—"a real pretty man," the women would say with a sigh.

On Friday morning about ten o'clock I went uptown to Henry's barbershop with my banjo, a small pasteboard suitcase, and well wishes and a kiss from my mother. She made the sign of the cross for my safe return from the "hellfying state of Miss'sippi." Outside the barbershop when I arrived stood Face-So Woods (drummer), George McCullum (cornet), Joe Gabel (bass player), and Freddie Boo-Boo (trombone). They looked at me real strange. I guess I looked funny to them. With the exception of George McCullum I had never seen these fellows before. I had seen George a couple of times, once when his band had a "battle" with Chris Kelly's band. Of course, Chris's band won the battle. I walked up, stood by the fellows and said, "Hello." They answered but seemed puzzled, because they didn't know me and were probably concerned about my playing ability. A banjo was important to the sound and body of a jazz band. They didn't say anything, but silently raised their eyebrows and hunched their shoulders at each other. I saw the action and just stared off into space. Henry came out of the barbershop with his horns and a fine suitcase. "Let's go fellas," he said, as he got behind the wheel of a car that was parked at the curb. We piled in and Henry drove off to the outskirts of town and onto the gravel highway. You knew when you got to the highway, because you could feel the bump as the car left the asphalt pavement of the city street and started down the unpaved open road.

I was seated in the rear of the car, jammed in beside a bass drum. It was an uncomfortable perch, but I hardly noticed. I was happy because this was another step up in the music world; these musicians were real pros. We had gone a good distance when the noisy motor calmed down and I could hear the musicians talking. Henry was saying, "My Daddy is hot as a six-shooter at the idea of me going to play music on Friday and Saturday, a barbershop's most busy days. He says I'm crazy, especially going to Miss'sippi." The musicians laughed. Then I heard him say, "Don't worry about that kid, he plays the hell out of a banjo. He's one of them Barbarins! That's Teeboy Barbarin's nephew! Big Eye Louie told me about him, and he's alright if Big Eye says he's alright."

One of the musicians remarked, "I was worried 'cause I ain't never seen him before. Yeah, them Barbarins, they good musicians! Yeah, I feel better now." I felt better too when I heard these remarks. We stopped on the highway a couple of times to stretch, and the fellows spoke to me kindly.

About five o'clock in the afternoon we arrived in Crystal Springs, Mississippi, pulled up in front of a cafe, and stopped. A crowd of the local loafers gathered in front of the cafe. We got out of the car and stretched our limbs. Henry and three of the musicians went into the cafe. I asked Joe Gabel, "Ain't you going in?"

He looked at me, his forehead wrinkled, and he spoke softly, "Hell no, I'm gonna watch my bass. These Miss'sippi monkeys will steal Christ off the cross and then come back later and steal the nails." He glanced at the crowd, which was getting bigger by the minute, then whispered to me, "These are the thievingest monkeys in God's creation." We both laughed, and this drew the attention of the crowd. In the fifteen or twenty minutes Joe and I had stood by the car about a hundred colored men, young boys, and a few girls had gathered. The cafe was on the main street and the folks gathered quickly when they saw the crowd, curious to see what had happened. As they hurried on the scene there was neckstretching and the question, "What happened?"

And the answer, "Oh, the band's here from New Orleans!"

"There's two of them standing by the car!"

"Yeah, this town gonna jump tonight!"

There were happy smiles on the faces of the crowd. A couple of the youngsters grabbed one another and started a comic dance, to the amusement of the crowd. Again, "Yeah, we gonna kick 'em up tonight!"

The crowd kept growing and there was the usual jabbering, greetings, laughter, and comments, everyone happily engaged in being the unofficial welcoming committee. There was a continuous jabbering, then, suddenly, the crowd became still and silent. No one moved and no one spoke. I looked about to see what had caused the sudden silence and noticed two white policemen slowly walking through the path the crowd made for them. There was nothing asked, nothing said; just silence. All eyes followed the police as they slowly walked into and through the crowd.

Then the people started to disperse and move on. In two minutes most were gone. Only a few stayed, but kept quiet. A T-model fire-red Ford coupe drove up and stopped behind our car. Out stepped a short, jet-black man with a nose just like Jimmy Durante's, maybe a bit larger and longer! He hurried out of the car and the men made a path for him. He had an air of importance and was dressed up like a dandy. He saw Joe Gabel and smiled a wide toothy smile, grabbed his hand and said, "Glad to see you, Joe! The band got here safely—that's great. Where's the rest of them?" Joe replied that they were in the cafe. The man said, "Come on inside, Joe." Joe shook his head, winked and answered that he was watching his bass and the rest of the instruments. The man winked, smiled and went inside. I asked who he was. Joe said he was Jack King the dance promoter. Jack King was a sight to see. He wore a light tan suit with a silver chalk stripe in it, a large panama hat, and light tan and white shoes. Jack King came out of the cafe and told one of the bystanders to watch the car and instruments. The man said, "Alright," and sat behind the wheel of the car. We went inside the cafe following Jack King. Henry and the other musicians were eating. Jack King hollered to the waitress, "Serve these two fellows in a hurry."

Henry said, "Jack, meet Daniel. He plays banjo." Jack King grabbed my hand, squeezed it, and shook it so hard I raised up on my toes. He let my hand drop and turned to Henry, saying, "I got some extra jobs for you. Three evenings, before the dance, we will play one hour in front of the Motordrome—that's in town. For that one hour of bally-hoo, from seven till eight, they'll pay you forty-five dollars; ten for you, five for each man, and of course ten for me for promoting the idea to the owner of the Motordrome. That's three evenings—Friday, Saturday and Sunday." Jack took a large gold watch from his pocket, looked at it and told Henry that we had about forty-five minutes. "We'll go to the Motordrome and get ready to start the ballyhoo. Get in your car and follow me." As we entered the car Jack said to the people standing about, "Folks, you all can get a sample of this fine Naw 'Leans music you will hear tonight if you come out to the Motordrome. The band's gonna ballyhoo for one hour. Come on out there!" Some of the people said, "Alright."

Jack got in his car and slowly drove off. Henry followed Jack's car to the outskirts of the town. As we drove we saw many people, colored and white, walking in the same direction. We stopped when the crowd of people blocked our path. Jack stopped his car, got out and disappeared into the crowd. He came back quickly with a policeman, who directed the crowd to open up so the two cars could drive through. We pulled up and stopped in front of a refreshment stand. We got out of the car and unloaded the instruments. Jack led us to a small platform in front of a tall wooden structure. It was circular, just like a huge coffee cup, about thirty feet tall, thirty feet wide at the top, and ten feet wide at the bottom. There was a four-foot wide stairway that led up to a platform about four feet wide that circled the top. The spectators paid the admission and went up the stairs, where they stood around the platform and looked down into the interior of the huge bowl.

There was the noise of a motorcycle which was inside the huge bowl. You could hear the motor accelerating to a high speed, and the atmosphere smelled of gasoline fumes. A man stood upon the platform with a megaphone, spieling to the spectators. The band tuned up and the huge crowd began to congregate around the platform. The man on the high platform with the megaphone leaned over and yelled to the crowd, "Ladies and gentlemen! You are about to hear a great band from 'way down yonder in Naw 'Leans! They're going to play some pretty music—some of that Basin Street lowdown music! Tell your friends that they will play here three evenings—Friday, Saturday, Sunday —admission free; don't cost you one red penny! I sent all the way to Naw 'Leans for this great band to entertain yer! So you're getting two sensational thrills for the price of one! OK, now this great jazz band will play."

Henry stomped off, saying, "Panama Rag." We played *Panama*. When we finished the huge crowd gave us a grand ovation. They whistled, clapped and yelled. I looked at the members of the band and everybody was smiling. After we had played a half dozen songs the MC yelled, "Friends, this great band will catch their breath for a few moments, and while they're resting, buy your tickets and come up here and see the sensational (so-and-so). He will thrill you with his daring lightning speed on the Harley Davidson motorcycle."

The people bought tickets and went up the stairs to see the daredevil. In front of me stood a white man with his arms folded. He had been standing there since we started to play, and never once did he take his eyes off me. He was medium height, blond, about thirty years of age. He was dressed neatly, his shirt sleeves rolled up. He stood three feet in front of me. He had the bluest blue eyes I had ever seen, and the thinnest lips—so thin they seemed just a thin line. He watched my every move. His eyes went from my strumming wrist to my face, back and forth. I saw his interest in my playing and smiled. He did not return the smile, just looked. When the MC said we could have a rest I stood the banjo on my knee and looked at the scene—the huge bowl and the people. I noticed his stare and looked at him solemnly. He looked at me with a straight expression on his face and said, "Boy, you sho' can whup det benjer!"

That Mississippi drawl struck me funny. I smiled on the outside but laughed out loud on the inside. I said, "Thank you."

"Yes, by Gawd, you sho' mastuhs det benjer," he said again. That was the first and last time I heard "banjo" pronounced "benjer." He said, "You boys are gonna be here three days?" I replied that I thought so. "That's nice," he said.

A white waiter came through the crowd with a tray of soft drinks in large paper cups. "Here's some sody pop," he said. Each member of the band reached for a cup. I drank the soda and watched the people crowd the stairs leading up to the top of the Motordrome. At the top I could see the MC moving the large crowd around the platform. The band was in a happy mood because the audience liked the music. Joe Gabel sat down next to me and said, "Kid, you play nice banjo. I was kinda leery when I first saw you this morning—I never saw you before, never heard you. A banjo is important to a band. But you're alright. You surprised me."

Suddenly the motorcycle inside the bowl started a loud racket. The motor speeded up and it sounded like it was going to explode. Then there was a lot of backfiring. You could hear the cycle speeding around the inside of the bowl. The strong scent of gasoline and the smoke caused some of the spectators to turn their backs to the speeding cycle. It was an exciting scene to witness—the speeding cycle, the fire from the exhaust pipe, the smoke and gas fumes. The speed kept up about three minutes, then the motor slowed down gradually to a stop and the act was over. The audience applauded again and some started to leave. The MC yelled through the megaphone for them to wait a minute. He leaned over the high platform and called, "Hey boy with that banjo, come up here!" I looked at Henry, who was talking to Jack the promoter. They both said, "Go 'head." All the spectators were looking as I carefully walked up the stairs.

The MC helped me mount the top of the Motordrome. I leaned against the railing and looked at the band and the people below; from up high they looked very small. The MC was a good-looking healthy young man with a big happy smile. He said, "Ah been humming and singing while the band was playing. I don't know the songs—never heard them before—but your music wants to make yer sing and dance, just holler, make noises, have fun. Now I want to sing a couple of songs with you playing the banjo for me." He said, "Do you know *California, here I come?*"

I said, "Maybe. I can follow you."

He said, "Ketch me."

I hit a cord—C. He started to sing, looking down at the spectators. He felt I was playing behind him; he smiled and sang louder—two choruses. The crowd applauded when he finished. He thanked the spectators, bowed, pointed to me and said, "I'll sing another. How's about the *Robert E. Lee*. I nodded, and he sang the *Robert E. Lee*. The crowd whistled and hollered, "More! More! More!"

He said later, "The next performance will begin soon. Line up and get yo' tickets." He looked at me and said, "What's yo' name?"

I said, "Dan."

He said, "Dan, you are a fine banjo player. You just what our show needs—some entertainment between the daredevil rides. You just what we need. Dan, can you travel? Would you like to join up with me and the Motordrome? I could pay you well—say fifty dollars a week, or sixty dollars a week—year round, even when we travel. Sixty dollars steady money. Next month we take off to the West Coast. We will talk the business over later. What you say?"

I said, "I'll have to go back home, explain to my mother. I'm for going out into the world, but I have to talk it over with my mother."

He said, "OK Dan, we'll work it out." The MC called Henry and we went down to where he stood. I noticed the thin-lipped white man come over and stand within hearing distance. Henry asked, "What's happening?"

The MC said jokingly, "I want to steal this banjo player from you."

Henry said, sort of puzzled, "You can't do that. He's a minor; his mother holds me responsible for him. I've got to bring him back to New Orleans right back to his mother like I promised her. And then if you still want him, you will have to get him with her permission."

The MC said, "He's just what the show needs. In fact, I would like to have your whole band. Out West, where I'm going, the people would go wild over your music."

Henry said, "I doubt it, because this is not an organized band. In fact we are just here playing together for these three days. Then we go back to New Orleans and disband until maybe Jack will book us again."

The MC said, "You mean you fellows don't play together all the time? That is, regular?"

Henry said, "No. Some of us have played on different occasions, but this is the first time Dan has played banjo with me or the other fellows."

The MC shook his head and said, "It's hard to believe. Maybe we can figure out a deal in the next couple of days." And he walked back up the stairs.

Henry said, "Let's go back, fellows!" as Jack looked at his big gold watch.

I went back to my seat on the bandstand and Joe Gabel whispered softly, "That cracker wants to hire you, huh?"

I whispered, "Yeah."

He said, "I figgered that these crackers sho' do like a banjo."

I noticed Henry and Jack in a serious conversation. Also the thin-lipped fellow returned and stood again in front of me, watching my every move. Henry mounted the stand and Jack shouted, "Two more hot numbers and that's it!" The large crowd gathered tightly in front of the band and we played *The Bucket* and *St. Louis Blues*. I looked up and the MC and the greasy motorcycle daredevil were looking down shaking their heads, seemingly annoyed. When we finished the last note the MC shouted, "Give this great band a real great ovation!" And the crowd complied. We all stood up and bowed thanks. Then Henry said, "Pack up, boys." Joe Gabel says softly, "Dan, I bet you ten dollars that white headed cracker standing in front of you plays a banjo, I bet yer. Watch and see; he's gonna tag behind you everywhere you go."

I put my banjo in its case and he was still standing. I looked at him and said, "See you." He did not answer, just looked. We walked through the large crowd to the car, and drove off, following Jack in his red car. We drove slowly through the many people standing around, then to the outskirts on the other side of town, to a hall. In front of this hall there was a large crowd of colored people. It was dark now and the front was not lit up like the Motordrome. We got out of the car and Joe Gabel, who was pleased at my playing, was friendly, saying, "This is it."

I said, "What?"

He whispered, "Dark Town."

We both laughed. We stood on the outside and looked about. The people started buying tickets, and then trucks and all sorts of ancient automobiles drove up packed with people. There were also wagons, buggies drawn by mules and horses. I watched as people got off the wagons. The men unhitched the animals, took off the harnesses and tied the animals to the back of the wagons. Jack came out of the hall and said, "We won't have to ballyhoo. The crowd is coming. We'll make money if the weather stays clear."

We did not play a ballyhoo in front of the hall. (A ballyhoo was a few songs played in front of a place of amusement. It let the patrons hear what sort of music the band would play for their enjoyment; a free sample.) We went to the bandstand, which was dirty, full of dust and cobwebs. It was a long time since a band had played on its crude planks. It was typical of the common annoyances to traveling musicians: dirty bandstands, out-of-tune pianos, rickety, wobbly constructions, poor lighting, no windows for ventilation or fresh air, and other nuisances.

We struck up our first song and the crowd gathered around the stand and watched us. They were happy, and soon the dance was on its way. Right from the beginning I noticed the women, six or eight of them, stood up real close to the bandstand staring at Henry. They ogled his every movement with pleasant, crafty smiles on their faces. In this group they were many sizes, colors, shapes, and dressed in their Sunday best, from cheap cotton to expensive satins and silks. Their expressions were, "I could go for you in a big way, daddy." I watched their moving lips say, "He's a pretty man." The band and Henry felt the eyes and actions of the group of women.

These people danced a peculiar sort of dance. Many, out of step, seemed like they did not dance much. But they danced slowly or fast and as best they could to the different tempos. Some just embraced and moved about the floor. Since there were no master dancers to watch, they just wiggled in any fashion. These sort of dancers are an annoyance to rhythm players in bands. If you watch them closely they will confuse and throw you off tempo. I wondered about these colored people dancing all around, ahead, behind the beat. I thought, "Well, these are country people in Miss'sippi, and they don't get to see much public dancing."

A time before I had played a dance in the Irish section of New Orleans called the Irish Channel. Being a banjo player and having been to all sorts of New Orleans dances, I was used to watching both the band for their rhythm and the dancers almost perfectly dancing to the tempo played by the musicians. I was completely confused watching the Whites dancing. They were dancing in complete disregard of the band's rhythm. They were just dancing in all sorts of irregular patterns; all actions were fast like a group of very young kids playing a nursery-rhyme game. For a long time I couldn't figure out their jumping and swinging about, until in New York City I saw some Irish people doing the Irish reel. These Irish Channel people just did not know or care about dancing to strict rhythm routines.

I watched the women standing in front of Henry. All night they stood there. They accepted requests from men who asked them to dance, but when the dance stopped they came straight back to the bandstand and stood to attention in front of Henry. Henry smiled at the women. I could tell which eyes he looked into because the woman's eyes lit up and a big happy smile covered her face. I heard, "There he is!" spoken by Joe Gabel, who was standing and playing beside me.

I answered, "Who?"

Joe said, "That cracker."

I looked, and there was the man who watched me constantly at the Motordrome. He was dressed the same, in his shirt sleeves, and stood on the long bench that lined both sides of the old hall. He was looking at me, no smile; I looked at him with no smile. Joe said slyly and quickly, "That white headed cracker is up to something." He just stood up on the bench looking at the band and me, ignoring the dancers. I wondered why he didn't come in front of the bandstand like at the Motordrome. Then I thought, "Oh, this is a colored affair. The Motordrome was for white people. They don't mix in Miss'sippi." Henry called an intermission, put down his horn on a dusty chair back of the stand. Joe Gabel and I stepped off the bandstand and walked to a small window. Joe said softly, "Here comes that cracker." I didn't look around; I just waited. Then I heard, "Benjer player, benjer player." Slowly I looked around. I said, "Hello."

He said, "Does yer drink?" I felt a soft hunch in my ribs, then two short ones; it was Joe hunching me. I answered, "Yes, sometimes."

He said, "I bought yer some likker." And he had a brown bag out of which he took a gallon jug of white liquid. Joe said, "What yer got there?"

He said, "Whiskey."

Joe said, "What about the police?"

He said, "Pay them no attention; they won't bother yer." Joe took the jug, pulled out the cork, lifted it and tasted, then gulped down a large drink, saying after catching his breath, "It's alright, tastes fine."

The man said, "I know you been seeing me watching you."

I answered back, "Yeah."

He said, "Rarely we folks here gets to hear and enjoy good music, specially a good benjer, and you whups the dickens outer yourn. I bought you the likker as a sort of 'preciation of the pleasure I've had watching you pluck the benjer."

I said, "Thanks."

Joe hunched me as he handed me the jug of whiskey. I took a drink; the whiskey was nice tasting and there was an aroma of black molasses. As I lowered the jug the man took it and swallowed, didn't wipe the mouth of the jug as I had seen people do when drinking with a group.

Joe said, "It's mighty nice of you to bring the likker. It comes in handy, hits the spot."

The man said, "Well, one favor deserves another."

Joe hunched me in the side three times. Joe said, "I sho' would like to take a jug of this nice whiskey back with me to New Orleans." And he hunched me once again sharply in the ribs. "Is it hard to git hold of?"

The man said, "No, not too much bother. I'll think it over."

Joe said, "It would be mighty kind of you sir, if you could get me a jug. I'll pay you for your troubles."

The man walked off a few steps and mounted the bench again, looking off and about the happy crowd of people. Joe put the jug inside the bag and stepped on the bandstand. I walked off and through the crowd. I saw Henry, and he was surrounded by the group of women who were talking and asking him many questions. He was conversing, not smiling, just talking. I wondered about his coolness to these female admirers. He saw me looking at the scene and said, "Let's go back." He was relieved to leave the women.

Back on the stand we started playing but the dancing didn't improve. These dancers now completely ignored the beat and rhythm. They were all now doing the slow drag, slowly moving about the floor embracing each other with their arms and hands clasped about all parts of the body, from the neck, shoulder, waist, hips, and as far down as the hands can reach. This affair was peaceful and orderly. At the door stood Jack and two burly blond policemen. Finally Henry said, "Let's play *Home Sweet Home*."

That done, we packed up our instruments and got off the bandstand. Joe Gabel was in deep conversation with two of the women who had stared all night at Henry. He said, "I don't know where we are going to stay at, but you all come on with me; we'll have some fun. I got a jug full of good whiskey."

The two women smiled and said, "Alright."

The white man was standing on the floor now, looking at me, and as the last group of people reached the door he came over to where I, Joe and the two women are standing. I noticed the two women's faces freeze as he approached us, and they turned their back when he arrived. The man said, "Benjer player, I would like to ask a favor of you."

Joe grunted, "Uh hum. Uh hooommm," then stepped aside and talked to the two women. The man continued, saying, "I heard you playing the benjer out at the Motordrome and I enjoyed it very much, so I went home and I told my pappy 'bout you. Er, he's got a benjer, used to play it all the time, but not no more. He's old and very feeble. When I told him 'bout you he asked me to fetch yer out to play a few songs and let him hear you. If'n it ain't too much bother, could yer come out to the farm and bring yer benjer? It would give my pappy some pleasure, I know it would."

I said, "When?"

He said, "Tomorrow."

I thought of him bringing the whiskey jug and Joe Gabel asking him for another one. I said, "What time?"

He answered somewhat happily, "Around noon time tomorrow. I'll come by and get you and the benjer."

I remembered that the band did not have rooms yet, and said, "I don't know where we are staying yet or the address."

He said, "I'll get the address from Jack King."

I said, "You know Jack King?"

He answered, smiling for the first time, "Everybody knows Jack King. Tomorrow I'll pick you and the benjer up around noon time."

No sooner did I say alright, than he walked off hurriedly, went to Jack King standing at the door, spoke a few words, and disappeared to the outside. Joe Gabel spoke, "What that cracker wanted?"

I said, "He wants me to go out on his father's farm and play the banjo for him."

Joe laughed, saying, "My mind don't fool me; I knowed that cracker wanted something, tagging behind you all night."

One of the women nearby grunted, "That's old Pappy's son. That bastard and his no-good old man are the worst of nigguh haters. I wouldn't play shit for that bastard."

The hall was empty when Henry called, "Let's go, fellows." The four of us walked out of the hall into the cool air. There was much activity, people getting into trucks and other motor vehicles. I laughed as I saw men hitching up mules and horses to homemade farm wagons. The group of musicians walked down the county road to a street where there were many houses. At a large house with a long porch stood Henry and Jack King, who were laughing at something. We mounted the steps and followed them into the house. The landlady greeted us, saying, "You all sho' did play some fine music tonight. The dance was fine—not even one fight. Generally there are three or four. Come on in the living room and have some supper. You all rooms are all ready; you all eat first."

In the living room there was an extra large dinner table. As the band sat the woman started bringing out platters of chicken, biscuits, milk, ice tea and other fine cooked food. There were lots of people sitting about looking on as the musicians, Jack King, and the buxom brown skinned landlady prepared to eat. Jack King said the blessing and we dived into the platters of food. There was much joking and laughter during the feast, and Henry was praised to the highest about his playing and the fine band. Suddenly he rose, saying, "Good night, folks, I'm retiring." And he left, walking up the stairs. A fine looking woman rose from her seat and said, "Well, that's that. I guess I'll go home." I saw she was one of the women who ogled Henry all during the dance. As she left the others followed out the house. The landlady laughed, remarking, "I can't figure Henry out: all these women after him and he pays them no attention."

Jack King grunted, "He iggs (ignores) them every time he plays here."

Joe Gabel laughed, saying, "Well, I ain't ignoring the fine Miss'sippi girls."

Jack King answered, "Well, Joe, you are an old man."

"I ain't that old and I ain't cold. Come on baby," shouted Joe as he took the jug of whiskey and put his arm around the woman's waist, and they walked out of the room. The other woman who came with us from the dance rose and said, "Goodnight folks." As the screen door slammed Jack King looked at me frowning, saying, "Didn't that girl come here with you?"

I said, "Yeah."

"Well why did you let her leave?"

"I didn't know she was gonna leave. I was just gonna go over and talk to her." Saying these words I felt simple.

The landlady interrupted. "Them gals been waiting for weeks for the band to come to town. They want to meet some out-of-town men. Boy, you got to learn to talk fast, talk up for yourself."

I shook my head and mumbled, "Uh huh," and slowly got up from the table.

She said, "Your room is the third one on the right."

I went to the room and sat on the bed. I heard Joe and the woman laughing. The laughter sounded simple—laughter of drunks.

The next day around eleven I got up, dressed and went downstairs and out on the porch. I sat in a large rocking chair and watched the scenery. The landlady came out and said, "If you want some breakfast, come into the kitchen."

I answered, "Thanks," and I heard Joe Gabel's voice, his laughing, as he and the woman came out on the porch. They looked at me, surprised. The woman said, "Where Mosella?"

I answered, "She left and went home when you all went upstairs last night."

She asked, "What happened?"

I answered, "Nothing."

"Well, she came here to be with you. Didn't you know that? It was all planned." Then she shook her head, looking at Joe Gabel.

I answered, defensively, "Well, I saw her looking and smiling at Henry Pagaud all night."

Joe laughed, saying, "Boy, I got to talk to you and wisen you up. Don't you know Henry couldn't handle all them women who was looking at him last night? Dan, listen: when you see a lot of women standing around the bandstand, all looking at one musician, you make it your business to get close or join them at intermission, because they are unescorted. Because if they were escorted, their men wouldn't let them stand there staring at a musician. They is what you call strays, little lambs ready for the slaughter." He laughed, real tickled.

The woman slapped Joe besides the head, saying, "You so damned smart. Come on, take me home." They both laughed and walked off. Joe looked back at me and shouted, "Dan, I've got to wisen you up to a whole lot of things."

As they walked out of sight I relaxed down in the big rocker, thinking of how I should have talked up real fast to the woman. A truck drove up in front of the door. I looked, and there was the white fellow slowly stopping the truck. I said to myself, "He's on time." He stopped the truck, got off, and casually walked to the porch. He walked up the steps, saying with his straight and smileless face, "Well, I'm here. Are you ready?" I looked at him with the same straight smileless face and answered, "I guess so, but I haven't had no breakfast." I got up from the rocker saying, "Wait, I'll be right out." I went inside, got my banjo. On my way downstairs the landlady comes out the kitchen and asks, "Boy, don't you want some breakfast?" Hearing her tone of voice I answered, "No, ma'am," because she sounded sort of sarcastic: "Fool, do you want some breakfast?"

I went outside and said, "Let's go." We got on the truck and drove off. He was a slow, careful driver, and after about ten minutes on the bumpy country roads we turned into a smaller road and pulled up in front of a large gate. There was a large arch over the gate which read "Mississippi Bloodhound Kennel." I thought as the truck came to a stop, "This ain't no farm." Kennel! I had never heard of the word before, or what it meant; had never seen a kennel. I thought, "What is a kennel? The man said, 'to his father's farm'; maybe this is a special kind of farm." We got off the truck and he said proudly, "This is it." I grabbed up my banjo and followed the man, who opened a gate under the arch and walked along a brown dirt path that led to a large white house in the distance (about a city block). As I walked, following the man, my mind sped on. I thought, "Mississippi Kennel. What the hell is a kennel?" Then I was shocked. As I quickly looked about I saw hundreds of dogs, bloodhounds, laying about in deathly silence, fat-bellied female dogs. I could barely see them breathing. These were fierce looking beasts, all brown and black, with huge ears and long tails. I had seen lots of dogs, but never this many at one time.

We came to the back porch of the old unpainted two-story house, and there on it sat old Pappy. He was sitting in a large rocking chair. His legs were long and he held his hands on his knees, his long bony fingers grasping the knees. Pappy was a huge man with a speckled face—large splatches—and high cheek bones. His hair was parted to the side. He resembled the serious face of Abraham Lincoln. He raised his right hand and pointed for me to come up on the porch. He said, "Come, sit here," pointing to a well-worn bench. I mounted the porch. His son said, "Pappy, this is Dan. I brought him here like I said." He walked off. Pappy never said a word, just looked, sizing me up with sky-blue eyes—his eyes rolling all over me. I went on taking the banjo from the case as Pappy's eyes rolled around me, on and on. I started slowly picking a song: *I wonder what became of Joe*. Pappy began to nod with pleasure. Made me wonder if he had ever smiled. Then I played the chorus of the *St Louis Blues*.

Pappy jerked nervously and grunted through the service door, "Tee ree saw." Pappy grunted three syllables, "Tee ree saw"; it was his crude southern way of pronouncing "Theresa." I had noticed this female figure standing in the doorway, behind the screen door; she came and went. Theresa came and said, "What is it sir?"

Pappy said, "Fix me a lemonade."

Theresa said, "Alright," and disappeared inside.

Pappy seemed to enjoy my playing the melody of the *St Louis Blues*, so I continued, getting a little louder. I noticed the dogs looking in the direction of the porch. Theresa came with the tall glass of lemonade, opening the screen door. She was a fairly tall, good-looking brownskin lady with a serious face. She said, "Good day."

I answered, "Good day."

Pappy took the lemonade and slowly sipped from the glass with his eyes glued on me. I thought, looking at the glass in his huge hands, "Could have offered me a glass of lemonade. But then," I thought, "my lips would ruin his glass." I had heard tales of white folks breaking glasses after Negroes drank out of them.

Pappy slowly grunted, "Kin yer pick the *Down by the Old Ribberside*?"

I said, "I guess so," and I went into *Down by the Riverside*. And I started to sing the hymn—really meaning the words, but also praying: wishing to the Lord to get my behind off this scene. I was sort of relieved as I heard Theresa singing a soft second voice with mine. I thought, "Oh yeah, she's Baptist." I sang and listened as she changed octaves, and yeah, she sings in the choir. I continued picking and singing as Theresa sang on, getting down into the riverside. Pappy listened to the voice of Theresa and turned his head and ear to the door very slowly, and then slowly lifting his sad old blue eyes right at me. I finished the hymn and and I heard Theresa say softly, "Thank you, Jesus." My body warned that I should go to the bathroom. So I said seriously, "Mr Pappy, can I use your bathroom?"

He said slowly, breathing deeply, "Sho' boy," and pulled a police whistle from his shirt pocket and blew it once. In a moment Jim Boy appeared. This man was smart looking, alert. I'd say nice looking and handsome, with a pleasant face. He looked at me and smiled a little. Pappy said, "Take this boy to the pissery back by the barn."

Jim Boy said, "Come on." I put the banjo down. Pappy reached for the banjo and I handed it to him and the pick. I got up and joined Jim

Boy. Pappy said, "Jim, how's the hounds? How the dog food holding out? I ordered more flea spray—real great stuff they say—kill them fleas and bugs—also a belly worm killer." Jim Boy just listened. No answer, just nodded. Pappy said no more. Jim Boy said, "Come on," and I joined him and we walked to the rear. We walked past dozens of hounds, all brown and black, some laying about, some playing. We passed a small plot of fenced-off yard, about ten by ten feet. I looked inside the enclosure and there stood a large hound, so I stopped to look at him. He growled and limped over to us. I saw he was in bandages, both of his hind legs were neatly bandaged in white cotton. So was most of his rear end. He stood looking at us, wagging his tail when he looked at Jim Boy and growling gruffly when looking at me. I said, "What happened to him?"

He said, "That's Stonewall. He got too big for his britches. Simon damned near killed him. Tried to chew his hind parts off."

I felt the call of nature again. We walked further into the rear. Jim Boy, seeing I was interested, went on talking his Mississippi country talk. "Yeah, Stonewall got too big for his britches. He ain't but eleven months old, ain't a year yet. He's very brave and courageous as hell. He'll fight, but he's no match for Simon yet. Maybe in another year. I don't doubt he'll whop Simon's ass, but not now." We reached an ancient lopsided outhouse and he said, "Here's the pissery." I went inside. In a moment I was out. "Tell me about Simon," I said.

He said, "Simon is the boss dawg here. All the male dawgs respects and fears Simon. Simon knows he's boss. None of the dawgs likes Simon because he has all the females to hisself. There's no love-making or whoring out in the open. Simon will tear up a dawg if he sees the slightest bit of fooling around. These goddamn dawgs is just like people—jealous, selfish, lowdown, sneaky. I'm telling you—just like people."

I said, "Well, is Simon the father of all these dogs?"

"No, but when we breed a pair of dawgs we match a couple and lock them up for a month or so, safe and away from Simon. But Simon knows what's going on because the male dawg always gits his ass whupped when we turn him back out in the open yard."

Jim Boy pointed to a large, very old hound lying under a tree. "That's Fitzsimmons. He was the boss until Simon growed big and strong enough to chew him up and take charge of the yard. He had his day. He ruled and reigned for many years. Now he just takes it easy and stays out of Simon's way. He's retired. Simon waited and waited until he was strong enough. You should have seen that battle. Simon damned near slaughtered Fitzsimmons. He ain't never really fully recovered. His balls was tore loose. We patched him up, but he ain't no good. I'm waiting for Stonewall to do the same thing to Simon. It's coming 'cause he ain't skeered of Simon. Just ain't strong enough yet. There's two other dawgs may whup him one day, but now they ain't got enough heart. They tag behind Simon. Just two punks. Simon is forever bulldozing them. But Stonewall's got heart and courage. From a li'l pup he took up following Simon. When Simon would go about sniffing the females li'l Stonewall would do the same, following in Simon's footsteps. Simon let him do it. Then I knew it was coming. Stonewall is big now and last week, while sniffing, Stonewall left the female that he was sniffing and went up and started sniffing the female that Simon was sniffing, and that did it. Simon leaped on Stonewall and tore his ass up. You shoulda seen that fight, boy. I had to throw buckets of water on them. That didn't stop the battle. I had to light newspapers and shove them under Simon's nose. The fire burned his nose and took the fight out of him."

We walked on and I looked over in the distance, still thinking about Simon. "This Simon is not no ordinary dog. He is a mean, vicious, prejudiced hound who hates for no reason." I thought, "Pappy had called his animals hounds, but Jim Boy called them dawgs." Simon was no dawg. He was a hound. I looked over amongst a lot of trees and I saw what looked like a convict in a striped uniform up in a tree. I started walking over to the trees. Jim Boy looked at me and a smile came on his face as he saw my curiosity.

Over near a barn stood two new Reo speed wagons—motor trucks very popular at that time. They were a sort of combination car and truck, the forerunner of the station wagon. The body of these trucks was large, long and built high on the chassis. There were signs on the sides: "Mississippi Bloodhounds." In one of the trees there were three dummy convicts. From a distance they looked real. They were stuffed convict uniforms—black heads, feet and hands. There were four or five hanging on the tops of fences; the pants of these were torn to shreds. The legs of a couple could be seen under a shack. I looked about in wonder to the silent amusement of Jim Boy. I curiously walked over to see what was in the barn. Inside there, on a clothesline, hung a few odd convict pants and jackets. Jim Boy said, "We train the dawgs in this section to trail and hunt down convicts. If'n it warn't so late I would let you see how it's done."

I said, "Don't the dogs attack you?"

"No. I feeds 'em and they knows me."

I said, "Do the dogs catch many convicts?"

He said, "Hell, yes. Just the yelping of the dawgs will scare the hell out of a scared convict who ain't never heered it. Come here. Let me show you something."

I followed and we went to another barn. Inside were small stalls like in a stable. Twenty stalls. In each was a huge chained hound, some standing, some sleeping. They were large, but not stout and robust like Simon and Stonewall. These hounds were vicious looking, lean and hungry. He said, "These are the pack hounds. We keep them lean, sparse and half-hungry all the time. Soon as Pappy gits a call from the penitentiary that there's a jailbreak we load the truck with these dawgs and speed to the penitentiary." I wondered about this bloodhound business and asked, "How often do you all get calls for the bloodhounds?"

"It varies. Maybe once a month or once a week in the spring, summer and fall when the chain gangs are out in the fields or working on the roads, but rarely in the winter because the convicts are locked up in the winter. But we are most busy in the summer when the sun gets too scorching hot. The boiling hot sun makes the convicts crazy and daring. That's when they take off to the woods and swamps. We don't git called much now, but years ago—say, maybe ten, fifteen years ago—we were forever on the go. Years back Pappy kept as many as two hundred dawgs on the leash ready for the call. Up until, I'd say, ten years ago, over in the railroad yards there was an engine and a caboose standing on a siding—the engine under constant steam day and night waiting for a quick call from the penitentiary. We'd get the call from the warden. I would rush the dawgs up into the caboose hooked to the engine, and off we would take to the penitentiary."

I said, "Whose train was it?"

"The State of Mississippi provided the train. Now the state, through the penitentiary, provides the two speed wagons for Pappy's dawgs. They pays Pappy well and he pays me well, because Pappy is the best hound-dawg man in the world. That's what the white folks claim. Once Simon sniffs the convict's scent, where the break started, he'll follow that trail till he comes to water. Then that slows us up, 'cause water moves and scatters the scent.

I said, "How can them dogs follow a smell like that?"

He laughed and said, "You see Dan, all convicts smell alike, because they're always caged up together, don't bathe properly, works hard like mules. So they stay strong and funky-smelling—different from other folks. They have a foul odor, a sickening odor. The penitentiary sends us those convict suits you saw in the barn and on them dummy convicts. The dawgs sniff these suits and are familiar with a convict's odor, so that's how they can sniff up a trail so quickly."

We were walking slowly now, and I saw Pappy sitting on the porch strumming on my banjo. I said to Jim Boy, "Where is Simon?"

He laughed, saying, "All that talk of Simon scared the shit outa you, didn't it?"

I said, not laughing, "It sho' did."

He said, "I fed him and put him in a stall with a young bitch that's in heat. Simon likes that. Dan, that Simon sho' hates a black man, a white one, too. White or black, if he runs yer down and you have on one of them funky convict suits, that's your fat ass. White or black, he'll chew yer ass up. I gits a big kick when we runs down a white convict. They rarely give a long chase, 'cause they don't know about black pepper or salt to throw in the dawg's eyes. Just don't know. Fust thing a nigger gits is pockets and hands full of dry sand, if they can't git pepper, to throw in the dawg's eyes."

We walked up to the porch. Pappy was strumming and smiling, and we continued to talk about Simon. Jim Boy said proudly, "That Simon has sunk his fangs in many a convict's ass! Glad to meet yer, Dan." And he walked off. I thought to myself I would love to have a white-hot, three-foot long fireplace poker in my hand and meet Simon on a lonely road. I'd fix his ass. I just pictured myself with that steaming hot poker whipping all the hair off Simon. Then, outside the screen of the porch I saw a big, red-eyed hound run up. He saw me and growled and snarled, pawing at the wire. I thought to myself, "That must be Simon. Why Simon has to get so mad at me?" He had never seen me before. I smiled sort of kindly at him. The only slight move I made was to carefully pick up my banjo and place it on my lap as a protection in case he got through the wire and attacked me.

The old man looked at the dog and grunted loudly, "Simon, git up and go on!" The dog looked sharply at the old man, then at me, and walked off, then went into a slow trot with the other hounds trailing behind him. I sighed, breathed heavily and said in relief, "I feel better now." I continued, "Do you raise these dogs to sell?"

The old man said, "Sell! Hell no. I'm in business for the State. It's a federal business. I raise and train these dogs for the state government to trail and track down convicts, escaped convicts. These dogs are the highest pedigree bloodhounds in the world. They will follow the scent and track and trail a man to the end of the earth. These are not dogs—these are hounds. The finest, smartest hounds in God's creation. These are bloodhounds! Bloodhounds! With these hounds I have trailed and tracked down many escaped prisoners. The very few convicts who have escaped me and my hounds got out of the open woods, swam streams, caught freight trains, went into towns and cities, where my hounds lost their scent. Once a convict leaves the open woods, swamps, forest, and gets in amongst other human beings, my hounds lose his scent. A smart convict knows that."

Pappy saw I was interested and started talking slow and careful of each word. "Two years ago there was a jailbreak. A flock of nigguh convicts flew the coop and took off into the swamps. The warden called up heah for me to bring my hounds to apprehend them nigguhs. We gathered the hounds, and in five hours we was at the scene. I unchained Simon and two dozen of my best hounds and turned 'em loose. In five minutes Simon snorted up the foul scent of them nigguh convicts and lit out on their trail. Now I'm old and can't follow my hounds as fast as before, but I followed the trail because I could heah Simon and the hounds' yelps. By my watch I had turned my hounds on the nugguhs' scent at 1 p.m. Nine o'clock Simon could be heard faintly in the distance yelping. The warden, myself and two dozen keepers were famished, exhausted and thirsty. They wanted to stop and rest a spell, but I urged 'em on. Those were the orniest bunch of nigguhs I ever tracked. I bet we must've covered thirty odd miles in swamp country, down in water, up outer water, over fences, under fences, through brambles, bushes, slush, soft sands—but we tracked on.

"10.30 by my Elgin watch we came upon some of my hounds. It was strange—they were not yelping. They were carefully moving about making a sort of nervous sound. I sensed trouble, and sho' 'nough it was around and about. There was the sound of a great nest of rattlers. Musta been five thousand rattle snakes rattling their tails. And that's a sound the bravest of men will take heed to—that's if he knows about snakes, especially rattlers. I called my hounds. They were scared shitless. The coward-assed warden and his spineless keepers backed off to a safe distance. I hate a coward son of a bitch. I calmed myself down, patted all the hounds and talked to them. The scene began to git sorta clear thereabouts. I looked over in the distance about thirty odd feet, and I saw the stripes of a convict suit. I looked good. Couldn't see the nigguh. Hard to see a nigguh in the dark, but I could make out the black and white stripes.

"I yelled, 'Nigguh, I sees you. Come on outter there.'

"The nigguh yelled pitifully, 'Boss, please don't shoot.'

"I said, 'Nigguh, come on outter them canebreaks.'

" 'I'm skeered, boss. I ain't lyin', boss. Cain't you hear them rattlers sizzlin'? Cain't you hear them? Boss, it's a million of 'em.'

"The scary-assed warden came tiptoeing back like one of them European ballet dancers. Made me sick to my stomach. And the keepers, the coward bastards, stayed put, just like statues. I yelled again, 'Nigguh, bring your black ass outter there. How many of you all in there?'

"The nigguh said, 'It's two of us, boss.'

"I raised up my shotgun and said loudly, 'Nigguh, I'm gonna count to three, and if you don't come here to me with your black hands reaching for the sky, I'm gonna blast your black asses to kingdom come.'

"The nigguh said, 'Boss, please don't shoot. I'm skeered to move. There's rattle snakes all around my feet. If I move they gonna bite me.'

"I said, 'Where's that other nigguh?'

"The nigguh yelled back, 'He's layin' on the ground. He's been bitten by a rattler and he's layin' on some rattlers. I think he's dyin'. He's shakin' all over from head to feet. He's dyin'. He cain't talk, won't answer. Just layin' here shakin' and shakin'. Down here on the ground. Come and see for yourself.'

"The warden hollered, 'What's your name, nigguh?'

" 'My name is Rufus, boss,' the nigguh answered.

"Boy, as I'm sitting here I've got to say it even if it chokes me," said Pappy. "I don't like nigguhs 'cause I can't figger out a nigguh. I thinks of nigguhs constantly. A nigguh is hard to understand. I works nigguhs, been working nigguhs all my life. You command a nigguh to do some work. He or she will do the work. You pay the nigguh Satiday. You don't see he or she on Monday and they might not come on to the job Tuesday or Wednesday. A nigguh's just plain trifling. But somehow that nigguh convict just got to me in the midst of all them dangerous rattlesnakes. And somehow I just had to take sides with the nigguh against serpents. Hearing all that constant rattling of all them snakes I knew the nigguh wasn't lying. Because my hounds has times before come upon pine forest and canebreaks infested with rattlers, and it's a terrible sight to see and hear all them snakes and all that continuous rattling.

"The warden yelled, 'I'll tell you what to do. Squat and leap and leap and leap in this here direction.'

"The nigguh said, 'What about this convict layin' here on the ground?'

"The warden said, 'You forget that nigguh. He'll be daid in a minute. You do as I command you to do.'

"The nigguh said, 'I plumb skeered, boss. I'm skeered. There must be a million rattlers around my feet.'

"The warden yelled, 'Nigguh, do as I command you or you'll be dying like the other nigguh.'

"The nigguh said, 'OK, boss, here I comes.'"

Pappy looked me right in the eye and then from head to foot. Seeing I was looking and listening with so much interest he shook his head and said, "Well, what happened is a miracle. Boy, do you know the nigguh was standing about thirty feet from me and I'm looking at the stripes on the convict suit. Of course I can't visualize the nigguh's face or head or hands 'cause it's dark. That nigguh squatted and leaped exactly and precisely three times, and each leap had to be twelve feet. The nigguh flew through the air with his arms outspread. His feet barely touched the ground, and he squatted with outspread arms and leaped again. He did that three times. He leaped through the air just like a bird, a fowl. Up until this day I wonder 'bout those leaps. It was just like a bird, a quail, that's been flustered. And do you know, when the nigguh got to us he fell to the earth. Generally the hounds leap on the convicts, both black and white, and start chewing them up. Do you know, my hounds did not lay a fang on that nigguh. They just stood there and looked at that nigguh in astonishment.

"Now my hounds are smart, and they saw what happened. It was something mystifying 'bout that. I just stood there. The warden stood there and my hounds stood there looking down at that nigguh—not the nigguh, but the striped convict suit, because like I said before, you couldn't see the nigguh in the dark. We just stood there about five minutes looking at the nigguh breathing heavy. We heard my other hounds yelping in the far-off distance, and that brought us to our senses.

"The warden told the nigguh to git up. The nigguh rose to his feet and reached for the sky. The warden said, 'Drop you arms, nigguh, and relax yourself,' which the nigguh did.

"The nigguh started moaning, 'Thank you Lord. Lord, Lord, I know there's a Lord. Lord, have mercy. Lord, thank ye. Thank ye, Lord.'

"The warden hollered, 'Shut up, nigguh! Stop that God calling,' but the nigguh kept on praising the Lord. The warden juggled his shotgun in the nigguh's belly and hollered, 'Shut up, nigguh!'

"The nigguh said, 'Gone kill me boss, but I got to thank my Lord.'

"Boy, you know, when the nigguh said those words about his God, seems like the swamp sort of brightened up a little. I'm sure we all saw it, even my hounds. My hounds did not lay a fang on that nigguh, and

I've trained my hounds to tear up a convict suit regardless of who is in it, a white convict or a black one. I heard my other hounds again in the distance, and I told the coward-assed warden to come on. The warden called them scary-assed keepers, who'd moved back further up on high ground. It took them minutes to come near. The warden said, 'Take this nigguh back.' All of them tried to grab the nigguh. The warden hollered, 'Just two of you!'

"One of the keepers hollered, 'Reach up, nigguh!'

"The warden juggled his gun butt in the keeper's belly and said, 'He's reached up enough. Take him back slowly. Don't lay a hand on him. I want to talk to him when I get back. Heah me?'

"The nigguh said to the warden nicely, just like a nigguh deacon, 'Boss, sir, warden, captain, what 'bout dat convict layin' yonder on top of dem rattlers. You gonna leave him dere?'

"The warden said to the nigguh, 'That nigguh is sho' dead by now, and I'm not going in that nest of snakes to git no nigguh. I'll resign first. I'll give up this job first. I'll not risk my life amongst no rattlesnakes to ketch no convict nigguh. That's final.'

"Boy, you know dat nigguh speaking like a deacon again said to the warden, 'Boss, good kind boss, I ain't skeered no mo',' and he dropped to his knees. Boy, I'm looking at this with my eyes popped open. That nigguh looked up to the sky. I see my hounds. They are looking at the nigguh, and do you know the whole bunch of them squatted down. The nigguh on his knees cupped his big black hands and spoke loudly, 'Boss, if you would trust me with a gun I will go back in the canebreaks and tote that convict on my back back here at your feet, 'cause as of right now I ain't fearin' nuttin on the face of the good God's earth, especially no snakes, no sort of snakes. That convict layin' on dem snakes is a Godfearing soul. He was forced to make this break for freedom. He prays all de time. He was—and if'n he's still breathin' the good God's air, he is—a church thinkin' soul. And in the sight of God a Christian man wouldn't leave a Christian man layin' at the mercy of snakes.'

"Boy, by this time I'm beginning to listen to what this nigguh is saying. The nigguh said, 'Boss, regardless of men's feelin's towards other men, the Good Book states in black and white that all men are created equal and all men are the same in the sight of Jehovah, and as Jehovah commands, thy is thy brother's keeper. And, boss, good kind warden, you is of now my keeper, and you is that convict dyin' over there's keeper.'

"The warden yelled, 'Shut up, nigguh.' I could hear my other hounds yelping. I'm now bewildered listening to all that nigguh church and Bible talk. I looked down and could see my hounds. It's sort of brighter now and my hounds are laying down and looking up sheepishly—in a row, like folks at church. Boy, the nigguh church talk got the best of me. Without my knowing I said to the warden, 'Warden, let's go and fetch that nigguh outter them canebreaks.'

"The nigguh said, 'Warden, please good, kind mister warden, please trust me with a gun so I'll go in dem breaks and fetch that soul out and from amongst the snakes. I'm not skeered any more. If you won't trust me with a gun, please let me fashion a branch offen one of them trees and I'll go amongst they snakes like the Archangel Michael and slay them and fetch that convict.'

"Boy, that nigguh's church talk aroused me and I went completely out of my senses and shot in the midst of them snakes. The warden and the keepers started shooting a path straight towards the direction that that nigguh leaped from. The way we shot up that earth you would've thought that all hell broke loose. About nine of us shot up a path in that swamp. Snakes, dragons, demons, 'gators tore ass and begone. It happened so fast and so quick I still can't believe it. As we shot up the ground it looked like New Year's Eve night. Before you could say 'Jack Sprat' the nigguh picked up the nigguh laying on the snakes, threw him over his shoulder, and ran out from the nest of snakes."

I said, "Was the convict dead?"

Pappy said, "When the country folks heard all the shooting, the menfolks came running to the scene with their shotguns. Of course everybody in the county by now had heard of the prison break. They lit lanterns and then you could see the nigguh's faces and what they looked like. The snakebitten nigguh was examined by a local vetinarian who was there with his gun. The vet said the nigguh would die 'cause he was badly bitten in many places by more than one rattler. One of the prison trucks came up and the keepers boosted the nigguh up on the truck and took the two nigguhs back to the farm."

After that, we got back to the banjo. I sang a song, *Li'l Liza Jane*. He thanked me. And he was looking at me with his sky-blue eyes. He said, "It's nice of you to come out here and sing and play for me." And he called Theresa and said, "Will you get my box for me? My tin box?"

Well Theresa took her time and went in and brought out the box. There was some money in there. The old man took out some bills and he gave me some. One side was yellow. I had never seen any bills like that. So I thanked him. He blew his whistle two long loud times, and his son came and drove me back in his truck. Back at my rooming house

I saw Henry Pagaud. I told him how I had been to the bloodhound farm, and about those famous bloodhounds that were known all over the South. And I told him how the hounds were sent out after convicts, and the stories of people who had the hounds set on them. And I told him how Pappy had given me some money.

"How much?"

"Fifty dollars. But strange—the money looks more like coupons to me."

So I showed Henry the bills. He said, "Man, these is dixies. These ten dollar bills are dixies. That's where the word dixie comes from: ten dollars—D-I-X—you understand? When soldiers in the Confederate War spoke of money, ten dollar bills, they spoke of dixies. And man, dixies are no good. They're Confederate money, used to pay the soldiers in the Civil War. And now it's no better than counterfeit. There's no money to back up the bills. So you can't spend that! He's pulled a fast one on you Danny." I thought learning about them bloodhounds and that convict and the snakes was worth the trip to the farm–kennel.

THIRTEEN

All them women belong to me

When I first started playing, an old bass player and I became very friendly. He hustled lots of gigs for me and I learned a lot from him. This musician's IQ averaged zero. All he was ever interested in was music, whiskey and women. Honestly, he did not know who was the president of the United States. I learned this listening to an argument he had with another musician who asked him just that question. He replied, "It don't matter to me who is the president, or what his name is, the rotten son of a bitch. What's the use of me knowing him? He ain't gonna do a damn thing for me or you either, and whoever he is, he can kiss my ass."

The band played a political rally in New Orleans in 1926. The politician was running for a high office. The band was hired to play on his tour of New Orleans and the neighboring towns and villages. The first night we played we sat on a platform behind all of the candidates. The platform was decorated with American flags, Confederate flags and bunting. There were about six thousand people in the audience listening to the speeches.

The leading spokesman got up and told the people, "I promise you all every road in this state will be paved. Every man and woman who wants a job to make an honest living, I'll see to it that they get a job. All the old people will get a pension." In the meantime we, the band, were given handbills and pamphlets to pass out to the audience. This politician spoke on and on of all the things he would do if elected. When we had finished passing out the pamphlets and took our seats again we were all acting half asleep. When he finished this long speech with all its promises he looked back at the band and said, "Boys, play *Dixie*." We played *Dixie*.

When we finished the crowd screamed, whistled and gave the rebel yell. During the next ten minutes he shook hands, and while looking at us he drank about four glasses of water. A few people who had been seated in the front row started to leave and so he walked to the front of the platform, raised his hands and yelled loudly, "Wait, my friends and fellow citizens. There is one thing I overlooked and forgot to speak of, and it is one of the most important issues of my platform." There was a pause and it became very quiet. He said, in a very dejected manner and bowing his head, "We have got to, and are going to keep them niggers in their places. There are some niggers who want to be even up with white folks, and them niggers is trying to start trouble. A nigger knows his place. There is some good niggers down here and there is lots of bad niggers. I can tolerate a bad nigger, but I'll go to hell with a smart nigger!!" The crowd went wild. While he spoke I silently observed the members of the band. No one seemed concerned or moved a muscle so I, from instinct, did likewise. In Rome do as the Romans do. When the politician stopped speaking and the crowd finally dispersed he and his group got into a huddle while we packed up our instruments. He came over to us and said, "Boys, you did a wonderful job. Here's five dollars tip apiece." Then he told us where the rally would be the following night.

While leaving I asked the old bass player, "Did you hear what that man said?"

He answered, "What the hell do you think I am—deaf?"

I said, "Wasn't that something!"

He said, "Son, all I'm interested in is the money. That ignorant son of a bitch, he ain't fooling nobody but them poor ignorant white folks. I'd like to meet that so-and-so in the desert someplace. I'd show him who to keep down—that so-and-so. Don't you know, to keep somebody down you got to stay down with 'em?"

We went to Pensacola, Florida, to play for a woman agent who proved a big disappointment. She did not have the engagements that she had promised, so she booked a weekend for the band in a small town called De Funiak Springs in Florida. We left for the town and arrived there early in the day so that the people in town would know we were there. That was how things were done in those days. The news spread around town very quickly and the dance was a success and a sellout.

I noticed that the sheriff stood by the bandstand most of the night watching everybody, looking solemn and showing no enthusiasm or emotion. All the ladies and girls seemed friendly, and quite a few of them flirted. The sheriff was just taking in everything. When the band took ten minutes off he called us in a corner and said, "Now listen heah. Kin all you all heah me?" He go no response. "So all of ya all don't heah me?" He became very stern and serious. "Is any of ya all dumb?"

We said, "No, sir."

"Is any of ya all deaf?"

We said, "No, sir."

"Is any of ya all blind?"

We said, "No, sir."

He said, "Well, all ya all kin all see me and who I am."

We said, "Yes, sir."

He continued, "Well, listen to me carefully. Ya all niggers is from Louisiana, and ya all thinks that ya all is smart 'cause ya all can play them horns. Well, listen now. I don't want to see or catch any of you niggers with any of these white men's nigger wimmen, and if I do it's going to be some dead Louisiana niggers shipped back to Louisiana."

There was a pause which lasted for a few minutes. Then my friend the bass player spoke up, "Mr. Sheriff, could . . . er . . . uh . . . you show us or point out these white gentlemen's lady friends to us."

The sheriff replied very curtly, "I ain't showing you niggers nuthin', but I'll tell you this: all them nigger women you see out there belong to them white men." And with that he walked away.

Back on the bandstand whenever any woman asked for a request, all I heard was, "Yes, ma'm." "Yes, ma'am." "Yes, ma'am." I have never heard so many "Yes, ma'ams." We stayed there for four days and I heard this remark many times. Those were the most polite bunch of music men I've ever seen. Even the children were told, "Yes ma'am."

The day we left the sheriff was there and came up to the car and said, "Well, boys, ya all got sense, 'cause when a white man tells you sumpin' ya all listen. And if ya all'll ever come this direction again, ya all is welcome; and if you have any trouble up the road send word to me, and I'll do what I kin to help you." Everybody nodded their heads but nobody said a word, and the car pulled off slowly, then sped away. The only sound in the car was the motor for the first twenty miles. Then my friend the bass player said, "When that sheriff was talking all that, I was so mad I could a punched him in the mouth, but it seems like a spirit or something powerful was holding my arm!"

The trumpet player then spoke up, "If you had punched that sheriff you would have met that spirit you said was holding your arm." We all laughed.

FOURTEEN

Dan and Lu's marriage

In New Orleans years back—say the 1910s and 1920s—the word and
the business of marriage was right before you. You saw and lived
amongst people who lived married lives. I saw couples living together.
I heard the talk and comments of elders, always discussing problems. I
grew up among relatives—aunts and uncles, great aunts and uncles,
cousins—most married. Solid marriages. Wives managing homes and
husbands working and providing for their families. I heard comments
of people, married couples and their families. I saw my relatives live
the poor black peoples' life-style, holding steady jobs at the same
location for a long stretch of years. Working, managing, not complain-
ing; contented and living within their means. The men earning the
money and the wives managing the house; the men bringing their
salaries to the wives, keeping their allowance and making do.

Now playing music only as a living, trade or profession was and is
today uncertain, shaky and unpredictable. But there are daily actions
in living that are constant and serious. First there is food: three or more
meals each and every day. Sleep: a clean bed. A house: the rent paid.
And a person or persons to maintain and keep the house. From the age
of twelve on I was aware of this house set-up, how the home func-
tioned. I saw the well-adjusted families, how they lived. And there was
a multitude of families to watch and pattern your life after. You saw and
heard of partings, break-ups, separations, and why they happened. All
sorts of disasters. I saw the married couples living nicely, working
steady on jobs—the low-salaried jobs, but managing to enjoy life.
Accepting jobs in service. Not skilled jobs, but important jobs, taking
care of the maintenance, cleaning of buildings: porters, watchmen.

Isidore Barbarin worked with the undertaking business as drayman
and carriage driver, with horses, until 1925, when the undertakers
changed from horses to automobiles. Isidore worked steady because
people die steadily. Dying is good business. My stepfather was a skilled
baker and worked steady. Bread is the number one food. Now at
sixteen I was playing music professionally. Isidore fathered nine

children and, I would say, managed a well-governed home. If you want a comfortable house you took care of your salary and gave your salary to your wife. My grandmother Josephine, Isidore's wife, was a very wise woman, and from close observance, prophesied the outcome of neighborhood happenings.

Now around the time when I first started playing with that little kid's band, the Boozan Kings, I would come in late at night, around eleven or twelve, which was after the curfew. I had an understanding mother, because she knew I was out there hustling, doing as many musicians did, playing in joints and honky-tonks and backrooms and house parties, all kinds of strange places where people wanted music. New Orleans then was a good-time town, and there was no real curfew. As long as people were spending money, the bartenders said, "Stay up! Stay up!" So at this time I began courting Blue Lu.

My mother was always telling me, "Mr Daniel" (that's what she called me), "You don't want to end up like your daddy, caught up in that night life. When you get through work, come on home. Don't stay up to make the money and then spend it, and be with those fast people. It's alright to play for them, but don't associate with them. If you want to make old bones, you don't want to die young. Having a bucketful of these wild, fast women, that's trouble. Them fast, wild young women are jumping from man to man. They's just wild. Ain't nothing to them. They with you tonight, Sam Monday night, Bill Tuesday night. You understand, they're fast and foolish. They're common. They're trash, garbage. Pick out a sensible young girl from a respectable family. Plan on getting married and living a normal life. Learn you a good trade and play music for pleasure. Take notice how your grandfather lives. You don't see him overdoing nothing."

I said, "Uh huh," but thought, "Isidore sure fathered a lot of children." And so I began to look out at the multitude of young girls around and about. And just at that time a couple of young aunts began scouting, figuring, and setting up a liaison—meeting—with me and a few well-chosen young girls. That was a New Orleans custom. The discussions, planning, campaigning as to what young people would make compatable mates. This was a serious matter. You knew who would make a good couple. My aunt Marie Phillips Barbarin, the drummer Louis Barbarin's wife, had observed Louise Dupont, a fine young pretty girl, and theorized that we would make a fine married couple. So she saw me and said, "Daniel, whatcha doing Sunday?"

I said, "I don't know yet."

She said, "I'm having a little soiree, a party, Sunday afternoon around three. Come by if you ain't playing music. I want you to meet a nice young girl. She's fine and pretty."

I said, "Alright."

In the meantime Louise was asked to come to the soiree party also. I went to the party and there I saw Louise before I was introduced to her. I was drawn to her like as if by a magnet, came on with the charm and started conversation. Louise and I talked, laughed, and I introduced myself. I told her who I was and she did likewise. My aunt called us and said, "I was going to introduce you two, but seems like I don't need to. You all look good together, a nice couple. Yeah, yeah." She smiled, satisfied at the meeting. Later Louise told me Marie had set up the plan for Louise and me to meet through Gladys Phillips, her sister. Gladys Phillips is big Billy Phillips's sister. Billy was a drummer and independent bandleader. He would get youngsters to play, get you going with jobs. And he was also a businessman, a vegetable seller, running his vegetable business from his house. Gladys met me, through Marie, and she liked me. She told me she knew a nice little girl she'd like me to meet. They knew I was straightforward—didn't get drunk or smoke reefers, always neat and clean, wore a collar and tie, always presentable. So she figured we would be a good combination, me and this little girl.

At the party, I asked Louise her age. She smiled and said, "I'm thirteen." But, I thought, a large thirteen—looked sixteen. My age was seventeen. I told her I was fifteen. During the party Gladys asked Louise how she liked me. Louise answered, "He's alright, but maybe he's older than me, and must have other girls.

Gladys growled, "Fool, that boy's got a job and he comes from a nice family. Make like you don't know how old he is."

After the soiree party I walked Louise and Gladys home. I asked Louise could I see her again. She said yes, and I began meeting her at Gladys's house a couple of times a week. But Louise told me, "My mother says if I'm going to be meeting you, to come to the house. Don't be meeting you at somebody else's house. She wants to see you, so come there—she's not going to bite you!" So we arranged it for Sunday evening, and she gave me the address. But I knew where it was, as by then I'd walked her home a couple of times, and her mother had seen me. She didn't come out to meet me, and I didn't knock on the door. Like all youngsters I was leery of her parents. So on the Sunday I knocked on the door: "Good evening, Mrs Dupont."

She said, "Hello, you're Danny, I presume. Well, come in." So I went in. And she told me she'd asked Louise to ask me to come to the house. She didn't want me meeting her in the street, as it wasn't respectable. I said, "Yes, ma'am, I understand." So she told me anytime I wanted to see Louise to come to the house, and if I wanted to take her to the theater, not to worry about Gladys, but to come to the house for her.

After that Louise called me to find how things had gone. She was afraid I'd never come back. But I did, and we struck up this courtship affair. I would see her when I could, but I was traveling, playing music. Her mother heard I was a musician and she asked Louise what else I did, as I surely couldn't make a living playing music. "All these musicians have two or three wives, and children scattered all over. And the music is haphazard, you don't know whether you're going to work or not, and it's hard to keep a family together. If you love your horn more than your family, well you put your family down, 'cause there aren't a lot of musicians going to put their instruments down." And she said she thought I should have a day job and only play when I felt like it, and be making a steady income that would provide for my family.

Now I had done a few other things. As well as having been a delivery boy, I painted—could have been a painter. I could have mixed paints, the turpentine, linseed oil, and all that business. But instead I tried to play music for a living. The youngsters I started with was people like Louis Cottrell and Arthur Derbigny, and we started in Dwight Newman's band (on the Roof Garden), which was two nights a week. In New Orleans. Then all of a sudden Don Albert came back to town, and Cottrell and some of the others left to play with his band. But they didn't take me, though I came up with Don Albert—his house was facing me as a child—they took Ferdinand Dejan for some reason. Maybe he was a better banjo player. They went to Texas. So that left me here. But I was glad I didn't go in that territory band with Don Albert; it never reached the fame or acclaim they should have had. They were a great band. But that was still the first let-down I had.

But I carried on playing, and getting tighter with Louise. This went on for three long years, and Mrs Dupont told Louise she was going to ask me my intentions. She wanted to know if I had the intention of getting married or just coming there to wear out her chairs. Mrs Dupont asked me my intentions with Louise. I answered, "I plan to marry Louise." She said, "That's nice, we will talk about it." We talked later and we started preparing for the wedding. That was in March 1929, and we got married on January 8th, 1930. We had a nice wreath and veil Catholic wedding and an exciting wedding reception loaded with jazz musicians blowing their horns. And we set sail on the great ship jazz on the sea of matrimony.

Now I had a wife and a home. Most of the other musicians had day jobs, real good money coming in, and they stayed alive with day jobs. I was still playing music for a living.

I met Lee Collins when I was working at the Alamo with Willie Pagaud. Somebody told Lee about me. I think it was Arthur Derbigny. This was the time I first heard of bands doing summer tours with circuses. Arthur recommended me to Lee Collins. So I went to a rehearsal. When I walked in I had on a pair of brand new shoes which were expensive. All the men round town wore this kind of shoes—the hustlers, the gamblers—they were something special. And later on Lee told me he kept me in the band because when I walked in I was wearing such high-powered shoes, and they looked so good on my feet. He said, "You must have had some sense. Those shoes sold you." So anyway, I walked into the rehearsal, knocked on the door. They said, "Come in." And there was the band: Joe Robichaux, Ernest Kelly on trombone, Arthur Derbigny, Lee Rouzan on saxophones, somebody Smith on bass, and Jim Willigan on drums. I'd never seen none of those guys. And when I came in Lee says, "Make yourself at home. Take your instrument out." So I took the banjo out. Ernest Kelly looked at me, I looked at him, and he said, "How's your mother?" That was playing the dozens. In New Orleans that was a thing they had. He didn't know my mother—why ask about her? It was a smart aleck thing to ask after my mother, playing the dozens. He was trying to see if I could take it. Having been raised in the seventh ward where all the do-wrong cats hung out, I'd heard people play the dozens all day: "Your mother don't wear no drawers," "Your mother fell in love with a police dog," and all that kind of real uncouth talk. So when Ernest Kelly tried to play the dozens on me I looked around—everyone was looking back at me—and I said, "How's yours? Give her my love." He shut up his mouth, because I'd put him back in the dozens, and from then on he always looked at me with a straight face. He never forgot that.

FIFTEEN

Jelly Roll Morton in New York

When I arrived in New York City in 1930 my uncle Paul Barbarin and my friend Henry "Red" Allen took me to the Rhythm Club, which was known for its famous jam sessions and cutting contests. The club was owned and operated by Bert Hall, a trombone player, politician and gambler, who had left Chicago for New York. Bert introduced many reforms in Local 802 that were for the protection of its negro members who, lots of times after working in clubs owned by racketeers, were doubtful of getting paid until the money was in their hands. (Before the coming of Bert there was The Bandbox, another club owned by a trumpet player named Major. And there was the Amsterdam Club, a relic of the old Clef Club.)

The afternoon I walked into the Rhythm Club, the corner and street were crowded with musicians with their instruments and horns. I was introduced, and shook hands with a lot of fellows on the outside. Then we entered the inside, which was crowded. What I saw and heard I will never forget. A wild cutting contest was in progress, and sitting and standing around the piano were twenty or thirty musicians, all with their instruments out waiting for a signal to play choruses of Gershwin's *Liza*.

It was a Monday afternoon and the musicians gathered at the club to get their pay for weekend jobs and to gossip and chew the fat. But this Monday the news had spread that the famous McKinney's Cotton Pickers from the Greystone Ballroom in Detroit were in town to record for Victor and start an eastern tour. At that time the Cotton Pickers, Fletcher Henderson, and the Casa Loma Orchestra were considered the best bands in the land.

This day at the Rhythm Club most of the famous leaders, stars and sidemen were there—the big names I'd heard and read about: Benny Carter, Don Redman, Horace Henderson, Fess Williams, Claude Hopkins, Sonny Greer, John Kirby, Johnny Hodges, Freddie Jenkins, Bobby Stark, Chick Webb, Big Green and Charlie Johnson. Around the piano sat three banjo players: Bernard Addison, Ikie Robinson and Teddy Bunn with his guitar. Paul told me, "See those three fellows? They are the best banjo players in New York City, and that guy standing behind them is Seminole. You watch him." Which I did.

After each of the banjo players played dozens of choruses the crowd yelled, "Seminole! Cut them cats!" And after much applause and persuasion Seminole, who was left-handed, reached for a banjo that was tuned to be played right-handed, and to my amazement he started wailing on the banjo playing it upside down, that is, playing everything backwards. I later learned that, being left-handed, Seminole did not bother to change the strings—he just taught himself.

After his solos the banjos were quiet; they just played rhythm. Then in rushed a comical little fat young fellow carrying some drums, which he hurriedly set up. Paul said, "That's Randolf. He plays with the Tramp Band, a vaudeville act." Randolf played eccentric and trick novelty drums; he was very clever with all sorts of rhythm and clever beats. Then the crowd yelled for Chick Webb, who washed Randolf away.

Paul said, "Watch this." Then it was a trumpet battle: Bobby Stark, Rex Stewart and Cuba Bennett. Cuba Bennett was the most highly respected trumpet player at that time in New York City. He is a cousin of Benny Carter, and the great bandleaders boasted with authority that he could play more beautiful and complex solos than anyone in the whole world. When he played everybody in the street and on the sidewalks rushed in. He was terrific. I'll never forget it, as I had never heard a trumpet played like that. He was everything they claimed he was. While I was listening someone said, "That cat is only pressing on the second and third valve." I never saw much of him after that as he went to Camden, New Jersey, to live. But any time trumpet players were discussed, Cuba Bennett was spoken of with reverence. I must have heard this about a hundred times from different musicians who had passed through Camden, New Jersey, on tours: "We passed through Camden, so we stopped at that gin joint where Cuba hangs out at. He still plays great. He's got a family and you couldn't pull him out of Camden for a million dollars."

At this session John Kirby, who had just bought a new bass, was playing and, like an amateur, was searching for the positions on the fingerboard of the bass. I asked Paul who was that cat trying to play that bass. Paul said, "That's John Kirby. He's the best tuba player in New York City; he works with Fletcher Henderson." I was amazed at his playing, because I had heard the greatest bass players: Chester Zardis,

Al Morgan, Albert Glenny, Jimmy Johnson, Ransom Knolling, Simon Marrero and dozens of fine bass players in New Orleans.

The crowd called for Pops Foster. Kirby handed him the bass and then stood by with all the other bass tuba players and watched Pops with pop-eyed interest as he slapped a dozen choruses of *Liza*. In 1930 Pops Foster and Wellman Braud were the only two string bass players in New York City other than a few Cuban and Puerto Rican bass players. The most renowned was Tizol, who was an uncle of Juan Tizol of Duke Ellington fame, who wrote *Caravan*. The bandleaders in New York City were finally convinced that the bass fiddle belonged and sounded better in the band than the tuba.

There were other bass players around, but they played with the West Indian gig bands and the negro show orchestras. They played the bass fiddle dignified, not with the barrelhouse beat. There were dozens of bands in New York City and all used sousaphones. This was different from the New Orleans scene. These bass horn players were called "Bass" this, "Bass" that, with emphasis on the word "bass": Bass Hill, Bass Turner, Bass Kirby, Bass Benford, Bass Aderhold, Bass England, Bass Taylor, Bass Smitty. When the bass fiddle caught on and sousaphones went out and all the bands and bass players used basses, the name "Bass" was dropped and the players were called by their given names, John Kirby, Billy Taylor, Wellman Braud. During the changeover to the bass fiddle Pops Foster had hundreds of students and imitators.

In the meantime, here's that Seminole seating himself at the piano and playing *Liza* like as if he had written it, as the crowd screamed his praise. In the next few years I learned that Seminole was a wizard at playing the banjo, piano and xylophone; but, like Cuba Bennett, he left New York and went to Atlantic City, New Jersey, and became a legend of the past.

I was watching the jam session with interest when Paul said, "Come over here and meet Jelly Roll and King Oliver." Paul led me through the crowd to where King and Jelly stood. I had noticed Fletcher Henderson was playing pool and seemed unconcerned about who was playing in the jam session, or who was there. Whenever I saw him at the club he was always playing pool seriously, never saying anything to anyone, just watching his opponent's shots and solemnly keeping score. All the other musicians watched the game and whispered comments, because he was the world's greatest bandleader. Paul told King and Jelly, "Here's my nephew; he just came from New Orleans."

King Oliver said, "How you doing, Gizzard Mouf?" I laughed, and Jelly said, "How you Home Town?"

I said, "Fine." And from then on he always called me "Home Town."

Jelly, who was a fine pool and billiard player, had been watching and commenting to Oliver on Fletcher's pool shots. King could play a fair game also. Jelly said (and he didn't whisper), "That Fletcher plays pool just like he plays piano—ass backwards, just like a crawfish." And Oliver laughed and laughed until he started coughing. The session went on and on, and I noticed that nothing—the ovations, comments, solos, or anybody or anything—moved Henderson in the least. That evening I went with King Oliver to his rehearsal. He did not play much as he was having trouble with his teeth.

Jelly Roll spent most of the afternoon and evenings at the Rhythm Club, and every time I saw him he was lecturing to the musicians about organizing. Most of the name and star musicians paid him no attention, because he was always preaching, in loud terms, that none of the famous New York bands had a beat. He would continually warn me, "Home Town, don't be simple and ignorant like these fools in this big country town." I would always listen seriously, because most of the things he said made plenty of sense to me.

Jelly was constantly preaching that if he could get a band to rehearse his music and listen to him, he could keep a band working. He would get one-nighters out of town, and would have to beg musicians to work with him. Most of the time the musicians would arrive at the last moment, or send a substitute in their place. I learned later that they were angry with him, because he was always boasting about how great New Orleans musicians were. Jelly's songs and arrangements had a deep feeling lots of musicians could not feel and improvise on, so they would not work with Jelly—just could not grasp the roots, soul, feeling. At that time most working musicians were arrangement-conscious following the pattern of Henderson, Redman, Carter and Chick Webb. Jelly's music was considered corny and dated. I played quite a few of these one-nighters with Jelly, and on one of the dates I learned that Jelly could back up most of the things he boasted of.

On one date the band met at the Rhythm Club about three in the afternoon and left from there in Jelly Roll's two Lincoln cars to play in Hightstown, New Jersey, at a playground that booked all the famous bands at that time. On the way we came upon a scene of much excitement. A farmer in a jalopy had driven off a country road right in the path of a speeding trailer truck. The big truck pushed the jalopy about a hundred feet, right into a diner. The diner was full of people who were having dinner. The impact turned the diner over, and the hot coffee percolator scalded the waitresses and customers. Nobody was badly hurt, but they were shocked and scared and screaming and yelling.

We pulled up and rushed out to help the victims, who were frantic. Jelly yelled loudly and calmed the folks down. He took complete charge of the situation. Jelly crawled into the overturned diner and called the state police and hospitals. They sent help in a very short time. Then he consoled the farmer, who was jammed in his jalopy and couldn't be pulled out. His jalopy was crushed like an accordion against the diner by the big trailer. The farmer was so scared he couldn't talk, and when the emergency wrecker finally pulled his jalopy free and opened the door and lifted him out, I noticed that he was barefooted. I remarked to Jelly that the farmer was barefooted. Jelly told me that happens in a wreck; the concussion and force cause a person's nerves to constrict and their shoes jump off.

Jelly talked to all the officials at the scene and they thanked him for his calls and calmness in an emergency. We got back in the cars and drove off. As we rode Jelly spoke on and on of how white folks are scared to die. I rode in the car with Jelly and I can't recall who it was, but it was either Tommy Benford or Ward Pinkett who kept on disagreeing with everything Jelly said, which was the usual procedure whenever he had an audience around the Rhythm Club.

We passed some men who were hunting in a field. They were shooting at some game that were flying overhead. Jelly said, "Them bums can't shoot. When I was with Wild West shows I could shoot with the best marksmen and sharpshooters in the world." Either Benford or Pinkett said, "Why don't you stop all that bullshit?" And that argument went on and on.

When we arrived at Hightstown and drove into the entrance of the playground and got out of the cars, I noticed a shooting gallery. So I said to Jelly, "Say, Jelly, there's a shooting gallery." Jelly's eyes lit up and he hollered, "Come here all you cockroaches! I'm going to give you a shooting exhibition!" We all gathered around the shooting gallery and Jelly told the owner, "Rube, load up all of your guns!" And the man did. Jelly then shot all the targets down and did not miss any. The man set them up again and Jelly repeated his performance again. Then he said, "Now, cockroaches, can I shoot?" Everybody applauded. Jelly gave me the prizes, as the man shook his hand. Then he and Jelly talked about great marksmen of the past, as his hecklers looked on with respect.

As he and I walked to the dancehall I asked Jelly how did he know the man's name was Rube. Jelly said, "Home Town, on circuses, carnivals, medicine shows, all concession owners are called Rube, and when anybody connected with the show gets in trouble with someone or people from the town, he hollers, 'Rube!' and the show people rush to his defense and rescue. Show folks stick together." From then on I had a sympathetic respect for Jelly. I also noticed that his hecklers did not dispute him in a vicious way like the cats on the corners in New York did.

As I look back on past scenes, situations, and the whys and reasons for many great musicians falling by the wayside to be forgotten by the public, that first Rhythm Club visit comes to my mind. The musicians played spontaneous, creative solos under critical eyes in competition with the world's finest jazz musicians, and many an unknown joined these sessions and earned an international reputation. Then I think of Fletcher Henderson's indifference to the activity there. He was the acknowledged king; his band was the greatest in the world. He knew it because he was being copied by everybody. His sidemen were the best and he paid the highest salaries. Every colored musician knew and read about his famous sidemen: Hawkins, Rex, Walter Johnson, Buster Bailey, Russell Smith, John Kirby, Jimmy Harrison, and the earlier ones—Don Redman, Benny Carter, Big Green, Louis Armstrong, Joe Smith, Tommy Ladnier. Fletcher had hired and fired the greatest jazz names in America. Then in the Rhythm Club Jelly and Oliver stood on the sidelines watching his pool game.

It was a new era. They had become famous with bands which were smaller and which gave the sidemen freedom to express themselves. But the sound that Fletcher presented to the jazz scene was stream-lined, big, powerful, and arranged especially to bring out the best in the instrumentalists of his band. The songs, scores and arrangements were copied and imitated by many of the big jazz orchestras (except Guy Lombardo and Ted Lewis). And as time marched on Jelly and Oliver stood on the sidelines with their plans and music, as the fickle public hurriedly paraded by.

Ten years later Fletcher Henderson, still cool and indifferent, stood on the sidelines as his fickle public hurriedly passed him by, rushing to hear Jimmie Lunceford and his youthful bunch of excellent soloists, novel arrangements, continuous music (intermission once a night). Lunceford gave his audience their fill of beautiful music. His band played; his sidemen did not wander off, as was the problem of leaders in the past. He popped the whip. In the past the leaders had around them famous soloists and sidemen and gave them publicity and billing on marquees and posters. But Lunceford's band was billed as "The Lunceford Special." No name but his.

Then came the great musical revolution. The new generation rebelled against the old system of being buried in a section and blowing tonal and rhythm patterns while the so-called stars, pets and musicians —the friends of bookers, agents, jive critics and magazine writers —got all the credit. The youngsters wanted to express themselves, and they did—they went right back to the old system of New Orleans: "You play your part and I play mine, so we'll both express ourselves. You don't tell me what you want and I don't tell you. We will all play variations on the theme."

In the meantime, during the 1930s, Red Allen had got quite a reputation in New York. Everybody was going to hear Red. He was the trumpet player who was playing on that third valve, which not too many others did. Red had practiced by listening to records. He was learning all kinds of things by listening to everybody on an old-time phonograph. And the phonograph would be sharp, or sometimes flat, and he told me if it was flat he would play to get in tune with it, and that's how he came to use all the valves. If the record was half a tone down he would play with it fingering all the valves, and that way he came to have access to doing all kinds of strange things with that horn. And we were tight. Now he was in demand then. Casa Loma sent word they might hire him if they could break that barrier. Isham Jones: they saw him, they liked him. The whole band came and listened to him play when he was with Luis Russell. They crowded round, asking for another chorus, "Do another one!" And Russell would let him play. They enjoyed all that.

He had a recording contract with Vocalion, where he made small-band records. I was on quite a few of them. He used me, sometimes, with the rest of the Russell rhythm section—Luis Russell, Paul, Pops Foster. As he had used me, when I came to record with Blue Lu I used him. Like I wanted the best musicians. So when I brought her to Decca I used Buster Bailey, Wellman Braud, Red Allen, Sam Price—later Lil Armstrong. And I played on them till I joined Cab and until I fell out with Decca over my royalties and my songs.

Now whenever Jelly Roll Morton appeared on the corner of Seventh Avenue and 132nd Street or in front of the Rhythm Club, or if he walked inside, he was sure to get an immediate audience. During the years 1929 to 1939 the Rhythm Club was always fairly crowded, especially in the cold winter seasons. The patrons were from all over America—mostly musicians, performers and petty gamblers. Jelly called them petty gamblers because he never heard of anyone winning large sums of money. I spent a lot of time there, for it was the focal point of contact for work in New York City. Sitting and standing about the place, as well as many famous names from show business, you would see people from the sports world and also many notorious Harlem characters. There were four pool tables always in use, and in the rear of the club were four green cloth-covered tables which were always occupied by musicians and hustlers playing blackjack, poker, seven-up, and other fast games of chance. In New Orleans I had seen gamblers on a winning streak have as much as five hundred dollars in chips before them and had seen gamblers at the Monte tables with money in the thousands, but at the Rhythm Club I never saw anyone at any time create the excitement of ever having won money in the thousands. I heard Jelly remark one day, "This is supposed to be a gambling house. These idiots ain't never seen the insides of a genuine gambling house. In fact, all them thieves back there wouldn't have the entrance fee to walk into a real house of chance!" From then on my opinion of the back-room gamblers at the Rhythm Club was a very poor one.

I've been asked many times why Jelly was so boastful, and why he even went so far as to explain that he had invented jazz. I have an answer to that. You see, Jelly Roll was part of an era that knew nothing of press agents and publicity build-ups. Most of the famous public figures blew their own horns. John L. Sullivan made many tours of barrooms and cafes and would challenge to a fist fight any man who expressed doubt as to Sullivan's right to the title of "the greatest fighter in the world."

Jelly was partly right in his claim that he invented jazz—that is, his type of jazz. His compositions *King Porter*, *Milenberg Joys*, and his recordings for Victor of *Shreveport Stomp* and *Shoe Shiner's Drag* were some of the finest, if not the best technically recorded jazz records at that time. If you collect records, just match his records with the records of those days. Most of the celebrities of that time were extremely self-centered and proud of their artistry and special talents. They were especially concerned with the billing which they were afforded on publicity posters and theater marquees. Yes, Jelly Roll felt that he was the greatest jazz pianist and composer, and he was just not concerned with any other talent but his own—that is, his own piano playing and composing.

It was the custom of celebrities in those early days to arrive in a city and immediately go to the main drag, where they would loudly start to boast of their ability, and then the mouth-to-mouth news would spread like wildfire that the great So-and-so was in town, and that would really draw a crowd. The gossip sounded like this:

First gossiper, "Man, did you hear the latest?"

Second gossiper, "No. What happened?"

First gossiper, "Man, So-and-so arrived in town this morning and he is down at the Blue Goose Cafe, running off his mouf. He was buying drinks for everybody. He threw a thousand dollars on the bar and said he was the greatest so-and-so in the world, and he'll bet anybody, and put up or shut up."

Jelly Roll pulled this stunt all along the Mississippi River, especially in Kansas City, Memphis, St Louis and Chicago. He pulled it on Fate Marable in St Louis. They admired one another greatly and were fast friends.

On many occasions I sit, drink and discuss jazz records with avid fans of early jazz who own large collections of records and who know their jazz. Beale Riddle of Baltimore, Maryland, had an immense collection of recordings by Morton, Ellington, Pinetop, Bessie Smith—more than I thought existed. During Jelly's last rough days in Washington, DC, Beale was his constant companion. In those days Beale had the forerunner of what is now a hi-fi set, similar to what is called stereophonic sound today. He had hidden amps all over his living room, and he nursed and cared for his immense collection of records as if they were infants. One year I went to Baltimore about fifteen weekends to play with a jazz band at Eddie Leonard's Spa Bar, promoted by Harley Brinsfield. The band was composed of John Alexander (piano), Tilden Street (drums), and Jerry Blumberg (trumpet). After the gig we would hurry to Beale's flat where I stayed and we ate, drank and listened to records, mostly Jelly Roll, Dodds, Ellington.

That's where I really absorbed Jelly's rhythm, beat, feeling, what he had to say musically: *Shoe Shiner's Drag, Wolverine Blues, Mamie's Blues*. Jelly's beat was his and his only; no other composer has it. It is the precise tempo to suit his compositions—not too fast or too slow. I guess that's why he screamed that he invented jazz. I wouldn't be surprised if he didn't take over the engineers and the control room, because his records in the twenties and thirties sound clearer acoustically than most of the jazz recordings of that era. Jelly had an argument with Wilton Crawley, a great performer who played clarinet as part of his act. Jelly played piano on that date for Victor. Crawley was very loud and boastful and Jelly became annoyed with him saying, "Listen, cockroach, the piano solos I'm puttin' on these records will sell the records, so be quiet and tune that poor instrument up, because I will show you how that instrument should be mastered." Crawley remained silent.

Jelly would drive up in front of the Rhythm Club some days, and when the musicians saw him they would start to laugh, for they knew they could anticipate a show and many laughs. As Jelly would stop his large high-powered Lincoln car and step out to the sidewalk, one of the group was sure to gleefully ask him, "Jelly, what's that you say about New York musicians yesterday?" Jelly would prop up his lips and exclaim crisply, "What I said yesterday and today and on Judgement Day and also my dying day is that it takes one hundred live New York musicians to equal one dead police dog." The group would laugh hysterically as Jelly went into his daily tirades and denouncements of the musicians.

I cannot recall one time when Jelly ever mentioned racial prejudice and discrimination. In the Lomax book *Mr. Jelly Lord* he proudly boasted that his ancestors had left the shores of France and settled in this country, but not once did he brag that he was a Creole as most of the light-colored downtown musicians would do. Jelly never used the title "mister" when talking of agents or record company and booking executives; a man was just a man, and when Jelly mentioned the name of a big wheel it was the man's surname that he used—no syrup or sugar tacked onto it. In his many speeches and tirades he never referred to his idleness as being the result of Jim Crow or color lines. It was the beef of most musicians that their color was a hindrance, and in most cases it was and is true. Jelly, however, would laugh at such remarks and discussions. He seemed real tickled and would be the only one to laugh and he would say, "If I could get me fifteen intelligent musicians who can play, I could start working tonight at the Waldorf Astoria." Most of the musicians would look at him with a sympathetic expression on their faces and think, "This man is crazy!"

At one time I bought a large chart which outlined the various sections of the human head and indicated the characteristics of the nose and nostrils, forehead, jaws, temple, chin, lips, cheekbones and mouth. I was particularly interested in the notes about the chin and the dozen or so differently shaped chins. These were titled weak, strong, jutting, etc. When I found myself in the immediate company of windbags I noticed that their chins were similarly constructed. Two celebrities in particular who possessed such chins and jaws were Jelly Roll and Bill "Bojangles" Robinson. Their chins were dimpled and under the skin there seemed to be millions of restless muscles and nerves that required constant action and exercise. Also they had what is called juicy mouths (very wet; you needed an umbrella if you stood within three feet of these mouths or you were showered with a steady stream of barely visible mouth juice). When you saw these men in the midst of a company of people they were always giving a lecture of some sort.

Jelly spied me standing on the corner outside the Rhythm Club. I was laughing and joking with a group of unemployed cats and I watched Jelly as he crossed the street and joined us. He said seriously, "Hello Home Town. How's you fellows?"

I answered, "Hello, Jelly," and the other cats stopped laughing and looked at him.

"Homey," continued Jelly, "I got a job to play this evening at a high-class club on Long Island. You think you can get a small band to play?"

I said, "Hell, yeah. How many cats you want?"

"Five," Jelly replied. "Trumpet, sax or clarinet, you, a bass and a drum."

I said, "I'll get 'em."

Jelly said, "Alright, have them here at four o'clock; I'll be here with my Lincoln. Tell 'em the job pays forty dollars and I pay them before they leave."

I said, "Don't worry, I'll have them here."

I found five cats and we left on the dot of four o'clock. Jelly was real pleased as he drove his big Lincoln out to Long Island. When we arrived at the country club and stepped out of the car Jelly said, "Wait a minute, fellows." He dug into his pocket and came up with a roll of bills saying, "Do you want your money now?" They said, "No," in unison and we entered the club. Jelly led us to the bandstand, told us to set up, and we did. A man who seemed to be in authority hurried up and shook Jelly's hand vigorously, smiling happily. He said, "Morton, I've been trying to contact you for months. How you doing my boy?"

Jelly said, "Doing great. Just can't get a band."

The man said, "Morton, I'm glad to see you. Take it easy, for the party will start late. So you and the boys will have dinner now. Anything you want; anything to drink. I'll send the maitre d' to take care of you." The man left and the maitre d' approached with a waiter, greeted Jelly, and placed a clean white cloth on the large round table. The club was really high class and everything spotlessly clean. The maitre d' said, "Sit down, gentlemen." We sat down, he handed us menus and he said, "Order anything you want." This menu read like a railroad train menu, only more expensive. No item was under a dollar.

Meals listed were all over five dollars and some as much as ten dollars. We musicians were cautious about ordering and the waiter stood by, looking on patiently. Jelly understood that we couldn't make up our minds and spoke up, "Fellows, get anything you see on the menu." Still no answer from us. Finally Jelly said to the waiter, "I think we will all have Long Island duckling dinners, soup to nuts." Then he looked at us and asked, "Is that OK, fellows?" We all said eagerly, "Yeah, yeah, yeah."

When the waiter left Jelly shook his head and as we sat there quietly he told us, "Fellows, this is a high-class place; please don't embarrass me. We will be served an eight-course dinner. Take your time and eat. Don't gobble up everything as soon as the waiter puts it on the table. The way you are all looking, I'm afraid you all might eat up the table cloth, the table and the chairs. I know these are Depression times, but if you all would stick with me, all them wrinkles would leave your stomachs and your pockets would be bulging with money."

The waiter brought the soup and then salads, and then each of us was served a nice-sized stuffed duck. Jelly was a very slow eater, but we watched him and we ate slowly as he talked on of all the places we could play if we would listen to him. Jelly was chewing his food for quite a while after the rest of the band had finished the dessert. During the meal I noticed that he had waved and smiled to a man who was seated at a table near a window which was not far from the table we occupied. The man was small, grey-haired and well dressed, and had a happy, sort of carefree expression on his face. He seemed happy in contrast to the other elderly men about the dining room. This was during the Depression and people smiled with an effort. The other men in the room were engaged in serious discussions.

When Jelly finally finished his meal he took the napkin from his lap and wiped his mouth saying, "Fellows, the repast should last you all at least a week!" We laughed. Jelly said, "Now, there's something very important I want to tell you all." He looked at the drummer as he spoke. (I'm not positive, but I think he was Tommy Benford. Jelly liked Benford's drumming and Benford had worked for Jelly on many occasions before. I have a good memory, but I cannot positively recall who the musicians on this date were.) Jelly continued in rather a serious tone, talking to the band and the drummer in particular. "You all see that little man sitting over there by the window?" We calmly looked at the object of Jelly's remark, who still sat there with the pleasant smile, and we all nodded. "He's a dear personal friend of mine," Jelly told us. "He is what is called a multi-millionaire; he's got money to burn. Also he loves to play the drums and I know that he is going to ask me to let him sit in with the band and play the drums —maybe three or four numbers. Now he is not going to hurt or break up them raggedy drums, and if he should accidentally break something he will buy you a brand new set." Now Jelly was speaking directly to the drummer. "When he comes over to me he'll be asking for permission to play the drums, and when you see that happen, do me a favor and get up from behind them dirty, raggedy drums and let him play. Now get a napkin from one of the waiters and wipe off them drums and the sticks so the man won't get his hands and clothes soiled. Will you do that for me?"

The drummer left the table and wiped off his drums. Jelly watched the drummer and said approvingly, "Now that's what I call common sense! The waiter is going to bring you whiskey-heads some high-class whiskey to smack you all's big lips on; take it easy and don't get drunk. What's left you can take home with you. Now, you watch when Mr Golet starts playing the drums. None of these other millionaires are going to laugh or poke fun at him, because as I stated before, he is what is called a multi-millionaire, and he can buy and sell all of them in this building. Nobody dares laugh at him because he is too powerful."

"Jelly," someone asked, "how many millions must one have to be a multi-millionaire?"

Jelly replied, "At least ten million, that is, in cold cash, not in property or real estate. You see, you must be a millionaire before you can become a member of this club. You have to have historical ancestors and historical background before you are admitted. No poor white man is allowed on the grounds unless he is in a servant's capacity—a waiter, cook or porter. No poor people are allowed; they might steal something." Jelly laughed, rose from his seat and said, "Let's play some music."

He adjusted the mike to his height and announced that the dancing would begin and that he would play all requests. When Jelly sat at the piano groups of well dressed women entered the room. It was a surprising scene, because I had not seen any women or heard any women's voices. They were seated quietly at the different tables occupied by the men, and some couples began to dance. For the first set just Jelly and the rhythm played; the horns were silent. The guests crowded about Jelly at the baby-grand piano and he played their requests, singing song after song. The people got a big kick out of Jelly's playing. They seemed to know him personally, for he joked and smiled as they asked for songs. Some of these he sang with his husky voice.

There was about an hour of just Jelly and the rhythm, and then Jelly stood and said, "Folks, we'll have a slight intermission." We left the stand and walked over to a table loaded with a dozen bottles of all kinds of high-class bonded liquors. This was a strange sight, for it was during Prohibition, and the only liquor we usually saw was bootleg booze. As we went for the whiskey Jelly cautioned, "Don't open all the bottles —just two. When and if they become empty, go for some more." We started to pour our whiskey. Jelly stood by watching the happy guests, but he did not drink. As I gulped down a glass he said, "Home Town, this reminds me of the good old days. This is what you call the elite. If I could get a band to play for me steady, we'd work forever." I just shook my head and wondered. I thought of the hour that had just ended, during which we had been on the stand and just Jelly and the rhythm had played. I watched everyone while Jelly entertained. He had played his style of piano with the melody and the heavy bouncing bass of his left hand. The guests had seemed thrilled by Jelly's playing, but when I looked at the musicians it was obvious that they were not moved or even interested. As far as piano players at that time were concerned, Earl "Fatha" Hines was the current rage.

The little multi-millionaire sent for Jelly by one of the waiters, and Jelly went over to join him at his table. As expected, during the next set Jelly told the drummer it was time to let the man play. The drummer turned over his sticks and the little man sat behind the drums, smiling. Jelly started a medium tempo and the horns started blowing. The guests all smiled as they watched the little man play, but no-one joked or made fun of him. He played well, kept good tempo and got real jazzy as we continued to play. When the dance was over the guests gathered around Jelly again, complimenting him and asking him for cards and where he was to play next. Jelly spoke to everyone nicely and then, as we packed our instruments I heard him say to himself sadly, "I wish I knew where I was going to play next!" As we were leaving the room Jelly handed each of us a brand new twenty dollar bill saying, "This is a tip from Mr Golet."

Jelly was forever beefing about and against ASCAP. He heard his many hit songs being played on the radio daily. It seems that he signed his songs over to some publishers and they became wealthy, but Jelly received no royalties as the composer, and there was nothing he could do about the situation.

When Jelly died in Los Angeles there were four famous negro bands touring the West Coast. None of these leaders attended the services or funeral or sent floral offerings. And, to top that off, an old underworld acquaintance of Jelly's, a dope fiend and a notorious thief, sneaked into the undertaking parlor during the night and, with a chisel and a hammer, removed the four-carat diamond from Jelly's front tooth.

While Jelly was bemoaning his failure to reach the pinnacle of success, there were many bandleaders who were doing quite well, and two who were world-famous, Duke Ellington and Cab Calloway. Jelly frequently tried to organize bands, with no success. Most of the available competent musicians did not understand Jelly or his music because it was considered old-fashioned and corny, especially the titles of his compositions: *Shoe Shiner's Drag, Milenberg Joys, Wolverine Blues.* During that period all the bandleaders were excited over the arrangements of Benny Carter, Edgar Sampson, Don Redman and Fletcher Henderson. Jelly's music sounded ancient compared to these new arrangements. Duke Ellington, Cab Calloway, Fletcher Henderson, Fess Williams, McKinney's Cotton Pickers, Luis Russell were creating much excitement. Also the Casa Loma Band, Bert Lown, Jean Goldkette. These leaders were the new sensations of a new era and they left Jelly arguing and standing by the wayside. The only two songs of Jelly's that I heard any of them play were *King Porter Stomp* and *Milenberg Joys.*

The last time I saw Jelly he was standing in front of the building where he and his wife stayed on Seventh Avenue. I was working with Lucky Millinder's orchestra and stayed on tour most of the time. On this particular afternoon I was walking down Seventh Avenue when I met Jelly and his little wife, Mabel. They were talking to the priest from the Catholic church around the corner on 132nd Street, between Seventh and Eighth Avenue. Jelly was engaged in earnest conversation with the priest, who was listening very attentively as Jelly spoke. Mabel and Jelly greeted me with smiles, and there was a big multi-carat diamond in each of their mouths, right up in front for the world to see. I'm sure the priest was aware of those diamonds and knew also they were the symbols of notoriety and of tenderloin characters. Mabel and I were friends. She liked me because she knew that I respected Jelly and had tried to help him get groups together for jobs. Jelly said, "Home Town, meet Father So-and-so." We shook hands and I noticed that he was a young man and seemed very much interested in Jelly. The priest excused himself shortly and left us. Jelly had noted my surprise at his association with a priest and then said, "Home Town, I have gone back to the Church; it is a great thing."

"That's wonderful," I said.

Mabel smiled and said, "Come have dinner with us." I told them I had just eaten, but I went up to their third-floor apartment with them, where I sat for a couple of hours listening to Jelly speak sadly of all the misfortunes that he had been through, and how completely disgusted he was with New York City as well as the music business. He told me that he was spending most of his time at the church and the rectory with the priests. Mabel said nothing as she served dinner; she just looked sadly at Jelly and then looked at me. I don't think she realized she was shaking her head as she moved about the kitchen and dining room. When I left the apartment I was real shook up.

A few days later I was standing in front of the Rhythm Cub with the usual crowd of musicians. I looked down the street towards the church to see Jelly there, talking with two priests. That was the last time I saw Jelly.

SIXTEEN

Louis Armstrong and trumpet rivalry

With the unanimous acceptance that Buddy Bolden was the king, the old timers would argue and argue and could never agree who was his successor. Only when the name Louis Armstrong was mentioned would they all become silent and listen as one would say, "Oh well, that's a different matter. Everybody knows Li'l Dipper is the greatest, but (it was always "but") you can't say he's the greatest, because if Louis met so-and-so when he was in his prime, then you could judge who was the greatest." And then they would relate many famous battle scenes.

Everybody had their favorites and personal idols. This keen rivalry continued until about 1928 or 1930. With the death of Chris Kelly and Buddy Petit the last great battles were gone too. There had been a half dozen bitter encounters between Henry "Red" Allen and Guy Kelly. At about that time (1928) Guy and Red were the most exciting trumpet players in America, with the exception of Louis Armstrong. King Oliver tried to get both of them. Fate Marable wanted them too, and he knew the ability of all the musicians in the Mississippi River Basin and the St Louis, Kansas City, Memphis, Cincinnati, and Pittsburgh areas. Of course there was the great Jabbo Smith—I'll say the phenomenal Jabbo Smith—who challenged Armstrong on one or two occasions. But Jabbo was out of the sideman category. He was a nationally famous musician, acclaimed, and above the approach of Oliver, Fate, or any of the famous bands. He appeared as an attraction; he was a star.

There was also Reuben Reeves, famous in Chicago, who played in Dave Peyton's Regal Theater Orchestra and who, on an occasion when Louis played the Regal, attempted some intrigue and serious planning in order to blow Louis down. Before the show started the house orchestra (Dave Peyton) always played a long five- to eight-minute overture, usually a classical or sedate piece of music. But Mr Peyton scored up an arrangement real hot and frantic this time, featuring Mr Reuben Reeves blowing his utmost, playing every technique and trick he knew. Blowing like this before Louis Armstrong was to appear on stage was a secret move designed to embarrass Louis; it was deliberate and most impolite—I'd say it was vicious.

Many in the Chicago area believed Reeves to be greater than Armstrong. When the Peyton Orchestra blasted out with Reeves's screaming there was much excitement in that theater as well as backstage. Louis heard the frantic screaming wailing horn and, as the story goes, he left his dressing room in his robe and peeped through the curtains down at the orchestra and watched as Mr Peyton dramatically directed Mr Reeves by flailing his arms while Mr Reeves screamed to the high heavens, trying to blow the roof off the Regal Theater. Armstrong watched the two, surprised. Backstage there were comments of praise concerning the greatness of Reeves. Louis heard these remarks. He returned to his dressing room. Generally shows close with that sort of wild and frantic playing. You are deliberately showing contempt by presenting such activity by one trumpet player when another has star billing on the program.

A witness says that Louis's feelings were deeply hurt, wounded beyond repair, and when he was grossly antagonized his nostrils had a great propensity to expand and he would get violently unconsolable. On such rare occasions his eyes became red and he sulked and breathed deeply, sucking up all the air in the room. Visitors generally used to leave at such times, for there would be very little air—it was all in Louis's lungs. It was wise to step outside, or suffocate. As the minutes passed before Louis's appearance on the Regal stage Louis was left alone, breathing deeply and huffing and puffing, like a raving bull in the arena charging Belmonte the bullfighter. When the stage manager knocked on Louis's dressing-room door telling him it was time to appear, Louis picked up his horn, walked onto the stage to a tremendous ovation, and bowed and smiled, glancing first at Peyton and then at Reeves.

The eyewitness says that Louis blew one or two hundred choruses of *Chinatown* (or *Tiger Rag*). The audience was completely spellbound; they had never heard horn blowing like that. They just sat there, electrified, and Reeves and Peyton sat petrified. I forgot to ask the eyewitness if Dave Peyton changed the overture to something less fiery.

And there was another time in Chicago when Jabbo's arrogance caused Louis's nostrils to expand.

Lil Armstrong tells of yet another occasion when the great Johnny Dunn told Louis, "Get up boy, and let the master show you how to play that horn." Dunn was seen sneaking out of the cabaret when Louis returned to the bandstand with his nose three times its size.

Another of my eyewitness reporters tells of a day when Louis appeared in the Savoy in New York City. One great trumpet player got so mad at himself after listening to Louis that he threw his horn up to the ceiling and demolished it. A different occasion at the Savoy concerned another noted trumpet player, Louis Metcalfe, who nightly wore a gold cardboard crown like kings wear. He was cautioned that Louis was going to appear and that he would look ridiculous with this emblem of supremacy on his highly greased head when Louis mounted the stand. Defiantly he retorted, "I'll wear this crown if Gabriel comes down from heaven." And like all of them, after hearing Louis play his first number, the man snatched the gold cardboard king's crown from his greasy head, and while no one was looking (he thought no one was looking) he slammed it under the piano like a nice little boy.

When the Armstrong Hot Five records were released about every six or eight weeks they created a sensation. Louis's sensational trumpet solos and his singing style opened the way for a new gimmick, or a new tag, for vocalists who were limited in their training as singers. Before Louis singers were classified as tenors, baritones, sopranos—with the exception of blues singers who were classed as sort of folk artists, and others who were considered comedy singers. Louis started the vogue of "song stylist."

After the voice of Armstrong was recorded everybody wanted to sing, and they did. In the thirties in New York City there was a joint called Reuben's where the Harlem musicians gathered to drink and socialize. Reuben was a frustrated drummer and he made a good living selling rot-gut whiskey. This was strong alcohol flavored with molasses or sorgum. He sold it as fast as he could mix up this concoction, and he called it "smoke" because it was cloudy and it gave off a barely visible vapor. It burned your mouth, throat and stomach until you drank enough to lose your senses and become simple, like the other patrons at Reuben's. In the early 1930s, the height of the Depression, the Harlem musicians (the greats as well as the near-greats) frequented this joint.

Now, to give an example of the great influence Armstrong had over the majority of trumpet players around the country, I recall one afternoon when I walked into Reuben's. It was bitter cold outside, five or ten degrees below zero. When I stepped inside I felt that it was just as cold inside. Reuben was cursing and swearing. I then noticed a half-dozen noted trumpet players, stripped to the waist, bare-chested, sitting in a circle by a wide-open window. The cold air was swishing snow flakes on them and all about the room. As Reuben was cursing I noted that the men were his best customers for that bad booze of his, and they were Ward Pinkett, Frankie Newton, Johnny Buggs, Preacher, Ted Colin, and two others called Red, one from Buffalo and the other from Washington, DC. What they were doing was trying to catch colds.

They had been listening to Armstrong records on the jukebox and discussing and arguing about Louis's singing. Ward Pinkett had convinced them that to get the sound of Armstrong's voice they should all catch colds. Reuben had said "no" to this idea, but they had threatened to leave his joint and boycott it. Reuben was overruled and told to go into the kitchen and sit near the stove. He allowed them to open the window, but started cussing when they refused to close it. Ward yelled, "I'll close it just as soon as we all start sneezing and coughing." It was as cold as the North Pole in that room, so I went to the kitchen and sat by the gas stove with Reuben and some women who were shivering there.

I am sure that Louis Armstrong has never had a fan that worshiped him more than Ward Pinkett; all his talk was Armstrong. He was forever singing Louis's vocals, and he would get so carried away by Louis's music that he would sit by the jukebox in joints in Harlem with his horn in his lap and cry in admiration of Louis. The last time I saw Ward he was living in a room at the building which housed Reuben's. The room was on the third floor. He had become a hopeless and chronic alcoholic. Reuben told me, "Dan, Ward is upstairs. Go up there and see him; he is very sick." I went upstairs and there found Ward sitting up in an iron bed. He was just a skeleton—all skin and bones. He wouldn't eat; he would just drink Reuben's fire-water. The musicians would send him that fire-water around the clock, twenty-four hours a day. There was a tremendous amount of this liquid consumed at Reuben's by the patrons, and amongst booze comedians the saying is generally, "Let him drink if he wants to drink. If that's the way he wants to die, that's his business. You don't live but once. He's a grown man. He knows what he wants to do. Everybody is always trying to tell somebody else how to live their life."

And when Ward Pinkett died it was up in the small, dingy room at Reuben's. When I had seen his condition I asked him, "Ward, you want some food?" His reply was a weak, "No, I want a drink." I said, "I'll buy you some whiskey if you'll eat some soup." He just looked at me, saying nothing. I went to the store and got a couple of cans of soup.

Reuben warmed it saying, "Ward ain't gonna drink this; you are wasting your money." I brought the soup up to him and tried to feed him slowly, but as the soup went down it came right back up. I'll never forget his efforts.

SEVENTEEN

New York clubs and the Harlem Renaissance

New York clubs were the haunt of the crafty night people. They used to put on the act: set a trap to catch the day nine to five people. I first saw the drama cleverly enacted at the old Nest Club, where there was not much action until after the big joints closed at the curfew time—3 a.m. Some officials were paid off and the after-hours joints stayed open until after daylight, not bothered by the police. It was a night when the place was empty. Everybody sat around like half asleep. At the door upstairs there was Ross the slick doorman. When he rang three loud rings on the upstairs door buzzer (it rang loud), it meant some live prosperous-looking people, a party, were coming in.

Like jacks out of a box the band struck up *Lady be Good.* Everybody went into action; the band swinging, waiters beating on trays, everybody smiling and moving, giving the impression the joint was jumping. (Fats Waller wrote a song, *The Joint is Jumping.*) The unsuspecting party entered amid finger-popping and smiling staff. ("Make believe we're happy.") This was kept up until the party was seated and greeted and their orders taken. Then on came the singers, smiling and moving; then another singer, a dancer. Then it was off to the races—action —"Let's get this money." Ross, smiling, looked on satisfied and went upstairs to watch and set the trap again.

The last great cabaret was Pod's and Jerry's—a jumping joint. This was the nightclub where many great performers, musicians, entertainers and notorious hip characters, as well as politicians and money moguls, all gathered to see and enjoy the last of the old-time Roaring Twenties.

At about 2 a.m., when the famous clubs, theaters and entertainment places closed for the night downtown and about town, it was the custom for good-time swinging people to come uptown: "Let's all go uptown to Harlem." There were songs composed about the happenings that went on uptown. Such songs as *Take the A-Train* by Duke Ellington; *Drop me off Uptown* by Anita O'Day and Roy Eldridge; *Underneath the*

Harlem Moon by Gene Krupa's orchestra; *Stomping at the Savoy* by Edgar Sampson; *The Jitterbug Waltz* by Fats Waller.

Pod's and Jerry's was a first-floor basement, one of the many hot spots located in New York City's brownstone and greystone buildings —row after row of identical four- to ten-story high apartment buildings. It was common to see people who got boozed up walking up the eight to ten steps and trying to unlock the wrong door—wrong key, wrong building! It happened to me a couple of times. Somebody would yell, "You live next door!"

"You at the wrong house!"

"Thanks bud." Then you tried to clear your head—back down on the sidewalk, looking for your house number or some house mark.

Now uptown really flourished before the bad publicity was purposely generated by widely read scandal-sheet columnists to wash out Harlem and its noted pleasure spots. There were in the 1930s three New York City newspapers: *The Daily News, The Daily Mirror* and *The Graphic*. These popular tabloids had three or four full-length columns written by famous news hawks, as they were called. They condensed very potent scandal. Tales of the doings of all the well-known show folks, sport folks, jet setters. Notorious names—just like the current scandal magazines. Their attitude was: rip your reputation to pieces, to shreds; put your private business in the streets for all to see. Now, what happened?

It was common to see taxi cabs roll uptown loaded with the bosses and the help. They would come uptown after closing for more good times. There the bosses saw Whites spending money like crazy after getting boozed up. Downtown these same wild spenders were tight-fisted and reserved—sober. So the bosses planned an area to keep the boozers' money downtown (these were the years 1930–1940). So, 133rd Street in Harlem had a raft of joints: the Nest, Jerry's, Tillie's, Mexico's, the Stable, the Mad House, and a row of dingy speakeasies and dives. You "dived in and dived out"—enjoying music, having fun.

Soon up arose 52nd Street, downtown. It had a long row of joints, but more elaborate: the Three Deuces, the Onyx Club, the Yacht Club, Leon and Eddie's, Jimmy Ryan's—a good dozen of sizzling clubs. There then appeared in the scandal newspaper columns in bold black print, "Be careful going to Harlem. You risk being mugged, beaten and robbed."

"Mugged." That's the first time I read and heard the word "mugged." I asked, "What was being mugged?"

They explained that one thief asked for a cigarette or match or some money; another threw his strong arm from the back around your neck and held you tight, choking you breathless; another rifled your pockets quickly. When you weakened and slooped to the ground they took off with your money, wrist watch and coat, especially if it was an overcoat. In the meantime the victim was on the ground, weak, helpless, out of breath. It was at least ten minutes before the victim could get his or her breath back to tell people what happened. The thieves might be a distance off, having quickly disposed of the loot, looking on. The papers kept up the mug warnings, and some thieves went into the Harlem mugging business and slowly scared off the white downtown spenders. But that did not completely stop the uptown safari: downtown swingers still came up in cabs and cars to the places they were known. They came in, enjoyed the fun, got in taxi cabs, and went directly downtown and home; they stopped roaming the streets.

Now in Pod's in 1930 the big attraction was the great, mighty Willie "the Lion" Smith and Mattie Hite, classed as the greatest cabaret singer; her great song was *Stop it, Joe*. And all musicians, that is jazz musicians—including Duke Ellington, Fats Waller, Tommy and Jimmy Dorsey—dutifully went to Pod's, where they sat, stood, watched, listened and learned sounds and riffs played masterfully by the Lion. You will hear snatches of the Lion in many great players from Duke to Mingus: phrases, turn-arounds, riffs, all used freely. The Lion knew his creations were being lifted, but never sued or complained or commented. The moneyed bandleaders tipped Willie well, also showered him with adulation and appreciation.

Then Milt Herth came uptown. He was a pianist, an organist, and he asked the Lion to record some songs for Decca. The Lion and O'Neill Spencer recorded. The records were instant hits, constantly played around the New York City clock. Milt Herth went into the Paramount Theatre on Broadway with a trio, but not O'Neill Spencer and the Lion. I wondered about that, but the Lion was not ruffled in the least.

Now, all entertainers at that time bowed and learned things from Mattie Hite. When the Lion played her introduction, all noises stopped and all eyes were glued on the great Mattie Hite. She was a slim, dark woman, who mastered the art of cabaret singing, slinking from table to table taking the green bills handed her as she sang *Stop it, Joe* and other sensuous, sex-provoking lyrics (*My daddy rocks me with one steady roll, Jelly Roll*, and *Salty Dog*.) Very spicy. I think Miss Hite created the novelty of slowly and carefully snatching thinly rolled greenbacks held protruding by glasses, or coke or whiskey bottles from the edge of tables. She slowly wiggled and rolled to the roll of the snare drum or the piano (watched by all) as she stepped up with her dress raised high, and grinded, taking the bills between her legs from table after table. Rarely did she miss snatching the bills. The women specially wanted to see the snatching performance. Some even got into the act as Miss Hite moved along, snatching and grabbing, putting the bills, many bills, in her brassiere or under her panties.

Many great popular performers and musicians frequented Pod's. There was a thing, an excitement, in New York cabarets—cabarets rather than nightclubs, as these had a sophistication, a coolness, which was enjoyable but restrained. These cabarets generated a sizzling atmosphere for four or five hours: two to seven in the morning. Pod's and the popular cabarets really cooked—singing, dancing, music; waiters, waitresses, bartenders moving. Action!!! When you stepped into the cabaret, smoke hit your nostrils—thick smoke and all kinds of smells. It took fifteen minutes or more to see who was sitting around you. You would hear familiar voices. Pod's and other cabarets had what was called "ups": entertainers getting on stage one after another and doing their act in friendly competition. The entertainers were closely tied. They were respected for their talent and ability. Envy and competition were cool and subdued. Do your thing and make that quick dollar.

Pod was the owner. "Jazz," a surly, no-nonsense guy, was head waiter; I called him "Shack Bully." The tables were strictly for spending guests only. If you did not drink and order frequently the first visit, you did not get a table the second visit. Jazz told you gruffly to go to the small bar with your party, where you were pushed about by the busy waiters. From two until seven or eight or nine, as the children passed by going to school, Pod's joint cooked, burned—night after night. That's where Billie Holiday got started. Billie was young, beautiful and sociable, eager for happenings.

Around 1931 the new craze came on for smoking reefers or "muggles"—"pot." Booze, the reefer-heads told us, made you make an ass out of yourself: you talked too much, you talked too loud. "Too much booze makes you ugly, nasty, foolish, ignorant." Smoke reefers, they said, and you kept your cool: "Amid all that noise, you can hear each voice. You can sit and concentrate and meditate. The singing and music sound so ecstatic and soulful. Everything is in a groove—so hip, so cool."

Billie joined the multitude of swinging night people who enjoyed New York City to its fullest. They hated going to bed—other than for romancing. You saw Billie and all these fast-moving young people around all night in joints. At the 3 a.m. curfew they went into after-hour joints. At nine o'clock they went back into the opening bars, cafes and clubs for breakfast. Twelve o'clock, noon, off to the many vaudeville theaters. There were dozens of theaters. Their attitude? Who the hell wants to sleep? You might miss something. On to the reefer joints to smoke, get high. So the reefer thing spread. And around 1938 I began to hear about so-and-so being "hooked with the habit" or "on H," on "horse,"—heroin. And then the long list of young, brilliant artists getting hooked, suffering and dying. There were so many. I heard many discuss the dope thing. They would condemn it, but later I would see them nodding and slowly sinking down in the cesspool. A hellhole of agony and death. There were many funerals attended by hundreds of celebrities, condemning and then getting it on in the arm—"the spike." I've learned that if you check out the serious talk of happenings with entertainers, musicians and show people, you will get the trend of the reality of things to come. Like with folk singing: Bob Dylan, Joan Baez, Woody Guthrie and the other pioneer folk artists, their songs tell of world happenings. These people are social scientists; they can feel calamities. When it came to reefers, Louis Armstrong had recorded *Muggles*, and Cab Calloway recorded *Minnie the Moocher* and *Down in Chinatown*.

After President Roosevelt cooled the rough Depression, things picked up in Harlem. Prohibition was abolished and a whole new era of clubs and amusements opened up. I found out that to survive in New York City you had to be alert and observant: watch and try to pattern after the life style of successful people. I saw in the TV news the action on the stock market. I saw all these very rich New York people doing big things in a big way, and wondered where and how they accumulated all this big money. Now in New Orleans, from my porch, I look at the long freight trains pulling hundreds of freight and tank cars. I see the thousands of names on the cars and the thousands of big trucks speeding on the wide smooth highway. There are offices in New York City, stock holders in New York City, well-paying management jobs in New York City. It was funny: in New York City, I (and I guess other entertainers) would see swinging people, big money people, at their businesses in the day time. On contact with you, they would not seem to recognize you. It seemed like they would be attending strictly to business, and they would be so involved they would completely black out Harlem and anybody from Harlem. Maybe Harlem doings was a fantasy or a dream trip. In reality, Harlem could be a farce. It was a place of wretched poor black people making believe they were happy, putting on an act, dancing and singing on the outside but all tangled up with misfortunes and degradation on the inside. Why were these black people so happy when the band was playing and the people were wild-eyed, looking on: "Come on monkey!"

"Entertain me!"

"Show me you!"

You were happy in spite of all the crap. Whites would come to Harlem to see this massive act of put-on make-believe. They would think, "I'll go to Harlem and sit back and watch how these many black people can and do survive. The sinful ones sing and dance the blues; the Christian ones sing gospel and scream at Jesus. That's what it is! The good book says, 'Suffer and come unto me.' So it's up to Harlem, the fantasy land, to recharge the battery and cleanse my mind, then come back downtown and attend to business."

When Blacks go to New York City they go to Harlem, generally, with the rest of them scuffling and struggling black people. If you go to black New York City, you'll see it's the same with Chicago, and the same with California: special slave quarters. Of course, today it's a little better than 1930.

In 1930 I had begun to meet and be introduced to celebrities in the Harlem hierarchy. Amongst them was Henry Saparo, or "Sap," the crown prince of the Harlem Renaissance. Sap was a strikingly handsome gentleman. I had noticed this good-looking, immaculately dressed man, sometimes carrying a guitar case. Then suddenly Jelly Roll Morton introduced me to Sap. He smiled when he was told I came from New Orleans. I had not heard of him in the New Orleans talk of jazzmen who had departed for the North and easier living. Henry assured me, "Dan, you'll do good here in New York City."

I said, "Thanks," at hearing those kind encouraging words.

As time went on I heard that Sap was one of the kingpins in the avant-garde intellectual society that grew out of the large group of talented young people in Harlem who were writers, poets, painters, sculptors, dancers, singers, athletes, political activists. They included the Lafayette Players, Andrew Bishop, Clarence Muse, Claude McKay, Countee Cullen. Marcus Garvey and his message aroused a sense of black culture.

The Harlem Renaissance was continued around and about Madame C. J. Walker's daughter Alelia Walker. She was loaded with money from the hair-straightening and color-lightening salves that swept the United States black communities in the years 1917 to 1925. It was popular to straighten the kinks out of the hair and bleach the dark skin, to lighten up to "a teasing brown! A peach-colored brown!" Miss Alelia Walker was a swinger. She sponsored the talented young artists and gave them encouragement and financial help. Her mansion on 139th Street in Harlem (called Strivers Row) was one of a row of beautiful greystone homes, clean and well maintained. There was much activity. There were parties and presentations galore. And so they used to say that Alelia was the royal princess, her mansion was the royal palace, and handsome Henry Saparo was his highness the royal crown prince. Alelia had arrived from Indianapolis, where the Walker pomade factory started and prospered.

Alelia took sick and fizzled out. I don't know the real full story; I only heard small talk about the trail Miss Walker blazed on Sap's arm. That must be an interesting story. But I did see many of these Renaissance people who walked the Harlem streets, frequented the lounges, very calm in manner, always silent, as if in sorrow of the passing of an exciting era—1915 to 1928. The beautiful bubble burst. Alelia passed away. The artists' incentive continued, and it was an era well documented by the writings and works of some of the creative artists. I had seen many of the important men and women and I noticed the way they moved about with a straight-faced solemn attitude: an attitude of superior surveillance and a deep inside disgust—a defeat, or helplessness. It was as if they had no personality. They would smile at nothing. Later I was to learn, seeing war movies, of defeated wounded soldiers trudging back from the battlefront. It was the same look in the faces of these Harlem Renaissance people. Some went on to fame and acclaim, but the majority just faded into the shadows, to zero.

I saw Sap, still dressed first-class, go on into the fifties. He lived in a large apartment building at 128th Street and Seventh Avenue. The old-timers knew him as the playboy of Miss Walker.

I saw Carl Van Vechten in the Nest Club, and what made me notice him was that he wore a carnation in his lapel, like Billie Holiday later wore a gardenia in her hair over her forehead. A waiter grunted, "That's that white son of a bitch that wrote that book *Nigger Heaven*." I was to see Mr Van Vechten many more times in and about Harlem. He was a part of Harlem. He wrote about its importance to the US, boldly telling the world's book readers about the greatness of Harlem people.

EIGHTEEN

Around the New York scene

Being a band jazz man, a band musician, my mind was centered in that direction—playing with bands. Now there were other musicians who played in combos, with novelty acts. Some were guitar players who became soloists and virtuosos. I checked on who were the great bands, the great musicians. Like today we know all the baseball stars: who's on third base, who's on second base. It was the same thing then in New York with musicians. You knew who was with the Cotton Pickers; you knew who was the banjo player with Fletcher Henderson's band, Cab Calloway's band; you knew who the drummers were, because their names were mentioned, because they recorded. You would read about this in the *Amsterdam News* in New York; the *New York Age*; the *Chicago Defender*, which was published nationally (a famous black newspaper), and later on there came the *Pittsburgh Courier*. They always had the bands: who was playing, who was appearing, and what band was in what city. Maybe there was some great affair, or a convention in Memphis or Los Angeles. They would tell you what band played, and that's how you knew. (These were the big bands, not the small groups like the Spirits of Rhythm, or Stuff Smith.)

There was eight years I paid my dues in New York, from 1930 to 1939, when I joined Cab Calloway's band. When I arrived in 1930 Cab had just made his fame at the Cotton Club. Cab's band included R. C. Dixon and Thornton Blue—a great clarinet player. You heard about Cab: the great money his band were making. They were doubling, working at the Cotton Club. Duke Ellington, when he worked the Cotton Club, did a double downtown at the Paramount, or the Gates Theater in Brooklyn. This was strenuous work. Their first theater show was twelve o'clock. Then they played four, five, maybe six shows. (A short movie was put on between stage shows if you were a sensation, like Duke and Cab were.) They played until 10.45, which was the last show. The band finished, rushed down from the Paramount, maybe with a police escort, to get to the Cotton Club, then they went directly on stage and did three shows that night. This would be starting about midnight, or around eleven o'clock—the first show.

You heard about these bands. They were famous. You would hear round the Rhythm Club what Fletcher Henderson, Cab Calloway, the Cotton Pickers were doing, what James P. was doing, what Fats Waller was doing. Gossip. Most musicians would give their right arm to go with Cab Calloway, because the money was great compared with New York club salaries. Buchanan at the Savoy said no musician was worth more than 35 dollars a week. That was their scale for seven nights. The union stopped that, and it became six nights, one night off.

Chick Webb was the star top band at the Savoy. He hired Ella Fitzgerald, who recorded *Tisket a-tasket*, and she and Chick went on to world acclaim. Chick Webb hired a director, a front man to MC, Bardu Ali. He was a dancer and actor from New Orleans. Then there was Abdul Ali his brother, who had a great act: a beachcomber, who did a kind of Apache dance where the cat beats the woman. He had whiskers like a wild man, a real raggedy cat. On a deserted island he sees this chick shipwrecked and lost, dressed ragged and fearful. Then a whole lot of chasing goes on, with snatching and grabbing like, with a whip. Exciting. Abdul Ali from New Orleans. Half Turk, half Pakistani or Indian.

Bardu Ali is still living, I think, on the West Coast.

You heard about Fats Waller's band around 1930. Fats Waller organized the band, got good management, a good recording contract with Victor records. And later his manager was Ed Kirkeby—I learned about him after I worked at Adrian Rollini's Taproom. I saw Kirkeby because he was a friend of Adrian Rollini. Rollini was a famous jazz bass saxophone player and vibraphonist who played with Red Nichols and that school of musicians. He was Italian, became famous. Had a little club in the President Hotel in the basement.

When I went to New York the Cotton Club was uptown, then they moved downtown for some reason. The main reason was that the bad publicity made Harlem a very unsavory place; they were trying to portray it as a mugger's den, to keep the business downtown. During the 1930s I played with a whole slew of bands. The first band I worked with was Harry White's band at the Nest Club. Then I joined Dave Nelson and went straight to Broadway in a show called *The Constant Sinner* with Mae West. That was 1930. She played the part of a swinging madam, a downtown, swinging, big-time chick who frequented Harlem. There was a cabaret scene in the show, and I was in the band, a five-piece band: me, Dave Nelson, Trent Harris, Slick Jones, and Lloyd Phillips (a piano player, who later worked with Pearl

Bailey). The show lasted about eight weeks; it flopped. Broadway wasn't ready for it. Mae West had a black lover, supposedly, in the play—a little advanced for the time for the attitudes of the Whites on Broadway.

So from there I left Dave Nelson and joined Wayne Talbot's band. I played the Madison Square Garden hockey game four nights a week with a fifty-piece orchestra of Harlem musicians. Mostly unemployed musicians, mostly from the old Amsterdam Club, old New York musicians. It was a sort of a concert band: cellos, french horns, baritone horns, about fifteen mice—that's what they call fiddles (violins). Fiddle players as a group, they take the beat from the leader and then go into their own thing, playing them syrupy sounds. Sensitive musical ears could feel them group up and take off. This Madison Square Garden must have been charitable, as you were payed five dollars. You worked from seven until nine. You played a little concert before the game, a couple of numbers at half-time. You played the *Saints* later, then cut out. For some of these old Amsterdam Club musicians it was like coming from under the rocks to get some fresh air, see what was happening.

Wayne Talbot was a no-nonsense, serious musician. You would see him around with a briefcase, going around from uptown to downtown, attending to business. Walking like he was in business. A smart, intelligent man. Wayne Talbot had been a personal friend of Pantages, president of the Pantages circuit of theaters, from Chicago. He had been a star on Pantages' vaudeville circuit for twenty years. And when old man Pantages got into trouble, that circuit sort of fizzled out. Talbot had played vaudeville with his act. He was a piano player, and he had an act, which was a big-time theater act. But the theaters had fizzled out too.

And you saw fighters who had been champs. Ex-champs. You would see them around, and they was battered and bruised. "One punch Willie, Knockout Brown . . . beat so-and-so, but never got a chance at the champs." You would see them with their flat noses and cauliflower ears. There was the musical equivalent of the same thing. There was Fletcher Henderson, not doing nothing, band broken up. He went with Benny Goodman, but before that, for a while, there was nothing happening with him. He would try it again, and another band would fizzle out. The last band he had, with Chu Berry and his tenor saxophone, went with Roy (Eldridge) to Chicago, and upset Chicago. He followed Earl Hines at the Grand Terrace, stayed there a few seasons, but came back to New York.

One time when I was walking on 116th Street, slowly, I heard a loud voice, "I'm Lloyd Scott, one of the greatest drummers that ever walked the face of the earth." I said to myself, "Let me hear more of this." So I backtracked and went inside the bar. I ordered a beer and stood half a dozen feet from Lloyd. The bartender said, "You are who?"

"I'm Lloyd Scott, a great swinging sensation, the greatest band that ever hit New York. I wrecked the Savoy Ballroom. People were running in all directions to hear me. I tore up the Rosemont Ballroom in Brooklyn, tore it to pieces. I blew the walls out the Roseland Ballroom down on Broadway. People had never heard music like mine before or since."

The bartender said, "You done all that? You blew down the walls of the Roseland? You blew the roof off the Savoy? And what you doing now? You doing nothing."

Lloyd said, "Well, well, well, well . . ."

The bartender said, "You had a destructive band, out destroying things, destroying people's buildings. They spend a million dollars on a ballroom, you blow the roof off. That's why you ain't working today. That's your trouble, I can see. If I owned the Roseland I wouldn't hire you. Where you come from?"

"I come from Ohio."

"Oh, that's where they have those tornados. You must be used to that kind of foolishness, blowing the roofs off ballrooms. You want another drink?"

"Gimme a double."

Lloyd Scott was one of the many musicians, leaders of great bands, that came to the Big Apple, and as fate would have it, tried for fame and acclaim, but fizzled down to zero. Lloyd drank that double whiskey and tears fell from his eyes; he acted like a man who had lost everything. I saw him on other occasions, shouting his name. He was a medium-sized, well-built man, about five feet four, clear brown skin, natural curly black hair and a well-shaped head. He had clear eyes, sharp, like an eagle's. When Lloyd spoke you looked straight in his mouth. His upper lip had a deep-cut cleave, a harelip. It seemed to me a pity, a tragic lifelong calamity. Everybody, on meeting Lloyd, looked up and down, at his eyes and the mouth and the harelip. Being the leader of the great Scott orchestra, the agents, promoters, club owners looked at Lloyd Scott's photos, and to a man, there would be the putdown. That lip on that face. As I watched the bartender badgering Lloyd, I saw his eyes shift up and down Lloyd's face. The harelip was his professional rejection. A pity.

There was his brother Cecil Scott, the great Cecil, who was a master musician. He was a great, respected tenor sax player and a master clarinetist—of the early school of tenor sax players, with a big, deep-toned sound. He was one of Coleman Hawkins's disciples. There were dozens of them on the New York City scene: Cecil Scott, Prince Robinson, Gene Sedric, Bingie Madison, Greely Walton, Jimmy Wright, Teddy McRae, Cass McCord, the Joe Beatus Brothers.

On the New York gossip scene, musicians were appraised, discussed. Generally the verdict of your appraisal concerning tone, technique, facility was just about correct. It was put up or put down around the Rhythm Club. You could, in a musician's absence, in a gathering mention a question on his ability and be sure to get a total analysis. I tried to get an appraisal of my rating. I asked Eddie William, a close friend of mine, a smart, aware young man. I whispered one day, "Eddie, when I split out, check on what these asses think of my playing." A while later Eddie said, "I asked the critics about you. They said you are OK—not great; good rhythm, man, you're alright, smooth, dependable. They say you are foxy, you know how to move in the right places."

I thought to myself, "Foxy. That's good!"

Then there was Fess Williams. I worked with him a couple of weeks and I fell out with him because he had a dancing act which was Clark Monroe and Gregory his partner. Clark Monroe who later had a club in Harlem. Jimmy and Clark Monroe were brothers. Clark was very business-like. He had a club on 52nd Street and he was in cahoots with the mob and the people who run that business. He was well liked. And he liked me. When I met him and his partner they were fanatics about Louis Armstrong. When a show played a theater we would talk: they were young, I was young (they were older than me, though). They heard I was from New Orleans, and we talked about Pops. They said, "Man, come over here, tell us about New Orleans." So I would tell them about the South. Now Fess Williams had a bunch of musicians nobody knew too well. You knew them, and they were around, but they were evasive. They would come in the Rhythm Club, then they used to walk out. They didn't stand still. In fact they looked like bush leaguers to me—they didn't mix well. Only one mixed. He was Kenneth Roane. He was a fine musician who later became a union executive.

So I was in the room between shows with Monroe and Gregory, talking. You could sense the resentment of the band. You see, they smoked reefers, them show boys—not all of them—and they had trumpets trying to play like Louis. They were interested, see. They would try Louis's solos between shows. They were all Louis's boys. They idolized Louis. Now I was in the room, and that smoke was seeping out of the dressing room, that reefer smoke (which I didn't smoke). But they assumed that since birds of a feather flock together, I was a reefer head too. I had taken a guitar player's place in the band, but after that theater engagement they didn't call me no more. That's New York. They hire you, they like you and what you do—then they might not call you again.

Fess Williams's band goes way back. Fess Williams's band had opened the Savoy Ballroom and then went to Chicago, and there he was a superstar at the Regal Theater for a long, long stay. All the schoolkids on the south side of Chicago knew Fess. He greeted his audience, "Hello gang!" And the audience answered, "Hello Fess!" He became a legend there with the kids—very popular. The Regal was the biggest theater in the central part of the USA and internationally known. Fess Williams goes way back to Freddie Keppard's days in Chicago. Fess told me he would never forget New Orleans musicians. He came up from Louisville, Kentucky, then worked in Chicago. He was scuffling round there trying to make it, and Freddie Keppard sent him on his job some nights he didn't feel like playing. "I'll never forget Freddie Keppard. He gave me his job on the nights he wanted to take off. And that's that."

Then I joined Orville Brown's band. It was a dancing-school band. Then there was the Lennox Club, next door to the Cotton Club, where I played with a series of bandleaders. These leaders were scratching the bottom of the barrel as far as work went. This was the Depression, and they were in the cats' scuffle for jobs. In New York City there was a practice called "making auditions" to let the owners of clubs hear the bands. These leaders would tell you, "I have connections. I can go into the Lennox Club. I'll get a band together, tighten up the band, and we can go downtown. We will be able to do this—we will be able to do that." Rather than staying home doing nothing I joined these leaders, and met so many great musicians who were throwing in the towel, as the fighters say—giving up. There was Leon Englund, Earl Scofidio, Earl Marco and Cliff Jackson, who was a great pianist from Washington, DC, and a contemporary of Duke Ellington; he was respected as a jazz great in the high echelons along with the Lion Willie Smith, the Tiger Willie Gant, Don Lambert the Lamb, the Beetle, Luckey Roberts the Octopus, Blind Steel and a few more super great piano players. Cliff Jackson had opened the Lennox Club in 1928, and stayed then until it slowly faded into a dustbin—empty. I heard half a dozen or more sermons before the death of several nightclubs. The owner called all the employees together and asked them to hang onto the sinking ship in order to keep it going. I sat with the bands of Leon Englund, Earl Marco, Cliff Jackson, and heard these pleas and saw quite a few tear-drops from the chorus girls and the ladies' room attendant.

Then I joined Tommy Jones's band, then James P. Johnson at Small's Paradise. It was a smallish big band. Jimmy Johnson had an orchestra —about twelve pieces. Small's Paradise was a big club. After that I was with Baron Lee's band. We played theaters, did split weeks: second-rate theaters in small towns like Erie, Chester and York, Pennsylvania —not the major cities. There was a great demand still for vaudeville. We did four days in one place and three days in another. Baron Lee—that was how they billed him: there was the Duke, the Count, the Earl, the King (that's Fletcher Henderson), and then there was the Baron. Irving Mills put that tag on him: Baron Lee. It was put together like Mills's Blue Rhythm Band: book this now, you get Duke Ellington next month. Theaters booked bands with a type of show—a show with dancers, a whole revue on the stage.

Albert Nicholas was around in New York. He had left Luis Russell's band. There had been a big change in personnel. And Albert Nicholas and I were friends. Albert Nicholas hired me following Bernard Addison for a job down at Adrian's Taproom. (Wingy Manone had been in there with four pieces.) So we went in with Albert: first Freddie Jenkins, later Ward Pinkett (trumpet), Joe Watts (bass), and myself. No drums. This was around 1935–6. And I worked there like maybe six, seven months. That was at the President Hotel. That was a musicians' hotel. We were the only band there; just a combo, four pieces. It was in the basement, a little niche on the right side of the hotel: Adrian's Taproom. Adrian had one bartender, two waiters, and a Chinese in the back cooking food. It was a musicians' hotel. The Casa Loma Band stayed there, Jimmy Dorsey's band, Tommy Dorsey's band. Most of the traveling bands that came through New York generally stayed at the President Hotel. You got good rates there.

So they had a little club down in the basement. We worked there from nine o'clock until around 3 or 3.30 in the morning. At night, most hotels closed round 1 or 1.30. The swinging musicians came to the Taproom, the ones who boozed and smoked. And there I saw and heard about reefers. I knew about it. I had seen them smoking. But at the Taproom they had a secret thing going for the musicians. There they had a door that led down into the bottom of the hotel. A subterranean place back down in there where they had all the pipes: air-conditioning pipes covered with this white cloth, like asbestos. That's where most of them went silently, under there with the pipes and pipes and pipes. There was one small light, a 40-watt bulb. You would go back up in there and get lost in the dark. I went down, and as my eyes grew accustomed to it I began to see the place had got like sixty or seventy musicians. They would disappear out of the Taproom, and they would all go down; take their time and go down to this subterranean dope dew dungeon—this basement. So I said, "What's going on?"

Nick said, "They're smoking." All you could see was smoke, and you smelt it when you went down there. Just didn't go for it myself. It made me feel kind of strange, feel helpless. You hear fifteen versions of what everybody's saying. Normally you don't pay it no mind, but it made me very sensitive. If ten people's talking you could focus your brain, listen at one particular voice. Normally you can't do that. It's a concentration thing, that reefer smoking. Well, I wasn't for that; I wanted to be fully aware of everything happening to me at all times.

So they would be down there smoking. All you could see was a flashing, the rising of the red light that diminished when they were drawing on a cigarette. You would see the puffing. They were all over the place, talking and laughing, laughing and choking from the smoke, and enjoying themselves. One night it was quiet in the place; nothing happening. A couple of white musicians came in. They said, "What's happening, Nick? What's happening? Sure would like to have a puff—take a drag. Y'all got them things?"

I said, "No, I don't have none."

They asked Nick. Nick said, "No, I don't have nothing." Nick knew them. I can't remember who they were, but he knew them; they were famous musicians. "Gee," they kept yakking, "sure would like to have a taste, man. It would lift my spirits."

So it dawned upon me. I thought, "I've seen one of them guys put a roach up on top of one of them pipes." You could reach up there and put a roach on top of one of the pipes either side; the roach of the cigarette—a reefer butt. So I said, "Nick, you know something? I seen them guys when they're smoking. They put their roaches down there, but I don't see 'em go back. There must be a whole lot of roaches down there."

He said, "You're damn right, 'cause I done put a lot of them up there myself."

Nick got some matches, a chair, and we went down there and looked with those two musicians. And we looked on top of the pipes. And Nick said, "You're damn right, Dan. Look at them roaches up there. Must be a thousand of them sons of bitches. Man, look at the roaches. Hold out your hands."

The two guys were all excited, and held their hands out like he was giving them twenty-dollar gold pieces, eyes popping, amazed at this treasure. So he started scooping up the roaches and putting them in them cats' hands. One of them dropped them. He couldn't get them fast enough to start lighting up, you know. They took their pick of about a couple of hundred roaches. They thanked me. Nick said, "You sure got a good mind, Dan, to think of it." So that was that. There must have been four thousand roaches if we had looked on the rest of them pipes. There must be roaches there yet, because the hotel's still there.

That's where I saw the last playing appearances of poor Ward Pinkett. Nick hired Ward. Freddie Jenkins left for some reason, took sick. He had been sick when he was still playing with Duke. He was still trying, but his doctor told him, strict orders, he ought to leave the horn alone, for ever. So Nick hired Ward Pinkett. Ward was kind of beyond rescue, a chronic alcoholic. But although he was drinking so heavily he could still play at that time, if he could stay sober two or three nights. But then he would get two, three drinks in him, sit on the bandstand, forget to pick up his horn on time. And we only had four pieces. So Nick told him before long, "I can't put up with this. The man wants a horn. You come here, get boozed up. So don't drink so much—stay sober through the night and go on home."

"OK."

But it went on. For about three weeks. Drunk. Nick said, "It's the last time, man, tonight. You got to go somewhere else. Not here." Ward used to bring his bottle and hide it. They got into an argument. He came drunk, couldn't play at all. Nick wanted to throw him off the bandstand. I said, "No, you're going to hurt him." He almost took his clarinet and broke it over his head. So eventually Nick hit Ward, he was so mad. He said, "It's unnecessary to come drunk every night." Ward went home crying. He stood in the street in front of the place crying. Finally he went home to his white girlfriend. I have to laugh, because recently a blind bass player here in New Orleans was telling me about all these chicks, who dedicate their life to these musicians. Hopeless cases: alcoholics, dopers. Helpless social problems.

Ward had a headstrong Italian girl. I had seen her around Harlem. There was a gang of them who would be with jazz musicians, white and black—they were mixers. So she came back to the hotel, called Nick on the side, and gave him particular hell about why he had hit Ward. He knew Ward was helpless, so why had he hit him? Why didn't he have mercy on him? Why did he have to hit him? "You know he's sick. He needs help, and you could help him. But instead of helping him you beat him and you hit him. And it's not right." And Nick had to bow his head and listen, like he was a criminal. And she went on and on: "Poor Ward needs help. I've taken all my time and energy to try to give him help and get him back so he could play again, and to try to help him. And you hit a poor defenceless man. You know he's sick—he can't help himself." She went on defending Ward. And Nick went on listening, bowed his head, and said, "Well, I'm sorry. I don't know—I can't use him."

"You give him a chance. Talk about black musicians needing a chance. He needs a chance, and here you won't give him one. You're Negro like him, yet you abuse him. But you should know better. You're a grown man, not a child."

But Nick didn't rehire Ward.

Later on, in the 1950s, I saw Lester Young when he was in his last stages. He was beat out and he was gone, and just drinking. Disappointed that he wasn't getting the money that other tenor players who were copying him were getting to play the clubs. Then it was standard about $900 for a quartet, and Stan Getz and Georgie Auld were getting that and more. They had quartets, these tenor players. Illinois Jacquet had a quartet. Lester Young had a quartet. Coleman Hawkins, Ben Webster—all had four pieces, and they went around the circuit.

Now, I saw this same chick with Lester later. He was drunk. He had been on one of them binges, looked like for weeks. And I saw him, standing up, eyes bloodshot-red. You could tell he was hanging over, see. And then I saw this chick with him, the same little chick that had been with Ward Pinkett. She was having the bartender fix a special drink for Lester: milk with an egg and a dash of something to revive him. And she said, "Lester, you must drink this. This will settle your stomach and clear your head."

There was a gaggle of chicks nursing these defeated musicians. These chicks would attach themselves to them, and look out for them, take care of them. Like Pee Wee Russell for a long time. He was a chronic alcoholic, walked like an old-time Chinese—looked like his feets was heavy. Big Bob Carroll. A great tenor player. He left Don Redman's band; didn't attend to business, or couldn't. His personality didn't help. He had a little delicate woman. He stood seven feet tall, but he got this little bitty woman. She would say, "Come on, get your food; sit down and eat. Take care of yourself. You live this life. You can't play this kind of music on an empty stomach." And all that. A whole bunch of chicks and a gang of musicians like that.

There's this old musician today here in town, in New Orleans, at Preservation Hall. Old. Forgets to zip up his pants, you know. He carries on a bunch of foolishness to keep people laughing. He's got a little white woman and she's very attentive to him: carries the instrument for him, gets him to the gig on time, sees he has a clean shirt, and really take care of him. This blind bass player asked me, "Where do these chicks come from?"

I said, "In my opinion they're what you call animal trainers."

Eventually I went with Lucky Millinder's band for three years. Had some ups and downs. With Millinder we played the Savoy, we played one-night stands, two or three steps below Calloway, the Duke, and Lunceford. Lots of times Lucky was a replacement for them. I think he was a threat for a while to all those bands. Irving Mills handled it cleverly: kept him working, but in another direction. While I was with Millinder I did other little gigs, making records, playing different groups. All very busy. Some I got paid, some paid less. Some I didn't fit with the combination—it didn't last. But you learn that in New York. You play with dogs, cats, bears tomorrow, gorillas the next day, acrobats, water-board people, electricians—you just get a tough skin. Have guitar, banjo—well, just guitar then—will travel.

Lucky Millinder had a terrific band: Charlie Shavers, Harry "Sweets" Edison, Tab Smith, Lionel Arnold Adams, Walter Johnson, myself, and Johnny Williams. We had a battle of music with Basie out in Baltimore and the band cut Basie's band. You tell people that and they say, "You don't know what you talking about."

They used to put bands on the road, sometimes three or maybe four bands, like Ike Dixon (out of Baltimore), Lucky Millinder, Zack White's band (out of Cincinnati). And you played in Baltimore at the Wheel. Then you played Chester, Pennsylvania; Richmond, Virginia; I can't recall the rest. But all of the places would be packed and jammed for these bands. They set up one after another, but sometimes the drummers had all set up their different drum sets first. Three or four sets. But often they used one. All them drummers used to hang out together. And then you left it to the public. Now this particular battle was Lucky Millinder versus Count Basie. Basie was big, but not as big as he became later, you know. The battle of music came, and we blew out Basie. That was before Harry Edison joined Basie. After Basie heard these musicians he hired Harry Edison, Eli Robinson (the trombone player), Tab Smith, Andy Gibson, for the arrangements Lucky was using. Nobody paid it no mind. You say something to musicians about that and they say, "That's talk." But Harry Edison still laughs about the night we cut Basie.

Millinder laid us off in New York. And he took another band —Frankie Fairfax's band, which was under the direction of Bill Doggett (the organist). Bill Doggett got the band for Lucky Millinder, because Millinder had heard his band. Dizzy had come out of this band, and Carl Warwick and Charlie Shavers. A gang of musicians came from Frankie Fairfax's band. It was a swinging band of the younger generation. And while we were laid off, Lucky went and took this band and played ten or fifteen one-nighters. While we were waiting somebody came back and said, "We saw Lucky Millinder out on the road."

"Where?"

"Lucky Millinder's band was swinging last night in Chester, Pennsylvania, man—a helluva band."

We were all waiting in New York. We all listened, so we all said, "Fuck Lucky Millinder."

So Charlie Shavers went with John Kirby, Buster Bailey (who'd been in our band), O'Neill Spencer and Billy Kyle; they all formed the John Kirby Band out of Lucky Millinder's band.

So I was around, and somebody said, "Benny Carter's organizing a band." Benny Carter used to organize bands and come up with a whole batch of new arrangements—forty or fifty. And he would be a sensation. And for some reason I don't know he would fizzle out. Been doing it for years, fizzling. Got discouraged because he couldn't keep on. Guess he didn't want to go on them one-nighters. But he had quite a name. And that opened doors for him in record companies; everybody knew him, because he arranged for everybody. So I saw him and went around to the hall for rehearsal. Somehow I had made contact. Johnny Williams got the leads and said, "Danny, Benny Carter needs a guitar player—you'll make it, won't you?" He told me he would play some theaters and things. So I went to see Benny, and that's how I joined Benny Carter's band. So, once you joined Benny Carter's band you could play in any band; that was the theory or belief in New York. When they said, "Benny Carter's rehearsing," everybody in Harlem knew it. They would ask, "Who's in the band?"

"Danny Barker's on guitar."

"Yeah?"

"They have Johnny Williams on bass."

I forget who was on drums. It was a great band. Prince Robinson was in that band. It was a beautiful sounding band with beautiful sounding arrangements. So we played the Apollo, the Savoy, then Baltimore (round the black circuit), Philadelphia, Newark, Washington, DC. Then back to New York and lay off.

When I was with Carter I ran into Jo Jones. He said to me, "How you doin', Section?" That's what he called me, Section, because of those big fat chords. We had a good rhythm section with that band, and we got the respect of musicians like Jo Jones. They figured if you could play Benny Carter's scores you could play anything. I didn't have regular scores of course. I had symbols written out—chord symbols—in the context of the rhythm. Most arrangers, in all the bands, wrote out chord symbols. A lot of writers wouldn't have known how to write for guitar any other way. It was the same in Cab's band. It would have taken an arranger too long to write those four or five notes out on the stave anyway, so they used letters or symbols. An augmented seventh with a flatted something or other would have taken a while to write out, so you got B♭7, with a plus or minus or whatever. You saw that and you knew you had to make a big B♭ chord; and your ears were trained—you knew which notes to put in to bend that chord, which inversion to use.

Not all the bands had everything fully arranged. They had certain arrangements, but there were some tunes everyone just played on: *Lady be Good, Honeysuckle Rose, Liza*. These were just straightforward tunes, and mostly they were played without scores.

Chu Berry and Roy Eldridge were buddies. They would roam about Harlem on a rampage looking for tenor players, and trumpet players, relentlessly. Roy would heat up a club, and the people would come down and hear them. Fred Moore played this joint on 140th Street and Seventh Avenue. Chu Berry and Roy Eldridge would be in there with a rhythm section, and would light up the place. After they left the Savoy, playing with Teddy Hill, they would go down to the clubs, about five to ten joints. They hired me to make a recording date. They wanted the big fat chords I played on the guitar, and I had been friends with them. Me, Roy, Chu, Clyde Hart, Artie Shapiro on bass, and Big Sid Catlett. So I made two records for Commodore, including *Sittin' In*. Those records made a whole lotta noise. So, I was cosy with Chu; we were friends. He liked what I did.

But before that my uncle Paul had started a band. Him and Luis Russell had had a disagreement, an argument about hiring me on guitar. So Paul got a band, and he had Chu in it, because Chu had been working as a superintendent in the basement of a building in Harlem,

playing sporadically. My uncle Paul organized this band and he went
working down the Strollers Club, which was a gangsters' club. We
worked there two nights. We went there a third night, and the place
was padlocked. They had killed some gangsters and bust the joint. So
Paul had trouble getting his drums outa there. He had to go to the
marshall to unlock the doors so he could go in, get his drums. But he
gave Chu the incentive to play, start again. Chu was grateful for that,
and we were chummy. Chu had come to New York with Sammy
Stewart's band, a great Chicago band that fizzled out, like many others.
Chu went to Teddy Hill, Fletcher Henderson, and then Cab Calloway.
Cab was making changes. From 1931 he had fired one Missourian of
the original band at a time. Rumor says he fired them because when he
first joined the band they resented him. Had a hard time getting them
to watch that baton. Lucky Millinder had done the same thing with the
Blue Rhythm Band—he fired one at a time. A process: to break up a
clique. You get a clique in a band, that's trouble.

So then we were laying off, and I met Yank Porter the drummer, who
said, "Say man, why don't you take your old lady down the Cotton
Club? They looking for a blues singer. Go down and tell them you want
to make an audition."

Blue Lu had sung this record *Don't you feel my legs*. So I asked Lu. I
said, "You wanna go down the Cotton Club, make the audition? You
might get the job."

"What job?"

"A singer to work with comedians." I said, "You tell 'em, *Go back
where you stayed last night*, you know, like they do on the Apollo stage.
You the lady—the sweetheart of the comedian; you do some lines with
him. Your chance to be a star."

So we went down to the club to make the audition. Bill Robinson and
Cab Calloway, they were rehearsing with all the chorus girls, all the
show girls. So we sat down. They said, "Who's next?"

I said, "Blue Lu Barker."

They said, "Who's Blue Lu Barker?"

I said, "She's a singer's gotta record." And all the chorus girls said,
"Yeah, she's that singer got the record *Feel my legs*." Now the record I
had composed, *Don't you feel my legs*, was a risqué thing at that time.
So everyone looked at Lu and I as we mounted the stage floor. Bill
Robinson and his wife were there. Cab Calloway's wife was there,
sitting up on the first balcony. They were all looking. I said, "I'll play for
her."

"Come on, OK."

So I went up with Lu. And there were all those people sitting around. Critics, artistes, promoters, newspapermen, electricians, contractors—they were fixing up the club for a new season. So I got up there, played the introduction, and Lu started *Don't you feel my legs*. Hughie Walk was the rehearsal piano player. A nice, pleasant, good-looking man. He was the pianist who also worked at the Apollo Theater, used to rehearse acts there. He worked on the production of the show. And he knew me, because I'd been through there with Luis Russell's band, Baron Lee's band, Benny Carter's band, Lucky Millinder's band, all those. He knew me, so he smiled and said, "I got you covered, man, I got you covered." He started right in; he anticipated what was coming. A good musician. Maybe he had heard the record on the jukebox. And we played it. I looked over.

"Don't you feel my legs . . . feel my thigh."

I seen Bill Robinson stand over there: "What?" His face was annoyed, all contorted, getting madder and madder. His wife was laughing. Cab's wife was laughing. Everybody was laughing, because it's a comic song. So I was playing the biggest, fattest chords I could find, and Lu was singing, and the chorus girls started singing on the second chorus. There were sixteen chorus girls started singing, the showgirls singing, it was like a full chorus. "Don't you feel . . ." And they were all singing, snapping their fingers, and everybody was enjoying it. We thought, "We got this gig." So we finished, got a big ovation. And we stepped down. And Cab's valet came on and said, "Cab wants to see you. Come to the back."

So I said, "All right, I'll be right back."

Meanwhile all the girls came round Lu. "Where you been? We didn't know where you was doin' your singin' in town."

Lu said, "I don't sing. I stay home. Stay home with my kid."

"But you're great."

So I went in the back. And there was Bill Robinson and Cab Calloway. Bill was telling Cab as I came up, "You imagine—that nasty motherfucker comin' in here an' singin' that nasty fuckin' song with my wife in here. An' your wife. Man, do you know, I could blow his fuckin' brains out. That'll learn him to come and sing about 'feel the bitch's legs and the bitch's thighs and her hips'—all that shit. What the fuck's wrong with the guy?"

And Cab said, "Man—shit—all them comediennes sing risqué songs. Bessie Smith sings them songs. Ethel Waters sings *Stop it, Joe*—ain't no worse than that. That's what the people want. They want a risqué number, so the man brought them a risqué number."

He said, "I still don't like it. The motherfucker."

You see, I think he was mad because I got too much of an ovation, and he didn't like that. He resented anybody getting a whole lot of adulation—a strange man. So I came up. He looked at me, cut his eyes at me. I gave him a little smile—like a con man. Instead of giving him the big bullshit I gave him a little smile of humility: "Good evening, Mr Robinson." Real sweet.

So Cab said, "Yeah."

I said, "How you doin', Mr Cab?"

He said, "Cut out that 'Mister' shit. That was great what y'all done out there. What you doin'? Where you workin'?"

I said, "I ain't workin'."

He said, "Want a job?"

I said, "Yes. That's why we come here, to get a job."

He said, "I'm not talkin' about 'we.' I said, do *you* want a job?"

I said, "Yeah. What kind of job?"

He said, "In my band."

I said, "That's a surprise to me. Sure, I'll take a job, play guitar in your band."

"Yeah."

"When do I start?"

"In 'bout a week. Speak to Rudolph, he'll give you the details." That was the valet. He was busy. So I was going out. He said, "That was nice, I liked that. Your wife's a nice singer. A helluva number. Who wrote it?"

I said, "I wrote it."

He said, "Yeah? Where you from?"

"New Orleans."

"No wonder."

I said, "I won't take up your time. I'll see you."

So I went on out. Bill Robinson was out there, looking in my direction and arguing with his wife. She was telling him, "Ah Bill, come on. That ain't necessary. I can tell people's behavior."

So Rudolph said, "Come by here, tomorrow, two o'clock, and I'll see about you getting your uniforms for you to join the band." He didn't say anything about salaries or nothing. But I understood it was OK.

NINETEEN

The record business

Lu Barker was singing around the house. Everybody complimented her and asked her to sing blues and popular songs. Some said, "Why don't you record her? She's got talent!" She had a great personality, likeable face, everything to go with the business. Someone said, "Why don't you make an audition for Decca?" So I went down there and met this guy Mayo Williams; he had an office there, a little cubby hole. He was in charge of a branch of Decca records which covered the area of blues, folk, and black popular music and ballads (different from white ballads). It was publicized as "race records" in publication and trade magazines.

There was a whole lot of black music that wasn't played on white jukeboxes, radio stations, theaters and Hollywood movies. This was done purposely through racism—prejudice. At one period this had happened with minstrel shows. There were ballads like *Honeysuckle Vine, Roamin' in the Clover*; a whole lot of music which was relegated as "black music." There was a period when they didn't want a male black artist to sing a love song on white stages. I experienced that with Chuck Richards, singer with Lucky Millinder, in Washington, DC, the USA capital. He had a beautiful voice. He sang *I've got a right to sing the blues* and *Sincere Love*. Dressed sharp; clean-cut under the spotlight. After the first show the theater manager came back and told Lucky to stop the singer singing those songs: "Sing a 'Mammy' song, or something about the river, like *Mississippi Mud*." There was much confusion between Lucky, Chuck and the manager. You had to sing a river song—the *Robert E. Lee* or *Swanee*—or you didn't sing at all. That was the racist custom down South—below the Mason–Dixon line. So Chuck sang *River stay 'way from my door* and three other songs pertaining to Dixie. That was the attitude of the time. Black artists had to do songs which were put on the black-race jukeboxes. Of the millions of jukeboxes around the country, many did not spin black artists. Many black jukeboxes only played two or three white artists; most were black—Ellington, Calloway, Lunceford, the Mills Brothers.

I talk about race records because black singers mostly had to confront these black entrepreneurs, who were subtle rip-off artists. And Decca had Mayo Williams, who was in charge of the race record department. I was going to Decca, but I didn't go to the office where Bing Crosby and the white artists go; I went to Mayo Williams's office, which is a cubby hole. He was in charge of the whole black artists' department. All deals to do with money done with Decca went through Mayo Williams. There was a woman at Decca, Miss Marks, a lawyer, in charge of finances, signing of checks and pay-offs. I didn't know, but I soon found out, that I was recording for Decca but I didn't talk to the Decca officials, I was doing business with Mayo. He was a wheel; very busy. Black artists came from all directions making records for Mayo.

Lu sang a song for him. I played, and a piano player; he liked it. Would we make a date? "Do you do something a little spicy, like *My baby rocks me?*"

I said, "I can figure something out." So I gathered some songs. I went and told Mayo about this tune, *Don't you feel my legs*, and he said, "That's fine." I told him I had another one, *Hot Damn* (we changed it to *Hot Dog*). Both titles are like what you would hear in a black cabaret, with the words and so on. So you could put it on a record. Which would be back of the tracks; slum, or in the gallion—where the black folks hang out. You would find those kind of titles on race records, strictly for the black market. Earthy things.

So the record was made. I got the best musicians: Red Allen, Buster Bailey, Wellman Braud, Sam Price, O'Neill Spencer. Good band. The tops. But there was engineering indifference in the Decca control room. Mayo Williams sat outside and did not concern himself with the playback sound, volume, overall proper sound-level for jukeboxes. I was not satisfied with the volume on Lu's records. I would have corrected this volume business, but I joined Calloway's great band that traveled.

Lu recorded, and while she was making these records I noticed some hangers around. Alberta Hunter was there. Perry Bradford, with his briefcase—every blues ever written, he claimed he wrote it; if anyone recorded, Perry was there: "I wrote that!" *Don't you feel my legs* (recorded as *Don't you make me high*) was a smash hit all over the place. Decca stopped pressing Guy Lombardo to press it, until the disaster that happened on Seventh Avenue, and the record stopped being pressed.

When we wrote *Don't you feel my legs*, it was during Franklin D. Roosevelt's second election. He was canvassing all over the country.

He was on a national tour, and word came he was coming through Harlem, which was quite a thing. Bill Robinson, Walter White, Miss Bethune, and all kinds of important people in Harlem arranged a rally for him. On 137th Street and Seventh Avenue there's a church called the Salem Crescent. It's famous, in the area where all the fighters came up, like Ray Robinson. There was a great gymnasium there.

So in the front of the church they put out one of those portable stands for people to sit on. It could seat say 500 people. All the streets round Seventh Avenue were waiting, full of people, because President Roosevelt was coming through. He was going to stop and make a brief speech on his way down to City Hall. Everybody was standing out there. I was standing out there too, waiting. And you could hear this buzzing of conversation, "Roosevelt's coming."

"When is he coming?"

"Which way is he coming?"

"Through the Bronx. And he's on his way here."

And everyone on the stand was sitting there polite and proper. Marian Anderson, Miss Bethune, Catherina Jambora—all the prominent black women. Society people, all the big politicians, office holders, were sitting up there, prim and proper. Mrs Eleanor Roosevelt, with FBI agents near to protect her, was looking on. And I was standing beside the stand with a bunch of musicians. And all of a sudden we heard a noise in the distance. The Savoy had a truck that used to come out and play the current record of the band which was playing there—whoever: Coleman Hawkins, Erskine Hawkins's band, Chick Webb's band. They would put on all the different bands and let the people in Harlem hear them—to advertise the Savoy attraction —with this big amplifier. All of a sudden, when it got almost to the stand, the driver put on Lu's record: "Don't you feel my legs . . ."

"Listen at that! Listen at that!"

That was all you could hear. Everybody was talking, most laughing; many were mad, especially the honored guest.

"It's a record!"

"Whose record is that?"

And he slowed down the truck and he passed by mischievously, and finally went by. And you could hear, "Listen at that filthy record . . ."

"It's filthy!"

"Get that record!"

Somebody shouted, "Stop that truck and get that record!"

Some of the people were laughing, some of them were embarrassed: a song like this showed the vulgarity of the black mind. It was a disgrace. Yet at their houses, probably half of them had that record, and played it at their parties. But they said, "Get that record!"

I backed off. There were poles and trees back there behind the stand, and there was a gate. There was a great big tall six-foot man in a blue suit—government man, secret service—standing round there. And from the stand the voices were going on, "Get that record, and find out who the hell wrote that record!" Well, when they said, "Find out who wrote the record . . ." I split through that alley and went on down Eighth Avenue. Behind me I heard, "Danny Barker wrote that record. He just was here. Where is he at?"

"He's gone!"

"Where's he at?"

"He was here."

"Where's Danny?"

"Danny who?"

"Danny Barker."

And the man wrote the name down. "What is he? A musician?"

"He's a musician, yeah."

And they went after the guy, made him stop the truck, give them the record. And told him he'd better not play that damn record any more. All the kids were around there. Well, once they heard this, they started to sing, and pretty soon everybody started singing it, like they were singing the National Anthem. The secret service man had got my name, not the address. "He must be in the phone book."

"It's a Decca record. That's the sonova bitches you've gotta stop. Putting out that filthy stuff."

Next day or so I got a call from Decca Records, "Danny Barker?"

"Yeah."

"How ya doin?" It was Dave Kapp, Jack Kapp's brother. He said, "Dan, I'm sorry. You had a smash hit here, but we gotta stop pressing them. United States say if we press one more of them records they'll revoke our license."

"Sorry to hear that."

So they stopped pressing the records. But the records became a collectors' item. You'll never find that record in a junk shop. Everybody who had bought that record kept it. Decca took it off the pressing machine, but there are many people, many houses I've been to, where they keep it in the armoire or the closet for special parties.

So I got my royalty check from Mayo, and he'd taken half the money. I called him and he said, "That's how we operate." I met Edgar Battle on Broadway (trumpeter, composer, arranger, could do anything involved with music—a survivor). He said, "I hear you having trouble with Decca over your money."

I said, "Yeah. Mayo's taking half my royalties."

He said, "I've got just the man to get your royalties. I'll get you to meet him, see you get a fair share."

I met Mort Brown, and he told me he can get my royalties. So I signed an agreement with him for 12% on the tune. And I signed the tune over to him. Mort Brown put out a cheap cover copy of *Don't you feel my legs*. When the next check came Mayo Williams had taken 50% of the royalties: and now he wasn't giving me the other 50%, he was giving it to Mort Brown. Mort Brown took 12% of that, so I was getting 38%. Mort Brown had said, "Don't worry about your royalties, I can get your royalties." So I was mad, because Mort Brown couldn't get my royalties for me. He had lied. After you hang around a little bit you find out a bit about the business—how they can flim-flam you. I said, "Didn't you say you can get *all* my royalties for me?"

He said, "But you had signed this thing. I thought I could, but I didn't know you'd signed this paper. What you signed has given Mayo Williams power of attorney. Decca gives Mayo Williams the money for all rhythm-and-blues or blues artists (the whole field).

Mayo Williams and Jack Kapp at Decca had hustled the record business in Chicago when they both were poor. Mayo and Jack were tight. They had started Decca, signed Kate Smith and Bing Crosby, and zoom! They were a major record company.

So, one night in Chicago, I met Brother Montgomery and Jack McCoy—a great blues singer. Mayo Williams had had hit records in the blues field—a whole bunch of people on those records. Jack McCoy was a big star. Well, he told me Williams had paid him for the dates and promised a bonus; no mention of royalties. So Mayo Williams had ripped off a whole lot of people. I asked him about my royalties. We got in an argument. I said, "You taking all my royalties."

He said, "I made your records. What do you think I'm here for? My health?"

I said, "Well, you don't have to take all the royalties. You could take it on one record or something. But long as I'm staying here you just going to take my royalties?" Because I had been getting the yackety yack from different people, saying, "He can't do that to you. Why don't you sue him?"

So I said, "Well, I ain't making any more records." But he had signed Lu up for twenty-four sides. In the meantime I joined Cab's band, so it became less important. Lu did the rest. Sammy Price directed some of the dates and Lil Armstrong some. She did quite a few songs for Lil Armstrong. Lil supervised some of the record dates. When I left, Lil used Ulysses Livingstone on the guitar. And she still used the best musicians, like Charlie Shavers and Benny Carter and Red Allen, Buster Bailey. That was some of the story of our Decca recordings.

On Broadway there is this multitude of do-gooders, willing helping hands. Hustlers, know-it-alls. They can get you out of a little hole and suddenly you find yourself in a bigger hole. So you are learning all the time. We were discussing music all the time. Lu was leery and reluctant to make auditions, which is a must in New York. You live, dream and die auditions. Somebody wants to see you—promises. We eventually decided to move, as it seemed as if you could wear yourself down to nothing in New York.

TWENTY

Cab Calloway's band travels

Cab Calloway's band was great, and Cab was an international institution. Cab's Cotton Club Orchestra and Revue, broadcasting from New York City on the national network, was an exciting big-time attraction. The band played top theaters, ballrooms, and the Sherman Hotel in Chicago, Illinois. Every year on New Year's Eve the band opened with a New Year's party and played a month-long engagement there. Cab used to give the band a paid Christmas vacation—two weeks—and a train ticket to Chicago, to arrive there in time for a 2 p.m. dress rehearsal on New Year's Eve day. It was more of a reunion than a rehearsal, as the band set up in its positions on the stand, tried out microphones, and so on. We left New York City on first class trains: the New York Central, the Twentieth Century Limited, the Broadway Limited.

Hugh Wright, our road manager, was a wonderful and understanding human being; he always made it a practice to get the band the best train transportation if it was possible. We played one-nighters and toured with the Cotton Club Revue, twelve to fourteen performers, a sixteen-piece band, three valets. Those fares were important money for the railroads, who were beginning to feel the competition of the bus companies and the airlines. The band knew all the names of the great and famous railroad lines and fast trains: the Katy (out of St Louis), the Southern, the Bullet, the Lark, the Cannonball, the Panama Limited, the Crescent Limited, the Pan-American, Sunset Limited, the Chief, the Super Chief.

I had remembered the green Jim Crow screens set aside for colored people on trains from Chicago to New Orleans and all over the South. But now the Cab Calloway Band sat all over the dining cars; the band members hurried to the dining room and sat at the first sound of the waiter's hitting the loud triangle as he walked through the coaches. We ordered, and ate watching the moving countryside, ignoring white passengers, only speaking if spoken to.

When Dizzy Gillespie joined Calloway's orchestra I noticed he wasn't dizzy at all, just young, vigorous, and restless. Some in the band resented some of the liberties he took. He acted restless, for the arrangements seemed trivial to him, as he had played at the Savoy Ballroom and heard the music of many great black arrangers. He would play and experiment with what seemed to me to be distant sounds and extensions—surprising things. You had to listen because his new sounds kept you off-balance until he came back in on time. His solos left the arrangement, traveled far, but returned in a split figure, correct musically. He went out through the front door, went round the house. You expect soloists to make a familiar pattern, but when you expected him to come in the back door, he came in the side through the window. During his solos the band would be listening, counting, with an expression of annoyance. Lots of times as Dizzy finished I'd hear, "Hot damn—he made it." But not in spoken words.

We played Kansas City and I and a few of the musicians in the band went to a rehearsal in the hotel's hall. It was Harlan Leonard's band, and there was a young pianist rehearsing and directing his arrangement. The band seemed annoyed at a passage he wanted played. So he went to the piano and played the sequence slowly, and after a while the band played his arrangement. This arrangement seemed difficult to them, and as he looked at the leader and the silent sidemen, a trumpet player fingering his horn said, "This fingering is funny and tricky; I'll get it, but it'll take me time." The piano player was a serious young arranger, Tadd Dameron. He did not say anything, but the wrinkle on his brow spoke: "What's wrong, can't they hear?"

Listening at Dizzy and playing in the Calloway rhythm section behind him I had the opportunity to listen seriously to what he was playing through his horn. The rhythm section was Benny Payne on the piano, Cozy Cole on drums, Milton Hinton on bass fiddle, and myself on guitar. Calloway had a fairly good book of arrangements: nothing too way out or extreme, mostly current popular songs with a dozen or more of Andy Gibson's great dance arrangements played in nightclubs and on the dance tours. Most of the year we played theaters, about thirty each ear, plus strings of one-nighters.

Dizzy would ask Hinton and sometimes myself to come into one of the empty theater rooms and play experiments. Hinton would always join Dizzy. After a while I would give an excuse, because the more we would jam and discuss music in depth I began to find myself sitting there listening and holding my guitar in my lap. Hinton and Diz would go in serious discussion, analysis, which was beyond my knowledge, using musical terms that I had seen on manuscript paper but paid no attention to. Calloway's rhythm section played strict to the arrangement. Benny Payne, a fine pianist, listened to Diz but didn't seem the least bit interested in what Diz and Hinton were doing when Diz played his few solos. Cozy Cole was only interested in Cozy Cole. Cozy's every minute when the band was not on stage was in his dressing room practicing with his sticks on a rubber drum pad. I have never witnessed anybody practice so intensely; over and over he played exercises. As soon as he came down from the stage and wiped off the perspiration he sat down at that drum pad, playing from books on drum techniques: ratamacues, paradiddles, flamadiddles. He practiced these monotonous rhythms to perfection. I doubt if any drummer living can master those cues, diddles, and other drum techniques like Cozy could. We heard the diddles on stage and off stage. So when Diz would be blowing his things to come, he was machine-gunned with Cozy's military diddles. It was an interesting thing to see Cozy's serious drum-technics. He was doing flamadiddles, explosions, and rimshots that Klook-a-mop (Kenny Clarke) was doing: bop—be-bop! In a different theory.

And Diz was playing extensions, exercises, in a whole new dimension. I would figure on playing chords that would be strange to some people, but would be correct with his extensions, chord-wise. I'd grip a tonic chord, listen, move up and down the fingerboard. He would say, "That's right what you're doing." But I had never heard it before. Neither the paradiddles, nor Dizzy's extensions, exploring extensions.

Cab had a big trombone section, four trombones: Keg, Claude Jones, Tyree and Wheeler. Claude left and Tyree left. Among the trumpets, Mouse Randolph and Doc Cheatham both left at the same time, which was when I joined, and Mario Bauza came, stayed a while, and went. (He joined Machito, his brother-in-law, and started that Afro-Cuban band.) Jonah Jones stayed until Cab disbanded.

It was the custom on the road that the sections stayed together: reed, brass, rhythm. It was interesting to see the actions of the series of young tenor saxophone players who came and went after Chu Berry. Illinois Jacquet, Skinny Brown, Ike Quebec, Bob Dorsey. Along the line there was Greely Walton, who had played with Luis Russell's band. Now the rhythm section—Hinton and I—we were buddies. Cozy left and J. C. Heard came. After J. C. came Buford Oliver. Then I left. Then Panama Francis joined. There was this cool, calculated turnover all the time.

They put the sections together so the musicians in different sections could discuss their own instruments. Birds of a feather flock together.

They know all the finer points on their instruments. And me, I attended to my own business, so I wasn't about to go over and get in any discussions. Or it would be almost time for them to leave before I found out somebody's got their notice. One of the trombone players left, or leaving, or got fired. It got monotonous on the road year after year after year. But Cab treated you decently. You never had to worry. You could go over to Mr Wright, get as much as $300 if you wanted. If it was real drastic, you had to "go speak to Calloway about that, son." Mr Wright called you "son," like he was your father. And he was a great man. We called him "Colonel." Maybe he was a colonel in the First World War. And he was just wonderful: he knew how to avoid all that Jim Crow shit, places you couldn't stay, or get something to eat. He knew all about that.

It was such a thing with all black show people having emergencies and hitting the bushes on the highways and byways, because the segregation laws did not allow black backsides to sit on the same toilet seats as white backsides. It would be mixing of the races. There was much trouble with many bands and troupes getting into hassles about using toilets which had signs above saying FOR WHITES ONLY. All colored performers knew this situation, as they were born with the laws, so hitting the bushes was generally something of a laugh. For a while, some years later, Blue Lu and I toured, doing one-nighters behind a record she recorded called *Little Girl from Jacksonville*. And Blue Lu had to hit the bushes two or three times. And it was annoying, embarrassing. But nature takes its course.

There was a funny incident that happened with Dizzy Gillespie. Diz and I rode the bus seated together. On this occasion he ate some jive food in Kansas. We were going through the countryside that night. Dizzy was sick. His stomach was hurting him. Something he ate—that jive Kansas restaurant food. The bus was swinging through Kansas. Dizzy called me, "Mose." Fondly. "Mose," he said, "I'm sick as a dog. I got to go to the toilet. I got this cramp. Never felt this bad before. Going to have to stop that bus. Go tell them to stop the bus, I got to get off."

So I went to the front and told Cab, "Dizzy's very sick back there. He wants to stop the bus."

Cab said, "We'll be in town in about ten minutes." So I went back and told Dizzy. He said again, "Mose, I ain't gonna last ten minutes. My stomach is coming down, I can feel it." And he started loosening his belt. I went back to Cab.

"You gotta stop. Dizzy's loosening his belt." The driver heard me and pulled on the side. So I told Hinton, "Help me with Diz. I gotta get him off the bus. Emergency. There's gonna be a disaster if I don't get him off in time."

So we got him to his feet and got him off the bus, and stepped off the highway into the bushes. I always kicked the bushes in case of reptiles. We hurried to get Dizzy's pants down and fix them so he wouldn't mess on them. And sure enough, things came down. And down again. "Get some paper to wipe him." So I went on the bus to get some, while they held Diz in a squatting position. I didn't see any newspaper around, but I had a new *Life* magazine I hadn't read yet. I rushed off to Diz with it. Tore off a page. And the paper was slippery, glossy. So I tore off another page. Nothing happened. So I tore another one, ruffled it, and passed it through the dust so it would catch a grip. That did it. Threw the paper in the bushes. Pulled up Dizzy's clothes, got him on the bus, and in two seconds flat he was snoring. "Do bop sh'bam . . . a klook-i-mop."

It was a serious thing how these owners of establishments where you wanted to use toilets (especially in the case of lady troupers, singers and so on) could tell you straight-faced, "No, you can't use our toilet," and not seem the least bit concerned about the comfort of a female. I watched these scenes many times and wondered about this attitude.

You would hear musicians coming back bitching, saying how they had been insulted, told, "You can't eat in here." Mr Wright knew all that shit. We would get to Canada, or to Boston and the East, where everybody's high-class and intelligent, they treat you according to your behavior: if you walked in like a gentleman, you was treated as a gentleman. You walked in as a bum—don't care what color—in the East, that's the way you were watched. Cautiously, because you're an incorrigible character, or obnoxious. All that New England area, all up into Canada. When you got up into the East and Canada, the ones who wanted hung out with white women. They were all around. Mr Wright never changed his face; it was alright with him. You know like some people can't stand to see it: black men with white women (or a black woman and a white man). A lot of white guys came round trying to pick up the girls on the show.

Mr Wright was cool to all that racial hassle. He was a straight man all the way. Wonderful man. Colonel Wright would see that all that baggage was getting there, getting to the train on schedule. I would go ask for a $50 advance. He would say, "You owe $200, Danny. You're overdrawn, see?" Then he would say, "OK. But don't tell nobody." I guess he heard that from everybody. Cab's band made money.

Cab Calloway was first-class all the way. I can't say nothing about him, nothing about him at all. He was a great performer and he knew what he wanted. His showmanship was carefully arranged. He learned his arrangements, and the band played them to perfection. And he is a helluva singer. Cab Calloway had good lungs. He could sing a ballad, sing a swing song; he could do a jive song. And he could dramatize a song. Then them dope-fiend songs: *Smoky Joe, Down in Chinatown.* And there was *Kickin' the Gong Around* and *Minnie the Moocher.* And on *Smoky Joe* he sung this long verse. At one time he had on the stage two of those bunks like you have for kids to sleep in; bunks, upper and lower. And he had four of the Cotton Club boys up in there, sleeping like they were dope fiends, and he would come out onto the stage into the light and say, sniffing and snorting, "And now a song about Smoky Joe, who was down in Chinatown." It was a smash thing. People didn't really know what the hell it was he was doing. He sang all these songs like *A Reefer Man.* Dramatizing. Nobody paid it no mind. But all the musicians knew about reefers. And there was jargon, like people round race tracks have in their jive talk around horses.

He was perfect, personable. And he had no vices other than, I think, them horses. He overdid nothing. And he was an athlete. He had a basketball team in the band, and a baseball team. With uniforms. And they would play against different bands in the theaters, and waiters and the hotel helpers. They would go out to City Park, early morning. Sometimes there was talk about him losing money on Wall Street. But he was always pleasant. Wore the best of clothes. Not loud—conservative clothes. Fine clothes, fine overcoats (we did a lot of winter traveling). British suits. British shirts. Sharp. Nice. And he had them Aquascutum coats: half a dozen of them, all different colors. And shetland wool coats. First-class all the way. He was pleasant with everybody. he called me "Mose" and "Stallion"; they were my nicknames. He would look at me and laugh. He got a big kick out of me, most times.

He came down to New Orleans when I was playing with the band. I put on a big feast; fixed baked red snapper at my mother's house for the whole band. And there was something about that food that gave them loose bowels. We were traveling by bus. One-nighters: Kansas City, down through Texas, down through New Orleans, but we didn't play there, we just stopped over. So I fixed a feast; my mother fixed a big feast for the band. Cab and Tyree Glenn just mopped up on that fish. Said they had never tasted nothing like it.

Next day we were traveling again, going up towards Mississippi.

Blue Lu and Danny in California, 1949: a Capitol publicity shot

Danny's band at Jimmy Ryan's in the early 1950s: Arthur Herbert (drums), Haywood Henry (clarinet), Red Richards (piano), George Stevenson (trombone), Doc Cheatham (trumpet)

Paul Barbarin's band at Sid Davilla's Mardi Gras Lounge, 1954 or 1955: Bob Thomas (trombone), Willie Humphrey (clarinet), Andy Anderson (trumpet), Danny Barker (banjo), Ricard Alexis (double bass), Joe Robichaux (piano)

Lucien Barbarin, grandson of Lucien Barbarin, Sr, who started on trombone with the Fairview Baptist Church Band

Charles Barbarin and Danny

Danny as assistant director of the Jazz Museum in New Orleans

Danny as grand marshall for the Onward Brass Band at Dillard University

Blue Lu Barker

Sylvia Barker, daughter of Danny and Blue Lu

Somewhere in Mississippi they hollered, "Stop the bus! Stop the bus! Emergency!" So the bus driver stopped. And Tyree and Cab Calloway broke for the woods. And just got their pants down in time. That fish had given them the diarrhea. And they had to hold Tyree up because he was fat, and the grass and brambles was scratching his backside. So then they say, "We gotta get some paper." There was none. So we got some dried leaves for them to wipe themselves. That was a funny scene. Both of them saying, "I never want any of that goddam fish no more!" So they told the bus driver, "When they say 'stop!'—you stop!"

Cab had a hell of a band at one period. A real swinging band, with Chu Berry, Jonah Jones, Dizzy and Shad Collins, Lammar Wright. That band was a swinging band. There are a couple of great albums, with a picture of Cab on them. I'm on them, Dizzy too. That was a helluva band compared to most of the bands at that time. With Chu on tenor. And he had Andy Gibson's great arrangements. Gibson really arranged them so they swung. The band would swing in the pattern of Basie, or Lunceford, or Earl Hines. This was a swinging band, and it was all pleasure alongside the wonderful Milt Hinton.

TWENTY-ONE

Bebop and how I left Calloway's band

Now in 1945 I was in New York with Calloway. I met Sir Charles Thompson, and he was very friendly. We met in bars, got to know one another. Now in those days they had what you would call *rhythm* sections. And rhythm men would go and listen to other whole rhythm sections, seeing how they would coordinate. The precision, which was like a machine. You used to hear Fletcher Henderson's section, with John Kirby, Walter Johnson and Fletcher, Clarence Holiday on guitar —they pulsed. Fantastic rhythm. They would shade it. Walter Johnson could shade a band, bring it up, bring the whole thing up, build up a feeling of exhilaration, make you feel good. See, down here in New Orleans they've never really had that concept of a rhythm section. It's just "I'll play my job, you play yours. Don't tell me how to play my drums, you just play your bass." But in New York everybody looked at one another. We got that feeling. Everyone would say to one another, "Where are we at . . . get in there!"

Now Sir Charles wasn't just a rhythm player—he could play any kind of piano from ragtime to modern styles. A masterful musician. He could arrange, and he had depth. A whole scope of music. He called me, "Dan, I've got a record date. Can you make it?"

I said, "Yeah. I could use the loot." So I said, "Who are we with?"

He said, "Charlie Parker."

"Charlie Parker! Man—I don't play bebop!"

He said, "It ain't gonna be a bebop record. It'll be sort of experimental, putting a rhythm section with these guys. It'll be a knockout. And besides, I've got you covered. I'll tell you what to press on."

I said, "You're sure? Charlie Parker? He'll be satisfied?"

He said, "We talked about it. Charlie digs you. He's seen you play."

I said, "Well, if you're sure. Because I'd hate to come down there and have the people look at me all funny because I don't know that music. I'm not a bopper."

He said, "They want a beat man, and big fat chords. You can do that."

So I made the date. I got there. It was a 9 a.m. date. Nine o'clock, I was there; one of the others too, and we were waiting. And I said, "What's the wait?" Charlie was there and Gordon—Dexter Gordon the tenor player, who had come to New York with Lionel Hampton. I didn't know him. Buck Clayton arrived. I knew Buck, and J. C. Heard, who was working with Cab Calloway's band.

Finally we got going, we played those big fat chords, and they seemed satisfied. Charlie was very friendly. But they didn't finally start recording until eleven o'clock, for they were waiting for the man to come with something. I was naive, still wondering what the hell this was. But somebody whispered—pulled my coat—"The man's coming with something for Charlie." So we made the date. I had the honor of playing with Charlie Parker when he was at his height. But that day, until those people came there, he was sitting around looking off into space, sweating.

I had played with Dizzy Gillespie with Cab's band of course. And so that's how I came also to play with Charlie Parker. Jimmy Butts sent me the picture of the session, which I cherish.

And then, of course, there was Minton's. The purpose in the beginning at Minton's was to manipulate the sounds and chord and harmonic structures of the songs played there. At Minton's, and in a few other back rooms, strategy was planned and plotted, gradually taking form, to cut out and eliminate inferior players. Thelonious Monk was the leader of the Minton's bandstand (a very small, tight one). He generally started playing strange introductions going off, I thought, to outer space, hell knows to where. I went there a few times in the formative stages of the new thing. Some nights Milt Hinton and Dizzy would grab a cab from the Cotton Club downtown on Broadway and rush up to Minton's. I went as an observer sometimes, because of Diz and Hinton. Chu Berry went a couple of times also, but this new innovation was not his thing; his bag was a rhythm section. He liked four men chomping a chord pattern. At Minton's Monk and Kenny Clarke ("Klook-a-mop") set up a mind-boggling diffusion of rhythms and sounds. It was like going into sudden fast rapids in a canoe on the river of sounds, daring and dangerous.

Monk and Klook, the other originators of the mental explorations, sat back at ease, pretending not to be confused, but watching the constant flow of confused would-be boppers. There was the intro, long or short, by Monk and Klook—Klook always looking straight ahead. Then a shot on the snare drum: that was the signal for the in gang

—"rim shot, bebop!" Then there would be maybe a short interval, then again, "bebop!" Somewhere in Monk's intro there was the melody of the song to be played. In Minton's there was complete quiet: very little talking, no glasses clinking, no kinds of noises. Everybody intense in observing and figuring out the music and the behavior of the players, especially of the musicians who dared to jump into the arena. Those who dared and played, started and finished the unknown song they played, had bopped and were now free to talk and join the small, but gradually building bebop fraternity.

Klook and Monk played. Monk started. Klook fell in, dropped in, dived in, sneaked in; by hook or by crook, he was in. A great many musicians who were trained to play to the swinging rhythm sections of the great swing bands—bass, guitar, piano, drums—a smooth, even, pulsating precision music, were first unnerved by the erratic bass-drum beats of Klook—a creation of his which he called "dropping bombs." This could happen any place, any time, at his own discretion, wherever and whenever he, Klook, pleased to indulge in the fireworks display. You would look, hear the off-, off-, off-beat explosion, and think "fireworks," and then the color patterns formed in the high sky of your mind.

At first there was no bass, no guitar, only the great master innovator of electric guitar playing, Charlie Christian. He sat in on many sessions when in town and off the road with Benny Goodman. Monk respected Charlie Christian because Charlie could join in any pattern, now, right now. He was a magician, a magic player. He would join in at once on a riff pattern.

Then I saw Milt Hinton jump in the rapids and play, highly professional. Right up to today I notice bop bass players play with their strings lowered to the bass fingerboard, and they seem to be feeling their way, going in many directions. Bass is a cheating, foxy instrument. Some swing bass players wanted to play that four beat. They couldn't get in the bag of make-believe, to and fro, up and down and around. The concentration: standing or sitting crunched up with the eyes almost closed like an African Congo river crocodile, saying to the public, "This bass man is into his thing." But many bass players slouched over, closed their eyes, played and became boppers.

Now in Cab's band I knew from the beginning to steer out of cliques and syndicates. I'm a Capricorn—a goat; and a goat sits back and looks. Sure enough, I saw cats come in Cab's band and go out again. Come in fast, go out fast; come in slow, be oh-so-happy to be in Cab's band—like I was, I guess. I could see it, you know. They would be extra nice to

Cab, smiling at him. Lighting up, like he was a messiah. He didn't take any notice of them. Friday we got paid: you got your envelope, your money in it, and another little envelope—there was your notice. And they were shocked. Like three or four of the guys broke down and started crying. Hysterical, like they had lost their mother. Yeah, because they got their notice from Cab. Crying. They would go in the dressing room, be unconsolable. "What did I do? Why's he firing me, huh? I did everything I could. I was a good enough musician to play with the band. Why would he let me go? Let me go . . . oh have mercy, oh Lord!" That happened to a famous tenor player: an old timer who had been in Luis Russell's band. Cab hired him, but for some reason they felt he was dated. The section grinned at him and everything. Somehow it got to Cab that he didn't fit the band. He was gone. Then Orville Brown, who had been with the band since the Missourian days. He got his envelope and there was a notice in there: "You're fired." He couldn't stop shaking. They sat him down in a chair. But he didn't stop shaking. I was fanning him, but he would go into periodical screams —loud screams, like a woman. And people said, "What's happening, man? What happened to Brownie?"

"He got his notice; they fired him."

And he talked about how this band was his family, this band was his life. He was in the Missourians at least five years before Cab joined the band. He had been with Cab up until now (1947)—from 1928 to 1947. He had been in the same band for 20 years. Came as a shock to him. So then they took him up and brought him in the dressing room, and he sat by the table and cried. Tears was all over the floor; never seen a man cry like that. Crying about what? He could get another job with another band.

When it came for my time to go I didn't have to leave. I was late, for sure, that Sunday morning. You stay on the road all them years. The Saturday night before we had a late show at the Paramount. After that I went to Harlem. Then home. Got high, stayed up until about seven o'clock. Had to get up at 10, catch the subway and get downtown for 11 or 11.15, 11.30. I woke up, must have been damn near eleven o'clock. I thought, "How am I going to get to the Paramount in time for the show?" I think I brushed my teeth; grabbed up my clothes and put them on. There didn't seem to be any cabs running on Sunday morning. Finally, when I got down to the theater, the band was on the stage. It was very embarrassing. And I looked, here came Bob Dorsey; he was late. I looked again and there was Shad Collins. There were six of us late. There were nine of the band on the stand. But they were playing like it was the whole band.

When the light went down on Cab I ran on stage and took my seat. There were people laughing in the audience who knew what was happening. Empty chairs. New Yorkers understand. I could have taken sick. When the curtain went up again Cab was facing the audience dead center. He turned around to direct the band. He looked dead straight at the band; straight back—right at me. Then he looked at me all disgusted, you know. But he was doing his act, so then he turned around to that audience and he put that smile on again. I know he had said nothing. Nobody said nothing. Friday came. We got paid, and in my envelope, a note: $20 fine. So I went to Mr Wright. I was rooming with Bob Dorsey. He was late too. I said, "Cab didn't fine Bob Dorsey."

He said, "No."

I went to the others and I asked them, "Did you get fined?"

They said, "No."

I'm the only one who got fined. I went back to Mr Wright. I said, "Mr Wright, I'm fined $20."

He said, "That's right son."

I said, "Why did Cab fine me and not fine the rest of the guys that were late. They were as late as I was—some of them later."

He said, "I don't know. I just was given orders to fine you."

So I went to Cab. I said, "I don't like what happened."

"What's that?"

I said, "You fined me $20 for missing the show."

He said, "That's right."

I said, "Well, why did you fine me and you didn't fine the rest of them monkeys?"

"I fined you because you know better."

"I know better?" I said, "I couldn't help it, man, I overslept." I said, "Why did you fine me and you don't fine them? Why don't you fine everybody?"

He said, "We don't want to go into that. You just take the fine—you buy four-fifths of whiskey." That's what he would do sometimes, buy four-fifths of whiskey, and everybody drink the booze. "Let's drink a toast to Danny Barker! Great tasting whiskey!" They didn't want your money—just the discipline. The band was laughing; they got some booze there—some fine booze from my fine. Well, I was mad about it. Why the hell did he pick on me when the rest of them were later than me? So I'm mad as hell. I thought, "I'll stay in New York." I was sick of being on the road; almost afraid to be home sometimes. I wasn't saving any money, with family expense at home and on-the-road expenses.

Barely breaking even. Then I went home and I told Lu, "I want to stay home anyhow, I'm tired of the road."

She said, "If you wanna quit, quit."

So I told Mr Wright and wrote my notice, and I brought it to Cab: "I am leaving the band. My time will terminate at the end of this week or the next week." He said, "You going to quit the band?"

I said, "Shit, yeah. I'm going to quit the band. You fine me. You didn't fine Shad, or Bob, or the rest of them."

He said, "I wouldn't quit, man. I ain't mad at you."

I said, "Then why you fine me and didn't fine everybody. Why the hell you pick on me? Man, you took my money. If you'd fined everybody, OK. But you pick on me."

He said, "Man, forget all that shit."

I said, "What about the fine?"

He said, "You're fined."

I said, "Well, I quit."

He said, "Well, you're still fined. But I want you to stay. I like what you do. You don't give me no trouble. You're one of the best ones I got in the band. Don't I pay you well?"

I said, "Yeah, you pay me well. But you fined me."

He said, "Well, the fine sticks."

I said, "Well, I'm gonna take you to the union. You can fire me, but you can't fine me. I'm going to get my money."

He said, "You don't wanna do that."

I said, "Well, give me my $20." $20 is $20. I went to the union, saw the delegate and told him, "I'm quitting Cab." I said, "I'm leaving Cab's band. He's fined me for being late, and I understand from the union if they fine you, you accept the fine—but if you leave he's got to pay you. I want you to come and get my $20."

He said, "Why do you want to leave that band? One of the best jobs in the music business."

I said, "Do me a favor: come there and tell Cab to pay me $20."

So he came there, and they called me in the room.

"You getting me my $20?" I asked. Cab was looking at me. Mr Wright was looking at me, straight-faced. The union delegate went through a great long thing: "Dan, why you leaving this band? This band's not mad with you. Mr Wright say you one of the most disciplined musicians, you give nobody no trouble. You do your work. Why you gonna leave?"

I said, "Will you get my $20?" I walk out the room. He's left in there with Cab. The delegate left. Pay day come. I didn't see my $20 in the envelope. I asked Mr Wright, "Where's my $20 Cab's supposed to give me because I'm leaving?"

He said, "It sticks, Dan. Cab says the fine sticks."

I don't want to hassle over $20; been over and over it. But I said, "I'm leaving. You'll have to get another guitar player."

"OK. I'll speak to Cab," he said.

See, when we were on Broadway, Cab was in and out, gone. He loved racehorses. He had agents; he'd got all kinds of people to see. So he called me the next day. "You're leaving, definite?"

I said, "Yeah."

"Can you find me another guitar player that plays like you, exactly the way you play?"

I said, "Yeah, I'll find you one."

"Well, try to do that for me. Somebody who can play, and got a disposition like you? Don't get into no arguments, don't argue, that kind of thing?"

"Yeah, OK." I went out. I was walking down 46th Street and I saw Smitty—John Smith. He was a messenger, see, at the Corn Exchange Bank. "Hey, Smitty."

"What you say, Danny. How's things?"

"What you doing?"

"I got a job as a messenger. Steele (Alphonse Steele) got me the job." Steele had sold the bank manager the idea of hiring musicians. He'd got about 150 musicians jobs as messengers with the Corn Exchange Bank. They liked musicians. Easy job. They say musicians know how to talk to people, how to wear a tie and collar. Disciplined. They do their job. They liked Steele very much at the bank as he found musicians work when things were slow. Musicians liked the job because they would get out of the bank and be round the Rhythm Club about four o'clock (as the bank closes at 3) and would have time to see about gigs. I said to Smitty, "You want a job?"

"What kind of job?"

"With Cab Calloway."

He said, "Ain't you with Cab?"

"Yeah, but I'm leaving."

"Why?"

So I told him, and the problem—fining me for being late. "And I want to stay home in New York and try to do something for myself. I ain't accomplishing nothing out on the road nine months of the year—never home. Got a child. I miss New York."

Smitty said, "I'll take the job. Can you fix it for me?"

"Yeah. Cab told me to find him a guitar player. I was going to call you, but since I see you. What you doing now?"

"Nothing."

"Well, come with me." So we went to the theater and asked, "Cab in his dressing room?"

"Yes, he's in there." So I knocked on the door.

"Who is it?"

"Danny."

"Come in, Stallion. What's wrong now?"

"Ain't nothing wrong. This is my very good friend John Smith. Plays guitar like me, but I play like him. Great rhythm guitar—fit perfect. After I'm gone you hear him and look over, you'll see me playing; same thing."

"You really leaving?"

"Yeah, got some things to do."

"You mad about the $20?"

"No, it's alright. Keep the $20. I'll get it later."

He say, "I know you're poor, got troubles . . ." We laugh it off. Cab said, "Well Smitty, see Rudolph." (Like they told me to see Rudolph, Cab's valet.) And Smitty stayed with the band until it broke up, when the big bands all fizzled out.

TWENTY-TWO

California, New Orleans and the Capitol sides

Lu was great, a great singer. Not a shouter. There are different kinds of singers. Like in the case of the Smith sisters. Any black woman with the last name Smith, especially if she was big, fat and Baptist, could automatically sing the blues. So you had thirty or forty women named Smith touring the country with medicine shows and circus side shows, singing the *Crazy Blues* and *Give me a pigfoot and a bottle of beer*. Bessie Smith was a shouter: she would scream, holler! Primitive. Old feelings about "When her man done her wrong . . ." or "Once I lived a life of a millionaire . . ." That kind of thing. Highly dramatic. Mamie Smith was as big as her—bigger than her at one time. And she was a sweet, sweet singer. So there were these various types. Nowadays you see all these singers—Patti Labelle and all—they're what you call shouters, screamers: they scream to the high heavens. Wonderful pipes.

But Lu was a sweet singer, a sweet, subtle blues singer. In her field there are people like Maxine Sullivan, that kind of singer. Ella Fitzgerald. Dinah Washington.

So I said to Lu, "Let's go to California." I had been to California and liked the weather. And I thought it was a whole new fresh area.

She said, "California?"

I said, "Yeah, California. Let's go out there, see what's happening." Albert Nicholas had been out there since 1949.

So we went to California. We stayed eleven months. Somebody told me the name of Freddie Webber, a fellow from New Orleans. We got a room with him. He had a rooming house. He was born in New Orleans, but had left there in 1922 or 1923. He was a wheel out there in the underworld: night life. And he took to Lu right away. He was going up away to northern California; we wasn't there but about a week. And he said to Lu, "I'm goin' away. Would you look out for my place here? Nobody's to go in there. You can go in there if you want. I'll get some phone calls. But don't let nobody else in there."

So that's what we did. When Lu heard the phone, she would go answer it. He went away and he came back. And we had all his phone connections written out, and he thanked us. We was real tight. And he had a friend called John McGee. He was a locksmith, had key shops—about three—in Los Angeles. We were friends with him. One of the neighbors in another room said, "You from New Orleans—you gotta be some helluva people. Freddie Webber do not let nobody be his housekeeper. Y'all must have somethin' special, 'cause Freddie don't trust nobody. But he trust y'all, lets y'all have his key. We was surprised to see you goin' in Freddie's house and Freddie not there."

Now Freddie would go to Chinatown, get in a huddle with the Chinese people. He would go over to other parts of the town, get in a huddle with the Jewish people. He would go down towards Mexico, down to all those little towns, and he would be in huddles with the people there. And he looked white—looked whiter than a white man; you couldn't tell he was colored. So he, Lu and I were tight until I left there to come back. But to me California's nothing. A beautiful place, a big flim-flam town. Nothing doing lest you're in movies and really a star. You scuffle like everybody else waiting to be an extra—waiting for somebody to call, talking about Hollywood. And the black community, as far as being stars at that time—well, you had to have some pull in the movie industry to let you be nothing but a porter or a menial. Every time you appeared in a movie you had to be in service: a street cleaner, a dish washer, a clothes washer. You could do nothing that would let you be equal with anybody else. And there were black people out there who had done all that business, like they had all them kids. Little black kids—they give them all nicknames: Farina, Pork Chops, Sunshine, Buckwheat—all kinds of things. Strange names: Sunshine Sammy, Li'l Smiley. And they had to pop their eyes. If you made a movie they said, "Let's see your eyeballs . . ."

I did a movie with Stepin Fetchit in New York around 1935. Stepin Fetchit was a big star. He had been in company with Will Rogers, who was a superstar. Stepin Fetchit came to New York, and they had this tune *Lazybones*: "Lazybones, sleepin' all the day . . ." So we did a movie on it—comic, a short. They had a machine where Stepin Fetchit was so lazy—he had a machine in his kitchen—a machine to lay an egg. He's sat in a chair, "Aaah . . . aaah." (Yawn.) It took him almost five minutes to raise up, but he kept the tension, and with slow mood music he said, "Aaah . . . time to . . . aaah . . . get me some breakfast. I'll fry me some bacon and eggs." And he slowly pulled a string, and three strips of bacon fell off the machine and into a frying pan, And he pulled another string and the gas came on. And he said, "I'll have me a coupla eggs with it." But he said this slow, man, slow. And he pulled another string and an egg came down a chute and fell in the frying pan, pop! Split open. And another egg did the same thing, fell into the pan. And it took him about all of a fifteen-minute short. And at the end he got up, had his breakfast, the music continuing with *Lazybones*.

So I made that short with him, and then I made a movie in Harlem. A guy came down to the Rhythm Club. He was standing around admiring my guitar case. I thought he was going to talk about going to play a gig or something. And the guy came up and said, "Say, fellows, I'm looking for a band."

"For what?"

He said, "We're making a movie down the street. A colored movie. We don't have much money, but we want five guys to come over and play. Just play about two minutes. Might take about twenty minutes to set y'all up. But just play one tune. I'll pay y'all five dollars apiece."

Well, that was a gig, see. So I said, "Alright." I looked around to see who was there. I think Ward Pinkett was on it. Me, Ward, Cripple Smitty, Geechie Fields, Bill Jones. And we went down the street to the next block. And they were shooting this movie up in an apartment on the third floor. They had the wires running out into the street, to somewhere they hooked them up to this machine on a truck. A generator. And we went up there, and there was a piano. A woman singer—a light woman I had seen around Harlem, but I didn't know her name. But she was an actress. And the name of the movie was *The Woman from Chicago*. We played the *St Louis Blues*. And she sang. There were a few cats at a table. It was a nice little scene. So we did that a couple of times. And then a guy came and said, "Thank you fellers, very much. Five dollars apiece."

We went back to the Rhythm Club and we said, "That's the easiest five dollars we ever made." No residuals, no nothing. A year later I was playing the Howard Theater in Washington, DC, with Lucky Millinder, and they showed this short. One of the guys went in to see the movie. He said, "Man, I seen you in a movie."

I said, "Where?"

He said, "In this theater. They're going to show it next show."

So I went up to see it. And sure enough, there I was. And they were showing that movie in all the colored theaters in the USA. Oscar Micheaux was the producer. He made movies specially for colored theaters. I get a letter from my mother saying, "They tell me you're in a movie playing at the Lyric Theatre and the Lincoln Theatre here in

New Orleans. You sure look good in that movie. You in moving pictures now? You must have made a whole lotta money . . ."

I answered, "Yes—five dollars!"

I have to laugh now. So that was the second movie I made. And with Cab I made two. And three Panoramas.

So here we were in California. A record came out, called *A little bird told me*, and it was a hit record. Somebody told Dave Dexter at Capitol that there was a singer from New Orleans in town. Blue Lu. So they sent for us. We went there and made a cover version of the record. *A little bird told me*—Blue Lu did it identical, like the record. And it ran up on the charts, you know, like about number 3. The *Billboard* charts. So then she made about twenty-seven sides for Capitol. And they wanted the risqué things, so she did some of them. They never released them. She had made some for Decca, and they wouldn't put them out either.

The most famous song from this California period was *Little Girl from Jacksonville*, and this is how it came about. Before we went to California, one day there were some kids in New York in front of my apartment. I came out of the building and heard the kids doing a nursery rhyme, dancing to it:

"Here's a little girl from Little Rock,
Let's see what she can do."

And they all did a little dance. Then:

"Here's a little girl from Alabam', Alabam', Alabam',
Here's a little girl from Alabam',
Let's see what she can do."

And they started clapping their hands, then they'd get out there and do a little time step, a little monkeyshine. And then: break! And I listened to them, and said to myself, "I'm going to make a song out of this." It was a song, somebody's song, I don't know whose—probably a girl made it up. But I went upstairs and I wrote the song down, and I put dances to it:

"Here's a li'l girl can do the Apple Jack, Apple Jack, Apple jack,
Here's a li'l girl can do the ring-dang-do . . ."

Just names of dances.

"Here's a li'l girl can do the Suzie-Q,
Let's see what she can do."

And it was good to dance to, because you could do all the dances when it came to the break. So the tune was alright. And I put one line:

"Here's a li'l girl from New Orleans,
She can drink a lot of Hadacol."

Now I'd been down to New Orleans before I went to California. And there was a patent medicine character, Doctor Dudley LeBlanc, Senator Dudley LeBlanc, who was a politician. And he had a patent medicine that was supposed to cure everything. It was made out of molasses, sugar, salt, honey, a little vinegar, a little turpentine— maybe something else in there too. And he mixed that up and made a formula. And he used to say, "One teaspoonful a night will cure cancer and cure acute tuberculosis." And all the people came and bought this medicine because he had a big advertising campaign.

My uncle Lucien had drunk a lot of wine one night, like one of them winos, and he said, "I'll go get me some Hadacol."

I said, "What the hell's Hadacol?"

He said, "It's that medicine that that monkey advertises on the radio every day."

I said, "How d'ya call it? Hadacol? Alcohol? Hadacol?"

He said, "We call wine Hadacol because it cures all pain."

It's a joke, so one of the first tunes I did for Capitol was *Here's a little girl from New Orleans*.

"She can drink a lotta Hadacol!

–Oh no she can't!

–Oh yes she can!"

And the record came out and became a hit in Louisiana and parts of the deep South.

Now there was a disc jockey here in New Orleans—Poppa Stopper. Senator LeBlanc, who owned Hadacol, the promoter of this medicine, wanted a commercial. Commercials just were coming in. And he wanted to publicize Hadacol. This segment of that record was perfect for him:

"Here's a li'l girl from New Orleans, New Orleans, New Orleans,

Here's a li'l girl from New Orleans,

Let's see what she can do.

She can drink a lotta Hadacol!

– Oh no she can't! (band answer)

– Oh yes she can!

She can drink a lotta Hadacol,

That's all that she can do."

So the disc jockey began to play this record. It was very popular. He played this record after every other record he played. He would say, "Now we're going to play the Hadacol record." And it was the perfect jingle for them. My uncle Paul wrote to me, "Man, you gotta record they play all day on the record program here. The guy has about a six-hour program. All you can hear is Hadacol, Hadacol, Hadacol, Hadacol, Hadacol . . ." So my uncle Paul said, "Why don't you come down here, man? We could get a little band, and we could tour all these little country towns. I think that radio station goes for about a hundred miles. And all that distance you can make it."

I said, "I'll ask Louise about it."

She said, "Yeah. We ain't doing nothing round here." California was like an oasis. Meantime Paul saw Poppa Stopper, because Poppa Stopper wanted to know who we were. So he enquired out and they had told him, "Paul Barbarin's his uncle." So he called Paul, said, "Where is Danny Barker?"

"Well," he said, "he's in California." Then Paul said, "By the way, he's coming here. We've been talking about a tour."

He said, "When he comes here, you tell him to get in touch with me. The man Dudley LeBlanc wants to meet him."

Paul said, "OK."

So Paul told me about Poppa Stopper and Dudley LeBlanc, and that made me want to come to New Orleans more. So I called up the station. And Poppa Stopper the white disc jockey said, "Mr LeBlanc will be in town next week. And when he comes to town I'll call you. He wants to meet you."

So next week we were rehearsing a band, me and Paul. We got kids, all of them kids: Wallace Davenport, Walter Lewis, August Dupont, and Percy Gabriel the bass player. Paul had a small station wagon, and he did the business, fixed a tour, and we toured jammed packed. And later we got a second-hand bus, an old railroad-station Texas Pacific railroad bus. I painted it white, with the name "Blue Lu Barker" on it. We toured the dozen small towns in Louisiana to small crowds—a couple of crowded dances.

Senator LeBlanc called me up. He said, "Hello Mr Barker, how are you? It's a wonderful thing you did with that record when you put that Hadacol thing on it. I'd been looking for a jingle, a commercial, and your rendition of that Hadacol song, using the name of my product, is just what I need. And if there's any way I can help you, I'd like to. I want to show my appreciation." Paul had told me who he was. He was from Lake Charles, Louisiana, and he had a company out there that made this product. A white building. And he had some trucks with Hadacol written on them to distribute it all through Louisiana, Arkansas, and Texas, and everywhere. Now you would expect him to have a big scientific plant with measuring instruments and all this business. But he had none of that. He used them big old abandoned slavery-time sugar-cane pots like a hat turned upside down—great big things; they used to boil molasses in them, and they would put fire under them, to make white granulated sugar. Well Le Blanc had about six of them in the plant. And he had some colored women in there, and they did the mixing—so much sugar, so much this—and they would mix it with broomsticks. And others would boil it, put coloring in it. It was a hand thing, like old salve medicine they gave to sick slaves. Well if you can cure a sick slave, you ought to be able to cure anybody!

Senator LeBlanc said, "To show you my appreciation young man, I want to take you and your wife to the Roosevelt for dinner. She's such a wonderful singer; I've been playing that record over and over."

I said, "Roosevelt Hotel? Senator, I don't think we can go to the Roosevelt."

He said, "What's stopping you?"

I said, "Senator, we are colored people. My wife's colored, I'm colored."

"Oh," he said, "that's a horse of another color." Then he said, "I'll tell you what to do. You come down to the hotel, and I'll have a present for you."

I said, "When d'you want me to come by?"

He said, "Come by tomorrow evening."

So I went by the next evening. He wasn't there. We had gone into the front door of the hotel, and a guy told us we would have to go out, round the side, and come in through the freight elevator, where they kept the garbage. So I went up on the freight elevator. No black people ever rode that front elevator—not even the help in the hotel. Lu said, "I ain't going on that dirty elevator." But the senator was out. So LeBlanc called back: sorry about the delay, he was attending to business. He said, "Come by tomorrow evening, I'll be there waiting."

I said, "I'll tell you what happened. It's embarrassing, because we had to go through the back door, and after we got up there, you weren't there."

Now Lu said she wasn't going again. "I ain't going through the goddam garbage elevator." So Paul, my uncle, he said, "I'll go with you." We went. We went to the back elevator. A colored porter from the front hall came round the back and got on the elevator with us. We went upstairs to the hotel room. The porter walked in the room; we followed. There were four guys with LeBlanc from Lake Charles and what looked like about six women, all of whom were necking. So me and Paul, we backed out, slowly, when we saw what was happening. And the senator came out with me and he said, "My boy, to show you my appreciation." And he went to his pocket, and he came up with five $20 bills. He was going to peel more, but something told him to stop. He said, "Here, this is for you." He said, "Now, your wife, I'm going to send her a watch. Give me the address and her name." I gave them. He said, "Thank you very much."

So we cut out. I gave Paul $40; I kept $60. Came back home, gave Lu $40 and I kept $20. I didn't hear any more from the senator. Except—I had said, "Senator, I got an idea of a promotion that could be a sensation for your business."

He said, "What is that my boy?"

I said, "We'd have what is called a Hadacol Caravan. It goes from city to city with a white band and a colored band. And one night we play for Coloreds, one night we play for Whites. We give them block dances. The admission will be small bottles for teenagers, and a large bottle for grownups. So if you're coming to the dance you buy a 75¢ bottle of Hadacol if you're a youngster, and you buy a $1 or $1.25 bottle if you're grown. So in other words you come in and you pay, but you're getting a show."

He said, "That's a wonderful idea. Write that down for me, all the details."

So I went home and wrote it all down, all the details. I said in my letter, "You'll have your trucks loaded with Hadacol. People go to the truck to buy the Hadacol bottle for their admission, and they pay when they get that bottle from the truck. And you have a whole caravan of trucks." I pictured that for him. "Maybe ten trucks, loaded with Hadacol."

I didn't hear anything again from the senator. We went on playing them one-nighters, but everything slowly fizzled down. Nobody came to the dances because maybe we had a little too much sophistication, and the Hadacol song was a one-round hit. All the people who toured Louisiana, like the Honeydripper, they had been around more than once, and they'd been playing the same thing over and over. Monotonous, jukey beat. And the people came again and again. But we had a real nice little band, playing different songs. So the people began to slow off, almost to nothing. And Lu was having trouble, having to sing every place, and often she couldn't use the ladies' room. All that kind of racial shit. So we stuck around a little while, and then we decided, "Let's go back to New York."

So we went back, and Percy Gabriel came with us, driving the bus. He wanted to leave New Orleans. He wasn't doing much here. He's doing real well now, so he's never forgot how I treated him—real nice.

Brought him up there with us, back to our apartment, which we had leased to a girl.

One day we were sitting at the house, and the radio was on. I'll never forget. Lu had cooked some fish and a potato salad, a big lettuce and tomato salad, and we sat down to enjoy this supper. And the radio said, "And from Hollywood! And from Hollywood! We present to you the fan-tas-tic Senator Dudley LeBlanc from Louisiana, and he's putting on the Hadacol Caravan at the Hollywood Stadium tonight! And the stars of the show: there's Mickey Rooney, Jimmy Durante, Betty Grable . . ." And they announced a whole slew of other people. "And the show will start . . . admission, a bottle of Hadacol!"

I said, "Hear this shit? Ain't this a bitch?"

So I got *The Billboard*, read about it. It said, "The great medicine man from the South, Louisiana Senator Dudley LeBlanc, signed a contract with Mickey Rooney, Judy Garland, Jimmy Durante." And they were going on a national tour. "Senator Dudley LeBlanc from the Hollywood Bowl to Madison Square Garden."

So I wrote a letter to the Hollywood Bowl saying, "Senator LeBlanc, remember me? Danny Barker? Wrote the tune *Here's a little girl from Jacksonville*?" No reply. But I said to myself, "I'll wait until he comes to the Madison Square Garden." The *Billboard* piece went on to tell you where he was: Los Angeles, Seattle, Utah, Denver. Now somewhere down the line while this was going on, he sold the company, sold it to a New York medicine company; several million dollars, I think. When those people finally went to the plant, they thought they was going to find all kinds of scientific stuff. When they got there, there were these six women there, colored women, mixing this thing with brooms and stuff, and putting it in the bottles. And they wanted to sue him for the money. Everything got tangled up. The Caravan didn't get to Madison Square Garden; the concerts were canceled. But he made a big splash. So I wrote another letter. "Senator LeBlanc, you remember me?" I haven't heard from the senator yet. So that's one of the disappointments you get. Imagine if I'd been on there and it had said, "Blue Lu and Danny Barker. Their jazz band." Or swing band, or whatever. But he had no intention of that.

That's a sort of horrible pill to take. After you know definitely you spoke to this man, gave him an idea, wrote it down for him; he uses it as a promotional gimmick—excites the whole West Coast—that's something of a blow. "The Hadacol Caravan"—and you know that's your brainchild. But the consolation is that you know you've got some intelligence, even if you didn't get the money. You know you're capable of promoting. So I have that satisfaction. And I put on little shows like at the 1984 World's Fair in New Orleans. But the papers killed the fair. I'd have told those newspapers to keep their damn mouths closed. "Don't kill the fair, printing the statistics daily: 'the attendance today was smaller than it was last week.' That's bad publicity for the public." Despite that I don't think I've eaten better, or slept better in my life than I have under my financial status today, or my earning ability. I couldn't live better than I do now.

TWENTY-THREE

New York dixieland revival

After the war jazz had been kept alive in the small clubs in New York. Condon's had kept going all through, and people like Rudi Blesh were getting a serious interest in jazz. East Coast college students, people with money, were taking an interest. Musicians like Josh White and Leadbelly found work.

Well, I got a call from Pops Foster. He said, "What you doin', man?" I said, "Not much."

He said, "Come over and play some jazz. You know them tunes. I'll recommend you to Rudi Blesh." And Rudi hired me on that show he started: "This is Jazz." And that's when I went back to playing the banjo. I had been playing guitar. Rudi Blesh said, "Danny, do you think you could play the banjo? I think there's a call for the banjo in jazz—the sort of thing Johnny St Cyr did, and Bud Scott."

I said, "I don't play the banjo. I haven't played it since 1930 when my banjo was stolen."

Rudi said, "Think about it."

Well, when he said, "Think about it," he meant, "Do it." He had something in mind. He was going to try and find somebody to play banjo. So I made efforts. I remembered seeing a banjo down in a pawnshop on the Bowery, the kind of shop where people borrow money and leave their possessions. Well people had pawned their instruments in this place. It looked like he had a thousand banjos in there. Every kind of banjo I'd ever seen. And among them were three or four six-string banjos. And I remembered Johnny St Cyr played a six-string. So I saw this one in particular and asked the guy. He wanted nine dollars for it. So I bought it. And in a week's time I surprised Rudi Blesh, because I had that banjo fixed, and I could play it straight away as it had six strings. But it was still a banjo, and I used it on the show.

The radio show went on for a year or more. This was 1947. On weekends. And with the band from the show we played many jazz concerts, and some sessions on Sundays at Ryan's. And that's where I came to meet Conrad Janis, who played trombone. And he liked the banjo. He persuaded the manager of Ryan's, Matty Walsh, to let him bring a band in there. Conrad was Harriet Janis's son, and she was a dear friend of Rudi Blesh. They promoted Circle Records. Blesh was also a writer, wrote a wonderful book with Janis, *They All Played Ragtime*. Conrad played trombone, and he wanted to get into jazz —before that he had been an actor in Hollywood. So he had a little band and asked me to join, me and Fred Moore. So we joined the band. Jimmy Archey was going out, going to Boston to the Savoy to play a job, and Ryan's needed a replacement, so I went in there with Conrad.

It was a good swinging band. Conrad was exciting and had a flair for show business; he was good looking, and had been to Hollywood. He was likeable and drew a young crowd. "The young kids with two veterans." But there was one thing annoying me and the piano player, Elmer Schoebel, who wrote the *Bugle Call Rag*. We were sitting next to each other, and we were playing the right chords (and we knew the old tunes), but we would hear the horns messing some of the harmony up. So Elmer and I would tell them after the show, "See that harmony y'all playing in there? Get that together—this is the way that verse should go." Elmer and I would hum it to them and they would listen, but continue to play wrong.

Elmer would say, "You can't leave it like that!" There would be musicians out there listening. And he would say, "You can't leave it—get it right." And they would glower at him, and I would say, "The man is right. That's a D7 chord y'all ought to play, and you're playing a minor chord." Whatever it was it didn't fit. And they did that on a half-dozen numbers. And we got so Schoebel would look at me, I would look at him, and we would say, "There they go again." Playing wrong; the wrong sequence. And I said, "Shit, I can't take this anymore." Playing that bad and that wrong, and all these great musicians coming there looking at you. And when the band did that you could see them flinching at the bar. They would be talking, but you could tell, you know, from their expressions. So I said, "I'm going to quit this."

Elmer said, "I think I'm going to quit too, man."

Pay day came, and we both gave in our notice.

After I left Conrad Janis I played with Wilber de Paris. I had played at Jimmy Ryan's off and on, before de Paris, for some years. Wilber de Paris, when he played there, thought the following he had was for him rather than for Ryan's, and he believed if it happened in one place it could also happen someplace else. Well, he had had some difficulties with the Ryan's management, and he left there. And Ryan's called me to bring a band into the club on 52nd Street. But their lease was up, and they were going to knock the building down, put something big up in its place. So the club moved to 54th Street, but roughly the same spot—between Sixth and Seventh avenues. I laid off for a week until they fixed up the new place, then we went over and started over there. We were there two or three months. And I got a call from Zutty Singleton, "They're nippin' at you, man! There's ten or eleven musicians, bandleaders, trying to get in there and get your job." He named them and told me these guys were calling the management almost every day.

Well I had just got an offer to go to Freedomland, which was a Disneyland they built in the Bronx. I was offered a job on the small riverboat and it paid three times as much as I was getting at Ryan's, so I left the club, and Tony Parenti went in there. But I had closed the old Ryan's and opened the new Ryan's. And that was a band with Doc Cheatham, and after he left, Herman Autry, Pete Clark, and later Haywood Henry. It was a good swinging band, a loose band, a foot-tapping band—not too bright so you would get out of breath.

Now when we went in the new place the manager, Matty Walsh, suggested two banjos, instead of a bass. So I hired Lee Blair to come in and open up the new place. He played beautiful banjo, solos like *The World is Waiting for the Sunrise*. We played features together sometimes: one playing chords, the other runs. We played *Mighty Like a Rose*, and we used to break up the place he played so pretty on that banjo.

Lee was offered a job paying twice the money at Ryan's. He explained it to me and left. Lee questioned me about why Luis Russell hired him and not me, since I was from New Orleans. I said, "You have a bigger name, having played with Jelly Roll—great banjo solos on *Shoe Shiner's Drag*—and you have a great reputation known in the four corners of the jazz world." So we laughed and went to the bar and got a double shot of Wild Turkey whiskey, no chaser, and toasted one another. Lee Blair had chronic colds and he contracted pneumonia and died. He was a real fine friend and I cherished his friendship.

From around 1955 to 1961 I had worked in Irish bars on the West Side, singing and playing as a soloist. Then I had also worked over in Hoboken, New Jersey. I wanted to do a single, which I did. I had seen Josh White and Leadbelly and folksingers working alone, so I went and worked for these Irish bartenders, and made a good buck. They would encourage you to have a drink—take a chaser, and another—but I was fortunate enough to survive. They were a bunch of nice guys—Paddy Flood, Johnny Mass, Willie Pascoe, Louie Leconte—over there on the waterfront at Twelfth Avenue and 42nd Street. The first job I got was for the mother of Daniel Patrick Moynihan, the politician. He was at Cornell, and all the college kids used to come down. The New England set. The ones who loved to ball would come to Moynihan's bar.

For the last few years in New York I worked all around. I made a few records with various people. I worked bars. The last job I had in New York was at a place called "Himself," owned by an Irishman from Galway Bay in Ireland, who had only been in New York a half dozen years. He was a big guy, about 220 pounds; a massive man with red hair and a big red mustache and beard. And the New York Irish toughies would come in and challenge him. He would pitch them out of the door, fighting three or four of them at once. No weapons, just fists. A brawl. A fracas. You would see him hang up his bartender's apron and shout, "One at a time! One at a time! I'll take you on, you muckers!" They would come at him two at a time. He would whip them, then two more would come and he would fight them, while I hid between the jukebox and the wall. The customers would depart through the side door in a hurry.

Apart from playing at Himself I did work odd gigs here and there. The couple of little joints I worked at over in Hoboken, for instance. They were little bars. On the weekend I played there: Friday, Saturday, and Sunday afternoon. And I made as much money as playing in the average band, most times more. I was offered a day job working for a company called American Management in the Astor Hotel on Broadway, a business school. The job was to put pitchers of iced water on the tables in the classroom, forty or fifty tables three times a day, morning, noon-time, and 2.30. That was my job, and then I served cocktails. I worked jazz joints at the weekends, like the bars in Hoboken; I played weekends in the Village at the Cinderella Club. And guys like Sam Parker and Johnny Windhurst, they called me for gigs. I was doing alright.

I had Oscar Pettiford work with me over in Hoboken, at a joint called Freddie Pisana's off Washington Avenue. I worked there for six or seven months. Oscar Pettiford was glad to get the gig. But apart from that he wasn't doing very much. Al Hall, Oscar Pettiford and Milt Hinton all worked over there with me: guitar, vocals and bass. The show consisted of half a dozen white girls singing off-key and out of tune.

But then my wife's mother took sick, and that made me decide to come back to New Orleans. For a long time I had been thinking about my status in music. I evaluated myself: "I am a musician, but what am I doing? Am I successful at it? Yes and no. I am playing sometimes, but where? At the bottom status, singing and playing in bars. In some my name is put out front for the world to see, but I have no drawing power. I can't draw flies at a molasses barrel. In New York City I've been to the top on other great musicians' bandwagons, so who's fooling who? Go back home." I laugh sometimes when I think of Blanche Mann, jazz music's Mother Teresa, a helping hand to many defeated, almost drowning musicians in the quicksands of whiskey and stimulants, both fatal. She said to me, "Danny, every time I see you, you're on some New York riverboat or in and out of various honky-tonks and dives." Blanche took care of, helped and consoled many jazz greats who were lost, in despair, hopeless and helpless. She supplied medicine, food, bookings and moral support, and you would see her at memorial services, funerals, wakes, sitting there off alone, looking on as the jazz musicians and fans slowly filed past the remains of the late great so-and-so.

So Lu went to New Orleans to be near her sick mother. She had been there three months when I decided to return myself. I was sick with diabetes, looking real frail, so I spoke to Lu about us moving to New Orleans. Lu said, "Yes, come on down, I'll look for a place." She found somewhere. I packed the furniture she told me to bring down and gave the rest away. Jack Bradley and Jean Fowler, our jazz friends who wanted to visit New Orleans, helped me pack, Jack drove a V-Haul extra large truck, and we took our time with a slow drive to New Orleans.

TWENTY-FOUR

Return to New Orleans and the
Jazz Museum

By the early 1960s there were only two clubs in New York City that used jazz bands regularly (that is for dixie—traditional jazz), and they were Jimmy Ryan's and Eddie Condon's. For the last fifteen years I had been thinking of just how the many great jazz stars survived—I mean many, many great talented jazz artists. Many of these men have never done any other kind of work, but you see them looking good, well dressed, and still smiling and joking when together—and that is the situation with so many colored actors and performers. I always managed to get some work playing, like playing at Freedomland, then opening at the New York World's Fair, staying there six weeks.

But eventually, in 1965, I decided to come to New Orleans, as the New York social scene was getting cloudy with the various militant rabble-rousers. Many places in the city I visited a lot seemed changed when I came around. I knew, because I would see and feel the draft; forced smiles, limp handshakes, silence. Here was Malcolm X the muslim telling off the important white leaders on the major panel-discussion shows, Adam Powell and all his legal entanglement and a sudden cluster of interracial marriages of celebrities—white and coloreds. I came to the conclusion that if New York City was going "southern"—with all sorts of racial uprisings, like minor riots all over, caravans of young colored folk in cars disrupting traffic at heavily congested traffic lanes, and the press stirring up the confusion—I felt I might as well be down South where it is the norm, and there's very little hypocrisy. The southern Whites have ways to save a colored person the embarrassment of being refused entrance and service. But other sections of the country—East, North and West—don't warn you beforehand. They brutally shock and embarrass you, while using the South as a scapegoat. There are places, many places in the North, West and East, where ordinary poor white people are not welcome, and will soon find out that they are out of bounds. So colored people are not the only downtrodden serfs in America; Mexican, Chinese, Indian,

American Indian and dark colored people all get the boot at times. This superior custom is a deep ingrained pastime.

So I came to New Orleans fully aware of the status quo and resigned to just about any sort of social abuse. I know it's national, not just the South, because I have been very observant and subjected to too much subtle, clever, hypocritical Jim Crow. One great thing about the South is that the politeness and greetings, especially in business dealings, are still carried on. In business transactions you are given in most cases the well practiced, "Thank you, suh. Pardon me." The other nasty salutations given to colored people are getting less common.

My job at the New Orleans Jazz Museum was pleasant, interesting, and very much to my liking. There are scores of jobs at the level of promoter or director in the large jazz and popular-music business. At times in past years when there were lulls and lay offs in the jazz scene I heard musicians say that they would like a job or a position in a business connected with jazz activities. Quite a few times I asked for jobs that I felt I was qualified to do capably. I asked people who I felt were very sincere and friendly, and every time I was given a well rehearsed reply, "Danny, I'm sorry, but I could not pull that job for you." And then I would see some youngster or somebody else, a stranger or a newcomer, not a musician or a performer, on the job, slowly and gradually learning the job while all the time acquiring that deep inner feeling of contempt for musicians and show people. "Oh, they're idiots—damned fools—suckers—puppets. Oh yeah, you respect them according to their box-office power, and just that."

When I came down to New Orleans I moved about meeting old friends, new friends, and lots of people in responsible jobs and positions in the arts. Among them was Dean Andrews, a smart lawyer whom I had met when he brought up Paul Barbarin's band to play at the New York World's Fair. Dean and I struck up a fine friendship. He loved jazz so much that he dug down in his pockets and helped it along. After the World's Fair job Dean had said to me, "Why don't you come down home? I can't promise you no job, but I'll help you keep out of jail!" We both laughed and shook hands, and that encouraged me to come South. As soon as I arrived in New Orleans Dean proposed that we produce a jazz festival. It was the first International New Orleans Jazz Festival, and—with a little annoying opposition—we staged the affair. I visited the New Orleans Jazz Museum and met Clay Watson, a fine person and a serious, dedicated museum curator. I heard Clay offer a young man an assistant's job at the museum. That soaked in, and I thought, "I would like a job like that." So I asked Clay for the job, and he said, "Great, I'll speak to the museum directors about it." Then I got a call from Clay Watson saying, "The job is yours." That simple—no nothing: "The job is yours." I went to the job and Clay explained to me the functions of a museum, its purpose, and what was needed at the New Orleans Jazz Museum. Then he said, "You are just what the museum needs—an experienced jazz musician."

Many times now I think of jobs I asked for in the business offices of jazz doings, and of how I was always given the refusal, and the plight of so many educated, sober, responsible jazz artists who have to seek employment out of music and show business. The people who became very wealthy in promotion, publishing, recording, and many other branches of the music business have a fear of giving musicians jobs that would enlighten them to the vast amounts of monies made in the profession, and particularly the intrigue and slick tactics—how to short change, such as in the royalty payments due to musicians and writers. They guard the inner workings very carefully. They see to it that creators get the minimum. Of course if the artist makes it real big, that's different: powers-that-be handle stars with more tact. One Christmas Eve a few years ago I decided to go and ask for long-due back royalties. At the publisher's office, a large outfit, the cold-blooded receptionist surprised me by looking in files and sheepishly handing me a check with a low figure on it. Then she said, "Mr Barker, do you know Mr So-and-so (a famous old songwriter of many blues hits, who lived out West and was in town)?" She explained he had come personally to try and get some royalties due him.

I answered, "Yeah."

"Well, he's been here a couple of times in the last week, and now we have found some money—royalties due him. If you should run into him, please tell him to come here and get the check."

Well, I had seen this elderly man in Beefsteak Charlie's, a gin mill, and in the front of the Brill building, swapping tales of woe with other elderly songwriters. The daily sight and sounds of the cluster of gatherings had a chorus that went, "We know the publisher has money—royalties—for us, but they say they don't, and there's nothing we can do," or "We know our songs earn more money than they gave us." I relate these situations from on-the-scene experiences, my immense backlog of eyewitnessed abuses suffered by creative people. So I am just not surprised at anything that's perpetuated by one person on taking advantage of another.

So I started work at the Jazz Museum. Also working at the museum was a smart, likeable youngster, George Finola from Chicago. George was undecided about continuing school or college. He lived jazz and played the trumpet surprisingly well; his idol was Bix Beiderbecke. And George and I became friends, and there was the constant talk and discussion of jazz music: figures, its state, its past, its future, and other jazz things. In a couple of months I cooled George off from some of his puzzled illusions about the jazz scene. I explained to him in detail much of what happens in jazz. "What you see is not what it is." "What looks like sugar from a distance could be salt," and vice versa.

Working at the museum I met all sorts of people from many places. Generally they would enter the small museum with a spirit of "Oh, I'm here at last," "This is it." The foreigners accepted the exhibits (which were limited because of space) with great relish, carefully looking and studying every object of interest. The students with limited funds usually asked, "Are there special rates for students?" Many times, noticing their special concern about their finances, I smiled and said, "Be our special guest." And what smiling gratitude glowed on their faces. I felt that helped jazz.

Then there was the couple. One would come in, look swiftly about, and then ask, "Is this all of it?" I would usually reply, "There's much to read, see and learn if you're interested in jazz." But nine out of ten of this type usually walked out to their husband or wife on the outside.

Then there were parties of people who would come in, see and read everything, and then sit at the listening phones for two or three hours, happily enjoying every note of music that came through the telephones.

Then there were the slickers who walked in past the admission counter, said nothing, then started looking and seriously peering into the instrument cases. I would watch for them at the exit, but many times I would miss them.

And there were the Bix fans: friends, schoolmates, distant relations, Davenport neighbors. They played in early bands with Bix. Some raved loudly that Bix was the greatest trumpet player who ever lived, and that there would never be another genius like him. Then they dragged down his person and character. "This fellow Bix drank himself right into the grave. He dissipated in excess. He did everything wrong that's humanly possible." I generally quieted these big mouths with this squelcher, "Bix was misunderstood. He was way ahead of his time, and the general public did not realize this man's great creative musical talent, so naturally he was in constant frustration. It's a feeling only genius can experience, and you don't drink milk or lemonade in that sad state of mind."

Then there were the ones who called out loudly, pointing to one of the large photo posters, "I don't see Ted Weems," or Louis Panico, or Clyde McCoy, or Wayne King, or Ben Bernie, or Vincent Lopez . . . and dozens of other famous names of thirty years ago. Some of those noted names never played pure jazz—couldn't play it. They recorded many records, but not one pure jazz record.

And there were the George Lewis and Jim Robinson worshipers, who shouted the two names as they entered, and continued until they left. According to them Robinson and Lewis were the all-time greatest on the trombone and clarinet. Sometimes I'd ask "Ever heard of Jimmie Noone or Johnny Dodds . . . Kid Ory or Miff Mole?" On occasions when I pulled that I would get the straight face, deep stare, and then the wandering eyes, deep thought, the pursed lips, the grinding teeth, silence, a quick turnabout, and the backside—not a whisper, look, or glance when they left.

Once a smart-aleck couple came in, and after a while softly asked me, "Who created jazz? Was it Jelly Roll, Nick LaRocca, or Stalebread Lacoume?" I thought for a while and answered, "Those three men came up in an era when there were few, if any, press agents handling jazz artists, so they blew their own horns, played their special kind of jazz, even had some success, and believed what they boasted. They were extroverts, maybe born under the same birth signs, I guess. They had lots of gumption, guts, heart, determination; they believed in themselves. They all had imitators catch on—and does that answer your question?" The couple both looked straight into my mouth and eyes as I spoke, and sheepishly grunted, "Uh huh!"

And there were the many who shouted in disgust, "Thank God for this museum. This music is gonna die; you rarely hear it anymore." I would then comfort them by explaining that the greatest jazz music of the 1920s and 1930s—the music of Morton, Oliver, Armstrong, Bix, Trumbauer, Nichols, Miff Mole, Hines, ODJB, NORK, is abundantly recorded, so the music of these great creative artists will live on. There were dedicated club owners in the past who operated nice clubs where jazz music could be heard, but these men—like Nick Rongetti and Jimmy Ryan—have passed on, and there are no new impresarios taking their place. Jazz fans now enjoy their vintage jazz at home, mainly because the clubs have lost the old happy, friendly atmosphere. Then I would ask if they had a record collection, and if so tell them to get a group of jazz fans at home and enjoy jazz. They would seem relieved, think of my revelations to them, and leave happy.

Then, before Louis Armstrong's death, there were the many who came in, looked at the Armstrong horn and Louis's historical dates before shouting "Armstrong is finished—playing all that commercial crap. He didn't have to do that. He clowns too damn much." I stayed clear of them because it was obvious they never did dig Louis.

Then the young ladies, who stared at the Storyville display cabinet, seriously ogling each object, straining their eyes trying to read the fine print on old licences issued to prostitutes.

In the years since I stopped working at the museum the New Orleans that was an exciting living experience to me has largely evaporated. There are just a few monuments—old benevolent halls converted into new Baptist churches and some spiritual Holy Roller and Sanctified churches. Quiet on the outside but deeply serious, metaphysical spirit calling and evoking of spirits on the inside—members screaming, shouting, talking to God. This is reality, no make-believe. Time brings on changes. These small black churches have replaced the atmosphere of the old-time booze-swilling tonks, dives and sin dens. You don't see young folks boozing to excess like before. The church members have meetings on the weekend nights and Sunday afternoons. The young church people get high on gospel music. There are multitudes of trained musicians: drummers, organists, pianists, tambourine slappers. The competition is fiercely intense. All the young church folk are aware of the holy war. This church war has replaced jazz. The singers and musicians who pounce on jazz chase young jazz entertainers to the side line. They have this spiritual attitude of looking heavenly while performing, building their doings into a scary madness: "Good God, help me do my thing." A good example is the actions and singing of Patti Labelle. New Orleans today has a bundle of Labelles. Look about and you gather that most of the young jazzers, shouters, screamers going back to Ella, Sarah, Billie, Dinah are all Protestants—Baptists. And about jazz—New Orleans jazz bands today generally play a limited repertoire of New Orleans jazz songs handed down. Very rarely do they go into the music of Jelly Roll (such as *The Pearls*), Armstrong's immense recordings of the Hot Five, Hot Seven. There is so much great music of the migratory pioneers up North that the New Orleans jazz players don't attempt or care to play. They just don't give a damn.

I had planned to, and still may, organize a jazz concert band or orchestra and get it into the works of Jelly, King Oliver, Clarence Williams, Spencer Williams, LaRocca, Paul Mares. For from what I see, all of jazz is periled. The USA is so highly geared to the newest innovations, or the in thing—what is great today. Big flash, slow fadeout. Rock-and-roll dancing is the sixties, seventies, eighties dance pattern; everybody do their own thing. Get up on the floor and get down with it. And you don't need no live and kicking musicians. There's the loud, wall-shaking amplifiers and the new MC, the rapper. This person makes a living replacing the small club bands and groups. He is cheaper to pay, plays all the latest record greats, keeps up a constant hip chatter, repeating the recording lyrics. There are many of these jazz replacements. Jazz playing, jazz singing, jazz dancing is old folks' old-time music. So you have to face it: time brings on changes.

Even so, there is much work for small groups in New Orleans and the rivalry and competition is cut throat. There are eight river boats, eight big new hotels, and a demand for jazz bands to travel over the USA and some places in Europe and Japan. Yet in my career the novelty and interest is on the wane. Clubs want you to stand and scream to attract tourists and visitors. I've explained the New Orleans straight face. And New Orleans people ask me, "Why did you come back down here when you had left New Orleans? Why didn't you go away and stay away? What's wrong? You were a failure where you were? Huh, answer me! We don't need you here." So I observe all in stride. In my travels about New Orleans I look about at the many places where musicians and sporting people used to gather. They ain't around any more. The jazz places are churches or open lots.

On occasion I gig with a group of talented fellows who can play and it is a pleasure. And when that happens you see the music's effect on the people: foot patting, finger snapping, head and body bouncing to the beat. That's a great pleasure for me and the people. So jazz will live on, because it digs down inside the body, the brain, the heart, the nerves and muscles.

Check out these small Baptist churches. That's where it started and that's where it's at. People don't plan to come to New Orleans and witness the Baptist and small Protestant churches to get a body blast. Get engulfed in spiritual music. Go to any place where there is a fine large group of underprivileged black people and, at the church services, you will steal away, steal away to Jesus! The city still practices burying the late deceased brothers and some sisters with the musical send-off. There are still brass bands, about a dozen, but they don't have the sound of the old Onward, Excelsior, Eureka. Well, jazz still lives in New Orleans in the churches, and in the future will come out and entertain the swingers under a new name.

Chronological Discography

a	arranger	g	guitar
as	alto saxophone	o	pipe organ
bb	brass bass (sousaphone/tuba)	p	piano
bj	banjo	ss	soprano saxophone
bs	baritone saxophone	t	trumpet
c	cornet	tb	trombone
cl	clarinet	ts	tenor saxophone
d	drums	v	vocals
db	double bass	vib	vibraphone
dir	director	vn	violin
f	flute		

This chronological list contains most known releases on which Danny Barker plays and sings. Titles are given as they appear on the record labels. Where possible, the first issue number is given, but the complexity of subsequent reissues is such that these are not shown. In preparing the list much use has been made of the works cited in the acknowledgment section as well as Stagg and Crump: *New Orleans: the Revival* (Dublin, 1973).

1931
June 9   New York
Dave's Harlem Highlights
*Dave Nelson (t, v); Clarence Brereton (t); Melvin Herbert/Harry Brown (t); Wilbur de Paris (tb); Buster Bailey (cl, as); Glyn Paque (cl, as); Charles Frazier (ts); Wayman Carver (ts, f); Sam Allen (p); *Danny Barker (bj); Simon Marrero (bb); Gerald Hobson (d)*

69905-1	Somebody stole my gal	Timely Tunes C-1587
69906-1	Rockin' Chair	Timely Tunes C-1576
69907-2	Loveless Love	Timely Tunes C-1577
69908-2	St. Louis Blues	Timely Tunes C-1588

*Danny Barker maintains he was not present at this session, and that the banjoist was Arthur Taylor.

1934
Dec 28   New York
Buster Bailey and his Seven Chocolate Dandies
Henry Allen (t); J. C. Higginbotham (tb); Buster Bailey (cl); Benny Carter (as); Charlie Beal (p); Danny Barker (g); Elmer James (db); Walter Johnson (d); Fletcher Henderson (a)

16445-1	Call of the Delta	Vocalion 2887
16445-2	Call of the Delta	Columbia 35677
16446-1	Shanghai Shuffle	Vocalion 2887

1935
Jan 23   New York
Henry Allen and his Orchestra
Henry Allen (t, v); Pee Wee Erwin (t); George Washington (tb); Buster Bailey (cl); Luis Russell (p); Danny Barker (g); Pops Foster (db); Paul Barbarin (d)

16671-1	Believe it, beloved (HA:v)	Banner 33337
16671-2	Believe it, beloved (HA:v)	Epic LN-3252
16672-1	It's written all over your face (HA:v)	Banner 33337
16672-2	It's written all over your face	Melotone 91940
16681-1	(We're gonna have) smooth sailing (HA:v)	Banner 33355
16682-1	Whose honey are you? (HA:v)	Banner 33355

1935
Oct 5   New York
The Little Ramblers

Ward Pinkett (t, v); Albert Nicholas (cl); Jack Russin (p); Danny Barker (g); Joe Watts (db); Sam Weiss (d)

95337-1	Everything is okey-dokey (WP:v)	Bluebird B-6144
95338-1	I'm on a see-saw (WP:v)	Bluebird B-6130
95339-1	Red sails in the sunset (WP:v)	Bluebird B-6131
95340-1	Tender is the night (WP:v)	Bluebird B-6131
95341-1	I'm painting the town red (to hide a heart that's blue)	Bluebird B-6130
95342-1	Tap Room Special (Panama)	Bluebird B-6193

1935
Dec 27   New York
The Little Ramblers
Bill Dillard (t, v); Albert Nicholas (cl); Jack Russin (p); Danny Barker (g); Joe Watts (db); Sam Weiss (d); Adrian Rollini (vib)

98398-1	The music goes 'round and around	Bluebird B-6220
98399-1	I'm building up to an awful let-down	Bluebird B-6232
98400-1	I'm shooting high	Bluebird B-6220
98401-1	I've got my fingers crossed	Bluebird B-6232

1936
Oct 12   New York
Henry Allen and his Orchestra
Henry Allen (t, v); Gene Mikell (cl); Tab Smith (as); Ted McRae (ts); Clyde Hart (p); Danny Barker (g); John Kirby (db); Cozy Cole (d)

20049-1	Midnight Blue	Vocalion 3339
20050-1	Lost in my dreams	Vocalion 3340
20051-1	Sitting on the moon	Vocalion 3340
20052-1	Whatcha gonna do when there ain't no swing?	Vocalion 3339

1936
Nov 17   New York
Henry Allen and his Orchestra
Probably similar personnel to session of Oct 12 1936

20267-1	Did you mean it?	Vocalion 3377
20268-1	In the chapel in the moonlight	Vocalion 3377
20269-1	Here's love in your eye	Vocalion 3389
20270-1	When my dream boat comes home	Vocalion 3389

1936
Dec 29   New York
Henry Allen and his Orchestra
Henry Allen (t, v); Tab Smith (as); Billy Kyle (p); Danny Barker (g);
?John Williams (db); unknown (cl, ts, bs, d)

20458-1 I adore you	Vocalion 3422
20459-1 He ain't got rhythm	Vocalion 3432
20460-1 This year's kisses	Vocalion 3432
20461-2 Let's put our heads together	Vocalion 3422

1937
Feb 11   New York
Mills Blue Rhythm Band
Lucky Millinder (dir); Charlie Shavers (t); Carl Warwick (t); Harry
Edison (t); Sandy Watson (tb); Wilbur de Paris (tb); Tab Smith (as);
Eddie Williams (tg); Ronald Haynes (ts); Harold Arnold (ts); Billy
Kyle (p); Danny Barker (g); John Williams (db); Lester Nichols (d,
vib); Chappie Willet (a)

M-1-2 Blue Rhythm Fantasy	Variety 503
M-2-1 Prelude to a Stomp	Variety 546
M-3-2 Rhythm Jam	Variety 546
M-4-1 Jungle Madness	Variety 503

1937
March 4   New York
Henry Allen and his Orchestra
Henry Allen (t, v); Buster Bailey (cl); Tab Smith (as); Sonny Fredericks
(ts); Billy Kyle (p); Danny Barker (g); John Williams (db); Alphonse
Steele (d)

20759-2 After last night with you	Vocalion 3524
20760-1 Goodnight, my lucky day	Vocalion 3490
20761-1 There's a kitchen up in heaven	Vocalion 3490
20762-2 I was born to swing	Vocalion 3524

1937
March 18   New York
Billy Kyle and his Swing Club Band
Charlie Shavers (t); Eddie Williams (cl); Tab Smith (as); Harold
Arnold (ts); Billy Kyle (p); Danny Barker (g); John Williams (db);
O'Neill Spencer (d); the Palmer Brothers (v)

M-278-1 Sundays are reserved (PB:v)	Variety 574
M-279-1 Havin' a ball	Variety 574
M-280-2 Big Boy Blue (PB:v)	Variety 531
M-281-1 Margie	Variety 531

1937
April 28   New York
Mills Blue Rhythm Band
Lucky Millinder (dir); Charlie Shavers (t); Carl Warwick (t); Harry
Edison (t); Alfred Cobbs (tb); Wilbus de Paris (tb); Tab Smith (as); Ben
Williams (cl, ts); Eddie Williams (ts); Harold Arnold (ts); Billy Kyle
(p); Danny Barker (g); John Williams (db); Lester Nichols (d, vib);
Chuck Richards (v)

M-429-1 The Lucky Swing	Variety 604
M-430-1-2 Please pity my heart (CR:v)	Rejected
M-431-1 Let's get together (LN:vib)	Variety 604
M-432-1-2 Since I've heard it from you	Rejected

1937
April 29   New York
Henry Allen and his Orchestra
Henry Allen (t, v); Glyn Paque (cl); Tab Smith (as); Harold Arnold
(ts); Luis Russell (p); Danny Barker (g); John Williams (db); Paul
Barbarin (d)

21070-1 Sticks and Stones	Vocalion 3564
21071-1-2 Meet me in the moonlight	Vocalion 3574
21072-1 Don't you care what anyone says?	Vocalion 3574
21073-1 A Love Song of Long Ago	Vocalion 3564

1937
June 19   New York
Henry Allen and his Orchestra
Same personnel as session of April 29 1937

21275-2 Till the clock strikes three	Vocalion 3607
21276-2 The Merry-go-round broke down	Vocalion 3594

21277-1 You'll never go to heaven (if you break my heart)	Vocalion 3594
21278-1 The Miller's Daughter, Marianne	Vocalion 3607

1937
July 1   New York
Mills Blue Rhythm Band
Lucky Millinder (dir); Charlie Shavers (t); Carl Warwick (t); Harry
Edison (t); Alfred Cobbs (tb); Wilbur de Paris (tb); Tab Smith (as); Ben
Williams (cl, ts); Eddie Williams (ts); Harold Arnold (ts); Billy Kyle
(p); Danny Barker (g); John Williams (db); Lester Nichols (d);
unknown girl (v); Eli Robinson (a)

M-545-1 Jammin' for the jackpot (ER:a)	Variety 634
M-546-1 The Image of You (v)	Variety 604
M-547-1 When Irish eyes are smiling	Variety 624
M-548-1 Camp Meeting Jamboree	Variety 624

1937
July 23   New York
Billy Kyle and his Swing Club Band
Charlie Shavers (t); Tab Smith (as); Ronald Haynes (ts); Billy Kyle
(p); Danny Barker (g); John Williams (db); Fran Marx (d); Leon
Lafell (v)

M-569-1 Can I forget you?	Variety 617
M-570-1 All you want to do is dance	Variety 617
M-571-1 Handle my heart with care	Variety 659
M-572-1 Girl of my Dreams	Variety 659

1937
Sept 7   New York
Henry Allen and his Orchestra
Henry Allen (t, v); ?Glyn Paque/Edmond Hall (cl); Tab Smith (as);
Sammy Davis (ts); Billy Kyle (p); Danny Barker (g); John Williams
(db); Alphonse Steele (d)

21630-2 I owe you	Vocalion 3704
21631-2 Have you ever been in love?	Vocalion 3704
21632-1 Is it love or infatuation?	Vocalion 3690
21633-2 Can I forget you?	Vocalion 3690

1937
Sept 10   New York
Chu Berry and his Stompy Stevedores
Irving Randolph (t); Keg Johnson (tb); Chu Berry (ts); Benny Payne (p,
v); Danny Barker (g); Milt Hinton (db); Leroy Maxey (d)

M-622-1 Chuberry Jam	Columbia 37571
M-623-1 Maelstrom	Columbia 37571
M-624-1 My Secret Love Affair (BP:v)	Variety 657
M-625-1 Ebb Tide	Variety 657

1937
Dec 10   New York
Cab Calloway and his Orchestra
Cab Calloway (v, dir); Shad Collins (t); Irving Randolph (t); Lammar
Wright (t); Claude Jones (tb); Keg Johnson (tb); De Priest Wheeler (tb);
Chauncey Haughton (cl, as); Andrew Brown (cl, as); Ben Webster (ts);
Walter Thomas (ts); Bennie Payne (p, vib); Danny Barker (g); Milt
Hinton (db); Leroy Maxey (d)

M-690-1-3 Every day's a holiday (CC:v)	Vocalion 3896
M-691-2-3 Jubilee (CC:v)	Vocalion 3896
M-692-1 In an old English village (CC:v)	Vocalion 3912
M-693-1 (Just an) error in the news (CC:v)	Vocalion 3912
M-694-1 A Minor Breakdown (Rustle of Swing)	Rejected
M-695-1 Bugle Blues	Vocalion 4019

1938
Jan 26   New York
Cab Calloway and his Orchestra
Same personnel as session of Dec 10 1937

M-743-1 One Big Union for Two (CC:v)	Vocalion 3970
M-744-1 Doing the reactionary (CC:v)	Vocalion 3970
M-745-1 Rustle of Swing	Vocalion 4144
M-746-1 Three swings and out	Vocalion 3995

M-747-1 I like music (with a swing
          like that) (CC:v)   Vocalion 3995
M-748-1 Foolin' with you (CC:v)   Vocalion 4019

1938
March 23 New York
Cab Calloway and his Orchestra
Same personnel as session of Dec 10 1937
M-787-1 Azure   Vocalion 4100
M-788-1 Skrontch (CC:v)   Vocalion 4045
M-789-1 We're breakin' up a lovely
          affair (CC:v)   Vocalion 4045
M-790-1 Peck-a-doodle-do (CC:v) Vocalion 4100
M-791-1 At the Clambake Carnival
          (BP:vib)   Vocalion 4437
M-792-1-2 Hoy-hoy (CC:v)   Vocalion 4144

1938
June 10 New York
Midge Williams and her Jazz Jesters
Midge Williams (v); Charlie Shavers (t); Buster Bailey (cl); Russell Procope (as); Billy Kyle (p); Danny Barker (g); Johnny Williams (db); O'Neill Spencer (d)
23054-2 Don't wake up my heart   Vocalion 4192
23055-1 Where in the world   Vocalion 4177
23056-1 In any language   Vocalion 4177
23057-1 Rosie the Redskin   Vocalion 4192

1938
Aug 11 New York
Blue Lu Barker, accompanied by Danny Barker's Fly Cats
Blue Lu Barker (v); Red Allen (t); Buster Bailey (cl); Sam Price (p); Danny Barker (g); Wellman Braud (db); O'Neill Spencer (d)
64432-A You're going to leave the old
          home, Jim   Decca 7560
64433-A New Orleans Blues   Decca 7538
64434-A He caught the B & O   Decca 7506
64435-A Don't you make me high Decca 7506

1938
Aug 30 New York
Cab Calloway and his Orchestra
Cab Calloway (v, dir); Shad Collins (t); Irving Randolph (t); Lammar Wright (t); Doc Cheatham (t); Claude Jones (tb); Keg Johnson (tb); De Priest Wheeler (tb); Chauncey Haughton (cl, as); Andrew Brown (cl, as); Walter Thomas (ts); Chu Berry (ts); Bennie Payne (p); Danny Barker (g); Milt Hinton (db); Leroy Maxey (d)
M-891-1 Miss Hallelujah Brown (CC:v) Vocalion 4400
M-892-1 The Congo-conga (CC:v)   Vocalion 4411
M-893-1 The Boogie-woogie   Vocalion 4400
M-894-1 There's a sunny side to
          everything (CC:v)   Vocalion 4411
M-895-1 Shout, shout, shout (CC:v) Vocalion 4369
M-896-1 Mister Paganini, swing for
          Minnie (CC:v)   Vocalion 4369
M-897-1 Jive (Page One of the Hepster's
          Dictionary) (CC:v)   Vocalion 4437

1938
Oct 27 New York
Cab Calloway and his Orchestra
Same personnel as session of Aug 30 1938
M-904-1 Do you wanna jump, children?
          (CC:v)   Vocalion 4477
M-905-1 I'm madly in love with you
          (CC:v)   Vocalion 4511
M-906-2 April in my Heart (CC:v) Vocalion 4477
M-907-1 Blue Interlude   Vocalion 4538

1938
Nov 2 New York
Cab Calloway and his Orchestra
Same personnel as session of Aug 30 1938
M-908-1 F. D. R. Jones (CC:v)   Vocalion 4498
M-909-1 Deep in a dream (CC:v)   Vocalion 4511

M-910-1 Tee-um, tee-um, tee-i, Tahiti
          (CC:v)   Vocalion 4538
M-911-1 Angels with dirty faces (June
          Richmond:v)   Vocalion 4498

1938
Nov 9 New York
Ethel Waters, accompanied by Eddie Mallory and his Orchestra
Ethel Waters (v); Eddie Mallory (t); Shirley Clay (t); Tyree Glenn (tb, vib); Castor McCord (cl); William Steiner (as); Reg Beane (p, o); Danny Barker (g); Charles Turner (db)
028387-1 You're mine   Bluebird B-10038
028388-1 Frankie and Johnnie Bluebird B-10038
028389-1 They say   Bluebird B-10025
028390-1 Jeepers creepers   Bluebird B-10025

1938
Nov 11 New York
Chu Berry and his Little Jazz Ensemble
Roy Eldridge (t); Chu Berry (ts); Clyde Hart (p); Danny Barker (g); Artie Shapiro (db); Sidney Catlett (d); *dialogue between Eldridge and Berry
23699-2 Sittin' in (*)   Commodore 516
23700-1 Star Dust   Commodore 1502
23701-1 Body and Soul   Commodore 1502
23702-1 Forty-six West Fifty-two Commodore 516

1938
Nov 22 New York
Blue Lu Barker, accompanied by Danny Barker's Fly Cats
Blue Lu Barker (v); Red Allen (t); Buster Bailey (cl); Sam Price (p); Danny Barker (g); Wellman Braud (db); (*) O'Neill Spencer (d)
64767-A I feel like lying in another
          woman's husband's arms Rejected
64768-A Give me some money   Rejected
64769-A I got ways like the devil (*) Decca 7560
64770-A That made him mad   Decca 7538

1939
Jan 30 New York
Teddy Wilson and his Orchestra
Roy Eldridge (t); Ernie Powell (cl, ts); Benny Carter (as, ts); Teddy Wilson (p); Danny Barker (g); Milt Hinton (db); Cozy Cole (d); Billie Holiday (v)
B-24044-1 What shall I say?   Brunswick 8314
B-24045-1 It's easy to blame the
            weather   Brunswick 8314
B-24046-1 More than you know Brunswick 8319
B-24046-2 More than you know CBS CL-2428
B-24047-1 Sugar   Brunswick 8319

1939
Feb 20 New York
Cab Calloway and his Orchestra
Cab Calloway (v, dir); Shad Collins (t); Irving Randolph (t); Lammar Wright (t); Doc Cheatham (t); Claude Jones (tb); Keg Johnson (tb); De Priest Wheeler (tb); Chauncey Haughton (cl, as); Andrew Brown (cl, as); Walter Thomas (ts); Chu Berry (ts); Bennie Payne (p); Danny Barker (g); Milt Hinton (db); Cozy Cole (d); Edgar Battle (a)
M-970-1 Long, long ago (CC:v)   Vocalion 4905
M-971-1 Afraid of love (CC:v)   Vocalion 4905
M-972-1 Ratamacue (EB:a)   Vocalion 4700
M-973-1 Ad-de-dey (CC:v)   Vocalion 4700

1939
March 28 New York
Cab Calloway and his Orchestra
Same personnel as session of Feb 20 1939
WM-1009-1 A New Moon and an Old
             Serenade   Vocalion 4767
WM-1010-1 One look at you   Vocalion 4767
WM-1011-1 The Ghost of Smokey
             Joe   Vocalion/OKeh 4807
WM-1012-1-2 Floogie Walk   Vocalion/OKeh 4807

1939
March 27   New York
Ethel Waters, accompanied by Eddie Mallory and his Orchestra
Ethel Waters (v); Eddie Mallory (t); Shirley Clay (t); Tyree Glenn (tb, vib); Castor McCord (cl); William Steiner (as); Reg Beane (p, o); Danny Barker (g); Charles Turner (db)

035355-1	Lonesome Walls	Bluebird B-10222
035356-1	If you ever change your mind	Bluebird B-10222
035357-1	What goes up must come down	Bluebird B-10207
035358-1	Y' had it comin' to you	Bluebird B-10207

1939
April 20   New York
Blue Lu Barker, accompanied by Danny Barker's Fly Cats
Blue Lu Barker (v); Charlie Shavers (t); Chu Berry (ts); Sam Price (p); Danny Barker (g); unknown (db, d)

65433-A	Scat Skunk	Decca 7813
65434-A	Nix on those lush heads	Decca 7588
65435-A	Buy me some juice	Rejected
65436-A	Georgia Grind	Decca 7588

1939
June 9   New York
Lionel Hampton and his Orchestra
Ziggy Elman (t); Hymie Schertzer (as); Russell Procope (ss, as); Jerry Jerome (ts); Chu Berry (ts); Clyde Hart (p); Danny Barker (g); Milt Hinton (db); Cozy Cole (d); Lionel Hampton (vib, v, d)

037614-1	If it's good (then I want it) (LH:v)	Victor LPM-6702-5
037615-1	Stand by for further announcements (and more good news) (LH:v)	Victor 26296
037616-1	Ain't cha comin' home?	Victor 26362
037617-1	Big-wig in the Wigwam (LH:d)	Victor 26296

1939
June 19   New York
Wingy Manone and his Orchestra
Wingy Manone (t, v); Buster Bailey (cl); Chu Berry (ts); Conrad Lanoue (p); Danny Barker (g); Jules Cassard (db); Cozy Cole (d)

037729-1	Royal Garden Blues	Bluebird B-10331
037730-1	Beale Street Blues (WM:v)	Bluebird B-10401
037731-1	In the Barrel (WM:v)	Bluebird B-10331
037732-1	Farewell Blues	Bluebird B-10401
037733-1	Fare thee, my baby, fare-thee-well (WM:v)	Bluebird B-10432
037734-1	Limehouse Blues	Bluebird B-10432

1939
July 17   New York
Cab Calloway and his Orchestra
Cab Calloway (v, dir); Mario Bauza (t); Irving Randolph (t); Lammar Wright (t); Doc Cheatham (t); Claude Jones (tb); Keg Johnson (tb); De Priest Wheeler (tb); Chauncey Haughton (cl, as); Andrew Brown (cl, as); Walter Thomas (ts); Chu Berry (ts); Bennie Payne (p); Danny Barker (g); Milt Hinton (db); Cozy Cole (d); Edgar Battle (a)

WM-1054-A	Trylon Swing	Vocalion/OKeh 5005
WM-1055-A	Utt-da-zay (CC:v)	Vocalion/OKeh 5062
WM-1056-A	Crescendo in Drums (EB:a)	Vocalion/OKeh 5062
WM-1057-A	(Hep-hep!) The Jumpin' Jive (CC:v)	Vocalion/OKeh 5005

1939
Aug 15   New York
Ethel Waters, accompanied by Eddie Mallory and his Orchestra
Ethel Waters (v); Eddie Mallory (t); Tyree Glenn (tb, vib); Castor McCord (cl); Benny Carter (as); Reg Beane (p, o); Danny Barker (g); Milt Hinton (db)

041552-1	Bread and Gravy	Bluebird B-10415
041553-1	Down in my soul	Bluebird B-11284
041554-2	Georgia on my mind	Bluebird B-11028
041555-1	Stop myself from worryin' over you	Bluebird B-11284
041556-1	Old Man Harlem	Bluebird B-11028
041557-1	Push-out	Bluebird B-10415

1939
Aug 30   New York
Cab Calloway and his Orchestra
Cab Calloway (v, dir); Mario Bauza (t); Dizzy Gillespie (t); Lammar Wright (t); Doc Cheatham (t); Claude Jones (tb); Keg Johnson (tb); De Priest Wheeler (tb); Chauncey Haughton (cl, as); Andrew Brown (cl, as); Walter Thomas (ts); Chu Berry (ts); Bennie Payne (p); Danny Barker (g); Milt Hinton (db); Leroy Maxey (d); Chappie Willet (a)

WM-1065-A	For the last time I cried over you (CC:v)	Vocalion 5126
WM-1066-A	Twee-twee-tweet	Vocalion 5126
WM-1067-A	Pluckin' the Bass	Vocalion/OKeh 5406
WM-1068-A	I ain't gettin' nowhere fast (CC:v) (CW:a)	Vocalion/OKeh 5195

1939
Oct 17   New York
Cab Calloway and his Orchestra
Same personnel as session of Aug 30 1939

WM-1101-A	Chili con Conga (CC:v)	Vocalion/OKeh 5315
WM-1102-A	Tarzan of Harlem (CC:v)	Vocalion/Okeh 5267
WM-1103-A	Jiveformation, please (CC:v)	Vocalion/OKeh 5195
WM-1104-A	Vuelva	Vocalion/OKeh 5315

1939
Nov 17   New York
Blue Lu Barker (v); accompanied by Henry Allen (t); Sam Price (p); Danny Barker (g); Wellman Braud (db); unknown (d)

66893-A	Blue Deep Sea Blues	Decca 7709
66894-A	Never brag about your man	Decca 7683
66895-A	He's so good	Decca 7695
66896-A	I don't dig you, Jack	Decca 7770

1939
Nov 20   New York
Cab Calloway and his Orchestra
Same personnel as session of Aug 30 1939

WM-1113-A	A bee gezindt	Vocalion/OKeh 5267
WM-1114-A	Give, baby, give	Vocalion/OKeh 5406
WM-1115-A	Sincere Love	Vocalion/OKeh 5364
WM-1116-A	Do it again	Vocalion/OKeh 5364

1939
Dec 13   New York
Blue Lu Barker (v), accompanied by same personnel as session of Nov 17 1939

66956-A	Handy Andy	Decca 7709
66957-A	Jitterbug Blues	Decca 7713
66958-A	You been holding out too long	Decca 7695
66959-A	Lu's Blues	Decca 7770

1940
March 8   New York
Cab Calloway and his Orchestra
Cab Calloway (v, dir); Mario Bauza (t); Dizzy Gillespie (t); Lammar Wright (t); Tyree Glenn (tb, vib); Quentin Jackson (tb); Keg Johnson (tb); Jerry Blake (Jacinto Chabani) (cl, as); Hilton Jefferson (as); Andrew Brown (as, bs); Chu Berry (ts); Walter Thomas (ts); Bennie Payne (p); Danny Barker (g); Milt Hinton (db); Cozy Cole (d); Andy Gibson, Benny Carter, Edgar Battle, Buster Harding, Don Redman (a)

WC-2983-A	Pickin' the cabbage (CC:v)	Vocalion/OKeh 5467
WC-2984-A	Chop, chop, Charlie Chan (CC:v)	Vocalion/OKeh 5444
WC-2985-A	Paradiddle	Vocalion/OKeh 5467
WC-2986-A	Boog it (CC:v)	Vocalion/OKeh 5444

1940
May 15   New York
Cab Calloway and his Orchestra
Same personnel as session of March 8 1940

27295-1	Calling all bars (BC:a)	OKeh 5731
27295-2	Calling all bars (BC:a)	*Jazz Archives 8*
27296-1	Do I care? No, no (CC:v)	Vocalion/OKeh 5591
27297-1-2	The Lone Arranger (BC:a)	Rejected

27298-1 Feelin' tip top (CC:v)   OKeh 5874
27299-1 Topsy Turvy (Hard Times)
    (EB:a)   Vocalion/OKeh 5566
27300-1 Hi-de-ho Serenade (CC:v)   Vocalion/OKeh 5591
27301-1 Who's Yehoodi? (CC:v)   Vocalion/OKeh 5566
27301-2 Who's Yehoodi? (CC:v)   Jazz Archives 8

1940
June 27 Chicago
Cab Calloway and his Orchestra
Same personnel as session of March 8 1940
WC-3160-A Fifteen Minute Intermission
    (CC:v)   OKeh 5644
WC-3161-A Rhapsody in Rhumba (BC:a)   OKeh 5644
WC-3162-A Come on with the "come on"
    (AG:a)   OKeh 5687
WC-3163-A A Ghost of a Chance (AG:a)   OKeh 5687
WC-3164-A Bye Bye Blues (CC:v)   OKeh 6084
WC-3164-B Bye Bye Blues (CC:v)   Jazz Archives 8

1940
July 27 Meadowbrook, Cedar Grove, New Jersey
Cab Calloway and his Orchestra
Same personnel as session of March 8 1940
Minnie the Moocher (CC:v)   Jazz Panorama LP-16
Limehouse Blues
I can't resist you (CC:v)
Hard Times (Topsy Turvy) (EB:a)
Fifteen Minute Intermission (CC:v)
Boog it (CC:v)
Cupid's Nightmare (DR:a)
King Porter Stomp

1940
Aug 5 New York
Cab Calloway and his Orchestra
Same personnel as session of March 8 1940
27801-1 Papa's in bed with his britches
    on (CC:v)   OKeh 5731
27802-1 Silly Old Moon (CC:v)   OKeh 5774
27803-1 Boo wah boo-wah (BH:a)   OKeh 5774
27804-2 Sunset (CC:v)   OKeh 5804
27805-1 Yo eta cansa   OKeh 5827

1940
Aug 28 New York
Cab Calloway and his Orchestra
Same personnel as session of March 8 1940
28513-1 Cupid's Nightmare (DR:a)   OKeh 6035
28514-1 Levee Lullaby   OKeh 5950
28515-1 Are you hep to the jive? (CC:v)
    (AG:a)   OKeh 5804
28516-1 Goin' conga (CC:v)   OKeh 5911
28517-1 Hot Air   OKeh 5950
28518-1 Lonesome Nights (BC:a)   OKeh 5827

1940
Oct 14 New York
Cab Calloway and his Orchestra
Same personnel as session of March 8 1940
28863-1 A chicken ain't nothin' but a
    bird (CC:v)   OKeh 5847
28864-1 The Workers' Train (CC:v)   OKeh 5874
28865-1 North of the Mohawk Trail
    (CC:v)   OKeh 5911
28866-1 Make yourself at home (CC:v)   OKeh 5847

1941
Jan 16 Chicago
Cab Calloway and his Orchestra
Same personnel as session of March 8 1940
C-3518-1 Run, little rabbit (CC:v)   OKeh 6084
C-3519-1 Willow, weep for me (AG:a)   OKeh 6109
C-3520-1 You are the one in my heart
    (CC:v)   OKeh 6391
C-3521-1 All you all reet? (CC:v)   OKeh 6035
C-3522-1 Ebony Silhouette (AG:a)   OKeh 6192

1941
March 5 New York
Cab Calloway and his Orchestra
Cab Calloway (v, dir); Jonah Jones (t); Dizzy Gillespie (t); Lammar Wright (t); Tyree Glenn (tb, vib); Quentin Jackson (tb); Keg Johnson (tb); Jerry Blake (Jacinto Chabani) (cl, as); Hilton Jefferson (as); Andrew Brown (as, bs); Walter Thomas (ts); Chu Berry (ts); Bennie Payne (p); Danny Barker (g); Milt Hinton (db); Cozy Cole (d); Andy Gibson (a)
29866-1 Hep Cat Love Song (CC:v)
    (AG:a)   OKeh 6192
29867-1-2 Jonah joins the Cab (CC:v)
    (AG:a)   OKeh 6109
29868-1-2 Geechee Joe (CC:v)   OKeh 6147
29869-1-3 Special Delivery (AG:a)   OKeh 6147

1941
July 3 New York
Cab Calloway and his Orchestra
Same personnel as session of March 5 1941
30835-1 Take the "A" train   OKeh 6305
30836-1 Chattanooga Choo-choo (CC:v)   OKeh 6305
30837-1 My gal (CC:v)   Columbia 32593
30838-1 St. James Infirmary (CC:v)   OKeh 6391

1941
July 24 New York
Cab Calloway and his Orchestra
Same personnel as session of March 5 1941
30838-4 St. James Infirmary (CC:v)   OKeh 6391
30938-1 We go well together (CC:v)   OKeh 6341
30939-1 Hey Doc (CC, Tyree Glenn:v)   OKeh 6354
30940-1 I see a million people (CC:v)   OKeh 6341
30941-1 Conchita (cares nothing about
    love) (CC:v)   OKeh 6354

1941
Sept 10 New York
Cab Calloway and his Orchestra
Cab Calloway (v, dir); Mario Bauza (t); Dizzy Gillespie (t); Lammar Wright (t); Tyree Glenn (tb, vib); Quentin Jackson (tb); Keg Johnson (tb); Jerry Blake (Jacinto Chabani) (cl, as); Hilton Jefferson (as); Andrew Brown (as, bs); Walter Thomas (ts); Chu Berry (ts); Bennie Payne (p); Danny Barker (g); Milt Hinton (db); Cozy Cole (d); the Palmer Brothers (v); Buster Harding (a)
31300-1 Blues in the Night (CC, PB:v)
    (BH:a)   OKeh 6422
31300-2 Blues in the Night (CC, PB:v)
    (BH:a)   Epic LN-3265
31301-1 Mrs. Finnigan (CC:v) (BH:a)   OKeh 6459
31302-1 My coo-coo bird (could sing)
    (CC:v) (BH:a)   OKeh 6459
31303-1 Says who? Says you, says I!
    (CC:v) (BH:a)   OKeh 6422

1941
Nov 3 New York
Cab Calloway and his Orchestra
Cab Calloway (v, dir); Mario Bauza (t); Russell Smith (t); Shad Collins (t); Lammar Wright (t); Tyree Glenn (tb, vib); Quentin Jackson (tb); Keg Johnson (tb); Jerry Blake (Jacinto Chabani) (cl, as); Hilton Jefferson (as); Andrew Brown (as, bs); Walter Thomas (ts); Ted McRae (ts); Bennie Payne (p); Danny Barker (g); Milt Hinton (db); Cozy Cole (d); the Palmer Brothers (v); Buster Harding (a)
31638-2 The Mermaid Song (CC:v)   OKeh 6501
31639-1 Who calls? (CC, PB:v)   OKeh 6501
31640-1 Nain, nain (CC:v)   OKeh 6547
31641-1 Tappin' off (BH:a)   OKeh 6547
31645-1 A Smo-o-oth One (BH:a)   OKeh 6720

1941
Dec 24 New York
Cab Calloway and his Orchestra
Same personnel as session of Nov 3 1941, plus the Cabaliers (v)
32037-1 The moment I laid eyes
    on you (CC:v)   OKeh 6574 (never issued)

32038-1 Virginia, Georgia and
    Caroline (CC, the
    Cabaliers:v)   OKeh 6574 (never issued)
32039-1 Blue Moonlight   Rejected
32040-1 Lordy (CC:v)   Columbia 36751

1942
Feb 2   Chicago
Cab Calloway and his Orchestra
Same personnel as session of Dec 24 1941
C-4179-1 I want to rock (CC:v) (BH:a)   OKeh 6616
C-4180-1 What's buzzin' cousin? (CC, the
    Cabaliers:v)   Rejected
C-4181-1 I'll be around (CC:v)   OKeh 6717
C-4182-1 'Tain't no good (CC, the
    Cabaliers:v)   OKeh 6616
C-4183-1 Minnie the Moocher (CC, the
    Cabaliers:v)   OKeh 6634

1942
July 27   Hollywood
Cab Calloway and his Orchestra
Cab Calloway (v, dir); Jonah Jones (t); Russell Smith (t); Shad Collins (t); Lammar Wright (t); Tyree Glenn (tb, vib); Quentin Jackson (tb); Keg Johnson (tb); Irving Brown (cl, as); Hilton Jefferson (as); Andrew Brown (as, bs); Walter Thomas (ts); Al Gibson (ts); Bennie Payne (p); Danny Barker (g); Milt Hinton (db); Cozy Cole (d)
HCO-884-1 Let's go, Joe   OKeh 6720
HCO-885-1-2 Ogeechee River Lullaby   Columbia 36662
HCO-886-1 I get the neck of the
    chicken   Columbia 36662
HCO-887-1 Chant of the Jungle   Rejected

1943
Jan   Los Angeles
Lena Horne (v), accompanied by Cab Calloway and his Orchestra
Probable personnel: Jonah Jones (t); Shad Collins (t); Russell Smith (t); Tyree Glenn (tb); Keg Johnson (tb); Hilton Jefferson (as); Illinois Jacquet (ts); Walter Thomas (ts); Dave Rivera (p); Danny Barker (g); Milt Hinton (db); J. C. Heard (d)
Diga diga dee   V-disc 126
There's no two ways about love   V-disc 126
Good for Nothing Joe   V-disc 126

late 1943
Hollywood
Cab Calloway and his Orchestra
Russell Smith (t); Lammar Wright (t); Jonah Jones (t); Shad Collins (t); Keg Johnson (tb); Quentin Jackson (tb); Tyree Glenn (tb); Hilton Jefferson (as); Irving Brown (as); Al Gibson (ts); Illinois Jacquet (ts); Dave Rivera (p); Danny Barker (g); Milt Hinton (db); J. C. Heard (d)
105 in the Shade   Palm POM1

with Bill Robinson (v, tap-dance)
Bojangles steps in   Caracol 439
Easy Joe
Ain't that something
Everybody dance

From the film soundtrack of *Stormy Weather*

late 1943
Cab Calloway and his Orchestra
Same personnel as previous session, without Robinson
Some of these days   Swing Treasury 107
Rose Room
Don't get around much any more
King Porter Stomp
Who can I turn to
Red Bank Bounce
Hey Doc
105 in the Shade

1944
July 22   New London
Cab Calloway and his Orchestra

Russell Smith (t); Lammar Wright (t); Jonah Jones (t); Shad Collins (t); Keg Johnson (tb); Quentin Jackson (tb); Tyree Glenn (tb); Hilton Jefferson (as); Irving Brown (as); Al Gibson (ts); Illinois Jacquet (ts); Dave Rivera (p); Danny Barker (g); Milt Hinton (db); J. C. Heard (d)
A Smooth One   IAJRC 17

1944
Sept 18   New York
Cab Calloway and his Orchestra
Russell Smith (t); Jonah Jones (t); Paul Webster (t); Shad Collins (t); Tyree Glenn (tb); Fred Robinson (tb); Keg Johnson (tb); Quentin Jackson (tb); Hilton Jefferson (as); Irving Brown (as); Al Gibson (ts); Ike Quebec (ts); Greely Walton (bs); Dave Rivera (p); Danny Barker (g); Milt Hinton (db); J. C. Heard (d)
VP947 I'm making believe   V-disc 338

1944
Sept 22   Broadcast
Cab Calloway and his Orchestra
Same personnel as session of Sept 18 1944, with unknown female (v)
The very thought of you   Caracol 439
Foo-a little-ballyhoo
Is you or is you ain't my baby
Frantic in the Atlantic
Blue Skies

late 1944
Same personnel as session of Sept 18 1944
The Honeydripper   Musidisc 30JA5153
Let's go, Joe
The Jumpin' Jive
The angels sing
The Birth of the Blues
Fiesta in Brass
I've got you under my skin
Lady Whistle Beat
Foo a little ballyhoo

1945
Jan 24   Chicago
Cab Calloway and his Orchestra
Cab Calloway (v, dir); Russell Smith (t); Jonah Jones (t); Paul Webster (t); Shad Collins (t); Roger Jones (t); Tyree Glenn (tb); Fred Robinson (tb); Keg Johnson (tb); Quentin Jackson (tb); Hilton Jefferson (as); Irving Brown (as); Al Gibson (ts); Ike Quebec (ts); Greely Walton (bs); Dave Rivera (p); Danny Barker (g); Milt Hinton (db); J. C. Heard (d)
CCO4323-1 Let's take the long way
    home   Columbia 36786
CCO4324-1 Foo a little bally-hoo   Columbia 36786

1945
April 19   New York
Cab Calloway and his Orchestra
Cab Calloway (v, dir); Russell Smith (t); Jonah Jones (t); Paul Webster (t); Shad Collins (t); Roger Jones (t); Tyree Glenn (tb); Fred Robinson (tb); Keg Johnson (tb); Quentin Jackson (tb); Hilton Jefferson (as); Bob Dorsey (as); Al Gibson (ts); Ike Quebec (ts); Rudy Powell (as, bs); Dave Rivera (p); Danny Barker (g); Milt Hinton (db); J. C. Heard (d)
CO34578 All at once   Columbia 36816
CO34579 Dawn Time   Columbia 36816

1945
July 8, 10   Club Zanzibar, New York
Cab Calloway and his Orchestra
Same personnel as session of April 19 1945
Foo a little bally-hoo   Unique Jazz UJ005
Russian Lullaby
I was here when you left me
St. Louis Blues
Frantic on the Atlantic
9:20 Special
The Great Lie
I can't give you anything but love
Rose Marie

I'm not ashamed of my tears
One O'Clock Jump
The Great Lie

1945
July 16   Club Zanzibar, New York
Cab Calloway and his Orchestra
Same personnel as session of April 19 1945
We the cats shall hep you   *Joyce LP1032*
If this isn't love
Zanzi
Can't we try again
Exactly like you
I'm not ashamed of my tears
Dinah
Gypsy Love Song

1945
July 20   New York
Cab Calloway and his Orchestra
Same personnel as session of April 19 1945
Foo a little bally-hoo   *Joyce LP 1032*
The more I see you
The Great Lie
Rosemary

1945
July 30   Broadcast, New York
Cab Calloway and his Orchestra
Same personnel as session of April 19 1945
I'll Pray for You   *Alamac QSR2407*
Cruisin' with Cab
Frantic on the Atlantic
Russian Lullaby
St. Louis Blues
9:20 Special

1945
July 30   New York
Oran "Hot Lips" Page (t, v); Mezz Mezzrow (cl); Sidney Bechet (ss); Sammy Price (p); Danny Barker (g); Pops Foster (db); Sidney Catlett (d)
KJ12-1   House Party   *Storyville SLP137*
KJ12-2   House Party   *Storyville SEP394*
KJ13-1   Perdido Street Stomp   *Storyville SEP411*
KJ13-2   Perdido Street Stomp   *Storyville SEP141*
KJ14-1   Revolutionary Blues, pt.1   *Storyville SLP153*
KJ15-1   Revolutionary Blues, pt.2   *Storyville SLP153*
KJ16-1   Blood on the Moon (OP:v)   *Storyville SLP136*

1945
July 31   New York
Same personnel as session of July 30 1945, plus Pleasant Joe (v)
KJ17-1   Levee Blues   *Storyville SLP136*
KJ18-1   Layin' my rules in blues   *Storyville SLP153*
KJ19-1   Bad Bad Baby Blues   *Storyville SLP141*
KJ19-2   Bad Bad Baby Blues   *Storyville SEP411*
KJ20-1   Saw Mill Man Blues   *Storyville SLP137*
KJ21-1   Minor Swoon   *Storyville SLP821*
KJ21-2   Minor Swoon   *Storyville SLP142*
KJ21-3   Minor Swoon   *Storyville SEP409*
KJ22-1   The Sheik of Araby   *Storyville SEP408*
KJ22-2   The Sheik of Araby   *Storyville SLP153*

1945
July   New York
Jonah Jones and his Orchestra
Jonah Jones (t); Tyree Glenn (tb); Buster Bailey (cl); Hilton Jefferson (as); Ike Quebec (ts); Dave Rivera (p); Danny Barker (g); Milt Hinton (db); J. C. Heard (d)
A4862   Rose of the Rio Grande   Commodore 602
A4864   You brought a new kind of love   Commodore 1520
A4865   Hubba hubba hub   Commodore 1520
A4866   Stompin' at the Savoy   Commodore 602

1945
Sept 4   New York
Sir Charles and his All Stars
Buck Clayton (t); Charlie Parker (as); Dexter Gordon (ts); Charles Thompson (p); Danny Barker (g); Jimmy Butts (db); J. C. Heard (d)
R1030   Takin' Off   Apollo 757
R1031   If I Had You   Apollo 757
R1032   20th Century Blues   Apollo 759
R1033   The Street Beat   Apollo 759

1945
Sept 11   New York
Cab Calloway and his Orchestra
Cab Calloway (v, dir); Russell Smith (t); Jonah Jones (t); Paul Webster (t); Shad Collins (t); Roger Jones (t); Tyree Glenn (tb); Fred Robinson (tb); John Haughton (tb); Quentin Jackson (tb); Hilton Jefferson (as); Bob Dorsey (as); Al Gibson (ts); Ike Quebec (ts); Rudy Powell (as, bs); Dave Rivera (p); Danny Barker (g); Milt Hinton (db); J. C. Heard (d)
CO35187-1   If this isn't love   Columbia 36894
CO35188-1   A Blue Serge Suit with a
                Belt in the Back   Columbia 36993
CO35189   Here I go just dreaming away   V-disc 585

1945
Nov 13   New York
Cab Calloway and his Orchestra
Cab Calloway (v, dir); Russell Smith (t); Jonah Jones (t); Paul Webster (t); Shad Collins (t); Roger Jones (t); Tyree Glenn (tb); Fred Robinson (tb); Keg Johnson (tb); Quentin Jackson (tb); Hilton Jefferson (as); Bob Dorsey (as); Al Gibson (ts); Ike Quebec (ts); Rudy Powell (as, bs); Dave Rivera (p); Danny Barker (g); Milt Hinton (db); Buford Oliver (d)
CO35420-1   The Honeydripper   Columbia 36894
CO35421-1   Afternoon Moon   Columbia 36893

mid-1940s
Danny Barker (g, v), accompanied by Haywood Henry (bs); Don Kirkpatrick (p); Johnny Williams (db); Fred Moore (d)
K100   Chocko mo fendo hey   King Zulu K0001
K101   Totie Ma is a big fine thing   King Zulu K0002
K102   My Indian Red   King Zulu K0001
K103   Corinne died on the battlefield   King Zulu K0002

This recording project was a disaster: when the records were printed the jukeboxes had changed over from 78 rpm to 45 rpm, so I could not put the records on the new boxes (Danny Barker).

1946
Jan 6   Stuyvesant Casino, New York
Bunk Johnson and his New Orleans Band
Bunk Johnson (t); Ralph Sutton (p); Danny Barker (bj)
Jada   *White Label (E)102*

plus Jimmy Archey (tb); Edmund Hall (cl); Fred Moore (d)
Muskrat Ramble   *White Label (E)102*
Someday sweetheart
Sister Kate

Bunk Johnson (t); Jimmy Archey (tb); Omer Simeon (cl); Ralph Sutton (p); Danny Barker (bj); Cyrus St. Clair (tuba); Fred Moore (d)
Baby won't you please come home   *White Label (E)102*
Basin Street Blues
Royal Garden Blues

Bunk Johnson (t); Jimmy Archey (tb); Edmond Hall (cl); Ralph Sutton (p); Danny Barker (bj); Fred Moore (d)
Jazz Me Blues   *White Label (E)102*
After you've gone

plus Cyrus St. Clair (tuba); Huddie Ledbetter (v); probably Omer Simeon (cl)
Finale (Untitled Blues)   *White Label (E)102*

NB: A limited edition of a 2-LP set: no details are to be found on the cover and personnel is from aural identification or from details given by the announcer. Errors may occur as the recording quality is rather unsatisfactory (Bruyninckx).

1946
Sept/Oct   New York
Blue Lu Barker (v), accompanied by Shad Collins (t); Teddy McRae (ts); Norman Lester (p); Danny Barker (g); Ernest Williamson (db); unknown (d)

R1050	You gotta show it to me baby	Apollo 399
R1051	Don't you feel my leg	Apollo 376
R1052	There was a li'l mouse	Apollo 382
R1053	That made him mad	Apollo 376

1946
Oct 3   New York
Blue Lu Barker (v), accompanied by unknown (t); Jerry Jerome (ts); Norman Lester (p); Danny Barker (g); unknown (db); Woodie Nichols (d)

R1066	I feel like laying in another woman's husband's arms	Apollo 382
R1067	Buy me some juice	Apollo 399

1946
Oct   New York
Oran "Hot Lips" Page (t, v); Earl Bostic (as); John Hartzfield (ts); Lannie Scott (p); Danny Barker (g); Carl Wilson (db); George Jenkins (d)

R1098	Birmingham Boogie	Apollo 411
R1099	Gimme gimme gimme	Apollo 411
AP3057	Open the door Richard	Apollo 1041
AP3058	Texas and Pacific	Apollo 1041

c1947
New York
Oran "Hot Lips" Page (t, v); probably Earl Bostic (as); John Hartzfield (ts); Danny Barker (g); unknown (p, db, d)

hu430-B	Kansas City Jive	Hub 3007
hu431-B	Buffalo Bill Blues (OP:v)	Hub 3007

1947
Feb 10   New York
Roger Jones (t); Earl Bostic (as); Jerry Jerome (ts); Ted Barnett (ts); Bill Clifton (p); Danny Barker (g); Vernon King (db); George Jenkins (d)

Richard's Answer, pt.1	Apollo 1042
Richard's Answer, pt.2	Apollo 1042

1947
March 1   New York
This is Jazz
Muggsy Spanier (c); George Brunies (tb, v); Sidney Bechet (cl, ss); Albert Nicholas (cl); James P. Johnson (p); Danny Barker (g); Pops Foster (db); Baby Dodds (d)

Slow Blues (Blues Improvisation)	Riverside RLP139
Baby won't you please come home	
Charleston	Riverside RLP149
That's a plenty	
I know that you know	

1947
March 8   New York
This is Jazz
Muggsy Spanier (c); George Brunies (tb, v); Albert Nicholas (cl); Charlie Queener (p); Danny Barker (g); Pops Foster (db); Baby Dodds (d)

Jada	Circle L423
Panama	

1947
March 22   New York
This is Jazz
Muggsy Spanier (c); George Brunies (tb, v); Sidney Bechet (cl, ss); Albert Nicholas (cl); Ralph Sutton/Art Hodes (p); Danny Barker (g); Pops Foster (db); Baby Dodds (d)

Black and Blue	Riverside RLP149
Sensation	Riverside RLP149
Buddy Bolden Blues	unissued
You're some pretty doll	unissued
Farewell Blues	unissued

without Spanier, Brunies, Nicholas

Summertime	Riverside RLP149

1947
April 19
This is Jazz
Sidney Bechet (cl, ss); Bob Wilber (cl); James P. Johnson (p); Danny Barker (g); Pops Foster (db); Baby Dodds (d)

Kansas City Man Blues	Kings of Jazz KLJ20033
Spreadin' Joy	unissued
Polka Dot Stomp Rag	unissued

1947
April 26
This is Jazz
Louis Armstrong (t, v); Wild Bill Davison (c); George Brunies (tb); Albert Nicholas (cl); Art Hodes (p); Danny Barker (g); Pops Foster (db); Baby Dodds (d)

Way Down Yonder in New Orleans	unissued
When the saints go marching in (LA:v)	Palm PC05
2:19 Blues (LA:v)	Palm PC05
Do you know what it means to miss New Orleans (LA:v)	Palm PC05
Dippermouth Blues	Palm PC19
Basin Street Blues (LA:v)	Palm PC19
High Society	Palm PC05
You rascal you (LA:v)	Palm PC19

1947
May 24
This is Jazz
Sidney Bechet (cl, ss); Wild Bill Davison (c); George Brunies (tb); Albert Nicholas (cl); James P. Johnson (p); Danny Barker (g); Pops Foster (db); Freddie Moore (d)

Ain't Misbehavin'	Riverside RLP149
Blue turning grey over you	Riverside RLP149

1947
June 12   New York
Nick and his Creole Serenaders
Albert Nicholas (cl); James P. Johnson (p); Danny Barker (g, v); Pops Foster (db)

NY35-B	Moi pas lemmé cas (AN, DB:v)	Riverside RLP12-216
NY36	Salée dame (AN, DB:v)	
NY37	Les oignons (AN, DB:v)	
NY38	Creole Blues (AN:v)	

1947
June 21   New York
This is Jazz
Wild Bill Davison (c); Jimmy Archey (tb); Albert Nicholas (cl); James P. Johnson (p); Danny Barker (g); Pops Foster (db); Baby Dodds (d)

NY69	St. Louis Blues	Riverside RLP12-211

1947
June 28   New York
This is Jazz
Wild Bill Davison (c); Jimmy Archey (tb); Albert Nicholas (cl); Ralph Sutton (p); Danny Barker (g); Pops Foster (db); Baby Dodds (d)

Shine	All unissued
Black and Blue	
Five O'Clock Blues (1)	
I can't stop (1)	
Struttin' with some Barbecue	
Tishomingo Blues	
I found a new baby	

1947
July 5   New York
This is Jazz
Wild Bill Davison (c); Jimmy Archey (tb); Albert Nicholas (cl); Ralph Sutton (p); Danny Barker (g); Pops Foster (db); Johnny Blowers (d); Bertha Chippie Hill (v)

Rosetta	All unissued
Save it pretty mama	

How Long Blues
Skeleton Jangle
Careless Love
Dill Pickles
NY71 Shim-me-sha-wabble   *Riverside RLP12-211*

1947
July 12
This is Jazz
Wild Bill Davison (c); Jimmy Archey (tb); Sidney Bechet (cl, ss); Albert Nicholas (cl); Joe Sullivan (p); Danny Barker (g); Pops Foster (db); Baby Dodds (d)
Dear Old Southland   *Riverside RLP149*
Sugar   *Riverside RLP149*

1947
July 16   New York
Sammy Price (p); Danny Barker (g); Pops Foster (db); Kenny Clarke (d); Monette Moore (v); Cousin Joe (v)
74006-4a Another Woman's Man (MM:v)   *Decca 48047*
74007-4a Please Mr. Blues (MM:v)   *Decca 48047*
74008   Bad Luck Blues (CJ:v)   *Decca 48045*
74009   Box Car Shorty and Peter Blue (CJ:v)   *Decca 48045*

1947
July 19   New York
This is Jazz
Wild Bill Davison (c); Jimmy Archey (tb); Albert Nicholas (cl); Ralph Sutton (p); Danny Barker (g); Pops Foster (db); Baby Dodds (d); Bertha Chippie Hill (v)
12th Street Rag   All unissued
Darktown Strutters' Ball
I'm sorry I made you cry
Oh, lady be good
Whitewash Man
Lonesome Road   Circle 12004
Muskrat Ramble   Unissued

1947
July 26   New York
This is Jazz
Same personnel as session of July 19 1947
NY43 Eccentric   Circle L402
NY44 Tishomingo Blues
NY45 Hotter than That
NY46 Big Butter and Egg Man
NY47 Baby won't you please come home
NY48 Sensation
      Everybody loves my baby   *FDC 1012*
      Alexander's Ragtime Band   *FDC 1012*

1947
Aug 2   New York
This is Jazz
Wild Bill Davison (c); Jimmy Archey (tb); Sidney Bechet (cl, ss); Albert Nicholas (cl); Ralph Sutton (p); Danny Barker (g); Pops Foster (db); Baby Dodds (d)
NY70 I never knew   *Riverside RLP12-216*
      Dardanella   *Riverside RLP12-216*
      China Boy   *Riverside RLP12-149*
      There'll be some changes made   *FDC 1012*
      Dear old girl   Unissued
      Wolverine Blues   Unissued
      California here I come   Unissued

1947
Aug 23   New York
This is Jazz
Wild Bill Davison (c); Jimmy Archey (tb); Albert Nicholas (as); Ralph Sutton (p); Danny Barker (g); Pops Foster (db); Baby Dodds (d)
      Ballin' the Jack   Unissued
      Four or Five Times   Unissued
NY67 As long as I live   *Riverside RLP12-211*
      Trombone Preachin' Blues   *Riverside RLP2514*
      Mandy   Unissued

Peg o' my Heart   Unissued
Nobody's Sweetheart   Unissued

1947
Aug 30   New York
This is Jazz
Same personnel as session of Aug 23 1947, plus Bertha Chippie Hill (v)
At the Jazz Band Ball   All unissued
Sometimes I'm happy
Some of these days
Just a Gigolo
Put your arms around me, honey
Blues
The world is waiting for the sunrise

1947
Sept 6   New York
This is Jazz
Wild Bill Davison (c); Jimmy Archey (tb); Edmond Hall (cl); Ralph Sutton (p); Danny Barker (g); Pops Foster (db); Baby Dodds (d)
NY59 Clarinet Marmalade   *Riverside RLP2514*
      Tishomingo Blues   All unissued
      'S wonderful
      Ol' Man River
      Maple Leaf Rag
      Georgia on my Mind
      Bugle Call Rag

1947
Sept 13   New York
This is Jazz
Same personnel as session of Sept 6 1947
      Crazy Blues   Unissued
      Jelly Roll   *Riverside RLP2514*
      I'm coming Virginia   Unissued
NY55 Can't we be friends   *Riverside RLP2514*
      Skeleton Jangle   *Riverside RLP2514*
      Blues   *Riverside RLP2514*
      Muskrat Ramble   Unissued

1947
Sept 20   New York
This is Jazz
Same personnel as session of Sept 6 1947
Indiana   All unissued
Sunday
Liza
I can't believe that you're in love with me
St. Louis Blues
All of me
Dippermouth Blues
Tiger Rag (1)   Steiner Davis Xmas 1949

1947
Sept 27   New York
This is Jazz
Same personnel as session of Sept 6 1947
      Jazz Me Blues   Unissued
      Royal Garden Blues   Unissued
      Take me to the ball game   Unissued
NY57 Avalon   *Riverside RLP12-211*
      Wrap your troubles in dreams   Unissued
NY58 Swinging down the lane   *Riverside RLP12-211*
      High Society   Unissued

1947
Oct 3   New York
Frank Galbraith (t); Fats Ford (t); Henry Glover (t); Eli Robinson (tb); Gene Simon (tb); Johnny Peck (tb); Burnie Peacock (as); Snookie Hubert (as); Frank Wess (ts); Bullmoose Jackson (ts); Ernest Purce (bs); Billy Mann (p); Danny Barker (g); Carl Pruitt (db); Alphonse Stirrup (d); Annisteen Allen (v); Paul Breckenridge (v)
74098 Don't hesitate too long (AA:v)   *Decca 24384*
74099 Tonight he sailed again (PB:v)   *Decca 24384*
74100 Berserk Boogie   *Decca 24495*

1947
Oct 4   New York
This is Jazz
*Wild Bill Davison (c); Jimmy Archey (tb); Sidney Bechet (cl, ss);
Edmond Hall (cl); Ralph Sutton (p); Danny Barker (g); Pops Foster
(db); Baby Dodds (d)*

Sensation		Unissued
Jada		Unissued
St. Louis Blues		Riverside RLP149
Laura		Unissued
Big Butter and Egg Man		Unissued
Sweet Lorraine		Riverside RLP149
Farewell Blues		Unissued

1947
Oct   New York
Dan Burley
*Jimmy Archey (tb); John Hardee (ts); Dan Burley (p, v); Danny
Barker (g); Herman Mitchell (g); Pops Foster (db)*

DB100	Chicken Shack Shuffle	Arkay 1001
DB101	Skiffle Blues	Arkay 1001

1947
Nov 8   Stuyvesant Casino, New York
Bunk Johnson and his Band
*Bunk Johnson (t); Ed Cuffee (tb); Garvin Bushell (cl); Don Kirkpatrick
(p); Danny Barker (g); Wellman Braud (db); Alphonse Steele (d)*

Please don't talk about me when I'm gone	Nola LP3
Peg o' my Heart	
You're some pretty doll	
Please	
Pagan Love Song	
Margie	
Royal Garden Blues	
Sweet Lorraine	
Darktown Strutter's Ball	
Tishomingo Blues (1)	
Tishomingo Blues (2)	

1947
Nov 18   New York
Mutt Carey's New Yorkers
*Mutt Carey (t); Jimmy Archey (tb); Albert Nicholas (cl); Hank Duncan
(p); Danny Barker (g); Pops Foster (db); Baby Dodds (d)*

MC101-3	Shim-me-sha-wabble	Savoy MG12050
MC102-1	Slow Drivin', pt. i	
MC102-2	Slow Drivin', pt. ii	
MC103-3	Ostrich Walk	
MC104-2	Cake Walking Babies	

1947
Nov 22   New York
Tony Parenti's Ragtimers
*Wild Bill Davison (t); Jimmy Archey (tb); Tony Parenti (cl); Ralph
Sutton (p); Danny Barker (bj); Cyrus St. Clair (tuba); Baby Dodds (d)*

NY49	Grace and Beauty	Circle 1030
NY50	Hiawatha	Circle 1031
NY51	Praline	Circle 1030
NY52	Swipesy Cake Walk	Circle 1031
NY53	Hysterics Rag	Circle 1030
NY54	Sunflower Slow Drag	Circle 1029

1947
Nov 27   New York
Mutt Carey's New Yorkers
*Mutt Carey (t); Jimmy Archey (tb); Edmond Hall (cl); Cliff Jackson
(p); Danny Barker (g); Pops Foster (db); Baby Dodds (d)*

MC111-D	Joplin's Sensation	Savoy MG12038
MC112-B	Chrysanthemum	
MC113-B	The Entertainer	
MC114-B	Fidgety Feet	
MC115	Indiana	

1947
Dec 23   New York
The New York Bunk Band: Bunk Johnson—The Last Testa-
ment
*Bunk Johnson (t); Ed Cuffee (tb); Garvin Bushell (cl); Don Kirkpatrick
(p); Danny Barker (g); Wellman Braud (db); Alphonse Steele (d)*

151	The Entertainer	Columbia GL520
152	The Minstrel Man	
153	Chloe	
154	Someday	

Dec 24
155	Hilarity Rag
156	Kinklets
157	You're driving me crazy
158	Out of Nowhere

Dec 26
159	That Teasin' Rag
160	Some of these days
161	Till we meet again
162	Maria Elena

1947
New York
Cousin Joe with Dickie Wells's Blue Seven
*Cousin Joe (v); Shad Collins (t); Dickie Wells (tb); Pete Brown (as);
Billy Kyle (p); Danny Barker (g); Lloyd Trotman (db); Woodie Nichols
(d)*

SRC-439	Come down baby	Signature 1013
SRC-440	Bachelor's Blues	Signature 1012
SRC-441	Don't pay me no mind	Signature 1013
SRC-442	I had to stop to conquer you baby	Signature 1012
SRC-443	Blues 1	unissued
SRC-444	Blues 2	unissued

1948
Jan 22   New York
Tony Parenti's Ragpickers
*Wild Bill Davison (t); Jimmy Archey (tb); Tony Parenti (cl); Ralph
Sutton (p); Danny Barker (bj); Cyrus St. Clair (tuba); Baby Dodds (d)*

NY73	Crawfish Crawl	Circle 1056
NY74	The Entertainer's Rag	Circle 1054
NY75	Lily Rag	Circle 1056
NY76	Cataract Rag	Circle 1054
NY77	Nonsense Rag	Circle 1055
NY78	Redhead Rag	Circle 1055

1948
Los Angeles
*Blue Lu Barker (v), accompanied by unknown band, including Danny
Barker (g)*

3527-2	What did you do to me?	Capitol 15308
3528-2	A little bird told me	Capitol 15308
3529	Here's a little girl	Capitol 15347
3538	Leave my man alone	Capitol 15347
3539	Trombone Man Blues	Capitol 70007

1949
Jan 10   Los Angeles
*Scatman Crothers (v), accompanied by Gerald Wiggins (p); Danny
Barker (g); John Simmons (db); Jesse Price (d)*

3839	Pretty Little Blue-eyed Sally	Capitol 15383
3844	Do something	Capitol 15431
3845	I'd rather be a humming bird	Capitol 15383

1949
March 21   Los Angeles
*Blue Lu Barker (v), accompanied by Ulysses Smith, Jr. (t); Dave
Cavanaugh (ts); James Jackson, Jr. (ts); Gerald Wiggins (p); Danny
Barker (g); Eddie Davis (db); Peppy Price (d)*

4102-2	Now you're down in the alley	Capitol 70007
4013-2	When the wagon comes	Capitol 70034
4104-2	I'll give you some tomorrow	unissued
4105-2	Loan me your husband	Capitol 70034

1949
Oct 25   New Orleans
Blue Lu Barker (v), accompanied by Earl Barnes (t); Joe Paris (p); Danny Barker (g); Percy Gabriel (db); Paul Barbarin (d)

5111-2	Boogie is the thing to do	unissued
5112-3	Low Low Down Blues	unissued
5113-2	Round and round the valley	Capitol 977
5114-1	That's how I got my man	unissued

1949
Oct 26   New Orleans
Same personnel as session of Oct 25 1949

5115-4	At the animal fair	Capitol 977
5116-2	Bow Legged Daddy	Capitol 807
5117-2	Love that man	Capitol 807
5118-2	Other People's Business	unissued

c1950
New Orleans
Danny Barker's Band
Albert Walters (t); Danny Barker (g, v); Percy Gabriel (db); ?Gilbert Erskine (d); Blue Lu Barker (v); others unknown

Honeysuckle Rose	All unissued
Some of these days	
Run, Joe	
That made him mad	
Panama	
Lily of the Valley	
Precious Lord	

1950
Nov 24   New York
Conrad Janis and his Tailgate Jazz Band
Dick Smith (t); Conrad Janis (tb); Tom Sharpsteen (cl); Bob Greene (p); Danny Barker (bj); Pops Foster (db); Fred Moore (d)

NY108	Tiger Rag	Circle L404
NY109	Yellow Dog Blues	
NY110	Bugle Boy March	
NY111	Kansas City Stomps	
NY112	Gettysburg March	
NY113	1919 March	
NY114	Oriental Man	
NY115	Original Dixieland One Step	

1951
Jan 23   New York
Jamming at Rudi's
Dick Smith (t); Conrad Janis (tb); Tom Sharpsteen (cl); Bob Wilber (ss); Ralph Sutton (p); Danny Barker (g); Pops Foster (db); Fred Moore (d, v)

NY116	Panama	
NY117	Weary Blues	
NY118	Maryland, my Maryland	
NY119	See See Rider	Circle L407
NY120	High Society	Circle L407
NY121	That's a plenty	Circle L407
NY144	Danny's Banjo Blues	GHB 50
NY173	When the saints go marchin' in, pt.1	Circle L407
NY174	When the saints go marchin' in, pt.2	Circle L407

1951
Jan 23, 27   New York
Dick Smith (t); Conrad Janis (tb); Tom Sharpsteen (cl); Bob Wilber (ss); Ralph Sutton (p); Danny Barker (g, bj); Pops Foster (db); Fred Moore (d)

When the saints (FM:v)	London LTZ-U15095
See See Rider	
High Society	
That's a plenty	

1951
Feb 10   New York
Oran "Hot Lips" Page (t); Tyree Glenn (tb); Bernie Peacock (cl, as);

Paul Quinichette (ts); Ken Kersey (p); Dan Burley (p); Danny Barker (g); Walter Page (db); Sonny Greer (d)

NY122	Blues no.1	
NY123	Blues no.2	
NY124	Dan Carter Blues	
NY125	Skiffle Jam	Circle L410
NY126	Moanin' Dan (OP:v)	Circle L410
NY127	Sweet Sue	Circle L410
NY128	Kersey's Boogie	Circle L410
NY129	I've got the upper hand (OP:v)	Circle R3003
NY130	Sunny Jungle	Circle R3004
NY131	Main Street (OP:v)	Circle R3004

1951
May 8   New York
Dick Smith (t); Conrad Janis (tb); Tom Sharpsteen (cl); Elmer Schoebel (p); Danny Barker (g, bj); Fred Moore (d)

NY134	Willie the Weeper	All unissued
NY135	Eh la bas (DB:v)	
NY136	When you and I were young Maggie	
NY137	Down by the Riverside (FM:v)	
NY138	Blue bells goodbye	
NY139	Weary Way Blues	
NY140	Just a closer walk	
NY141	Creole Belles	
NY142	Maryland (2 takes)	
NY143	Alabama Bound (2 takes)	
NY144	Danny's Banjo Blues	
NY145	Mahogany Hall Stomp	
NY146	Over in Gloryland	
NY147	Ain't gonna give none of this jelly roll	
NY148	Snag it	
NY149	Sobbin' Blues	
NY150	When are you gonna pop the question	

1951
June 7   New York
Dick Smith (t); Conrad Janis (tb); Tom Sharpsteen (cl); Elmer Schoebel (p); Danny Barker (g); Fred Moore (d)

Willie the Weeper	London LTZ-U15095
Eh! La-bas	
When you and I were young Maggie	
Down by the Riverside	

c1953
New York
Dick Smith (t); Conrad Janis (tb); Gene Sedric (cl); Dick Wellstood (p); Pops Foster (db); Danny Barker (bj); Arthur Trappier (d)

Tailgate Blues and Eh la bas	Jubilee JLP1010
Snag it	
When the saints go marchin' in	
South Rampart Street Parade	
Milneburg Joys	
St. James Infirmary	
Waiting for the Robert E. Lee	

1954
Aug 13   New York
Louis Armstrong and Sy Oliver's Orchestra
Louis Armstrong (t, v); Charlie Shavers (t); Taft Jordan (t); Abdul Salaam (William "Chiefie" Scott) (t); Alfred Cobbs (tb); Elmer Crumbley (tb); Paul F. Seiden (tb); Barney Bigard (cl); Omer Simeon (ss); Dave Martin (p); Danny Barker (g); Arvell Shaw (db); Barrett Deems (d); Sy Oliver (a)

86652	Skokiaan (South African song), pt. i	Decca 29256
86653	Skokiaan, pt. ii	Decca 29256

1954
Dec   New York
Paul Barbarin and his New Orleans Jazz Band
John Brunious (t); Bob Thomas (tb); Willie Humphrey (cl); Lester Santiago (p); Danny Barker (bj); Paul Barbarin (d)

Hindustan	CHJ 10006
Gettysburg March	CHRC 1205
Tiger Rag	

Careless Love
The Second Line
Screamin' the Blues
Mon chere amie (LS:v)
When the Saints (JB:v)
Lilies of the Valley
First Choice
Li'l Liza Jane (WH:v)
Big Bad Bully (PB:v)   Gld de J J710

1955
Jan 7   New York
Paul Barbarin and his New Orleans Jazz
*John Brunious (t); Bob Thomas (tb); Willie Humphrey (cl); Lester
Santiago (p); Danny Barker (bj); Milt Hinton (db); Paul Barbarin (d)*
Eh la-bas (DB:v)   *Atlantic 1215*
Bugle Boy March
Sister Kate
Bourbon Street Parade
Sing on
Just a little while to stay here
Someday sweetheart
Crescent Blues
Walk through the Streets of the City

1955
Jan 24   New York
New Orleans Shufflers
*Jack Fine (t); Bob Thomas (tb); Tony Parenti (cl); Hank Ross (p);
Danny Barker (g, bj); Arny Hyman (db); Arthur Trappier (d)*
Tishomingo Blues   *Kingsway KL700*
That Da Da Strain
Milneberg Joys
Gee baby, ain't I good to you?
Buddy Bolden Blues
Someday sweetheart
See See Rider
Do you know what it means to miss New Orleans?

1955
Nov   New Orleans
The Doc and his Patients
*Harry Shields (cl); Raymond Burke (cl, ss); Jeannette Kimball (p, v);
Edmond Souchon (bj, g); Danny Barker (g, v); Johnny St. Cyr (g);
Chink Martin (tuba); Sherwood Mangiapane (db); Monk Hazel (d);
Blue Lu Barker (v)*
Southland Blues (BLB:v)   *Southland SLP218*
Sister Kate (BLB:v)
All the wrongs you've done to me
Somebody else is taking my place (JK:v)
Rose Room

1956
May 28   New York
George Wein's Dixie Victors
*Ruby Braff (t); Vic Dickenson (tb); Bill Stegmeyer (cl); Ernie Caceres
(bs); George Wein (p); Danny Barker (bj); Milt Hinton (db); Buzzy
Drootin (d)*
G2JB4574 Squeeze me   *Victor LPM1332*
G2JB4575 Struttin' with some Barbecue
G2JB4576 The Magic Horn
G2JB4577 A Monday Date

Same session: Peanuts Hucko (cl) replaces Stegmeyer
G2JB4578 Sugar   *Victor LPM1332*
G2JB4579 Dippermouth Blues (1)
G2JN4580 Dippermouth Blues (2)
G2JB4581 Ain't gonna give none of this jelly roll
G2JB4582 On the sunny side of the street

NB: For (1) Jimmy McPartland (t) added
     For (2) McPartland replaces Braff

1956
New York
Dixie by The Seven
Jack Fine (c); Bob Thomas (tb); Tony Parenti (cl); Hank Ross (p);

Danny Barker (bj); Arny Hyman (db); Arthur Trappier (d)
Da Da Strain   *Queen JLS5000*
Someday sweetheart
Gee baby, ain't I good to you
New Orleans
Milneberg Joys
Tishomingo Blues
See See Rider
Buddy Bolden's Blues

1957
Dec 5   New York
Henry Allen and his Orchestra
*Henry Allen (t, v); Rex Stewart (c); Vic Dickenson (tb); Pee Wee Russell
(cl); Coleman Hawkins (ts); Nat Pierce (p); Danny Barker (g); Milt
Hinton (db); Jo Jones (d)*
CO59469 Wild Man Blues   *Columbia CL1098*
CO59470 Rosetta   *Columbia CL1098*

1957
Dec 5   New York
Jimmy Giuffre—Pee Wee Russell
*Personnel includes: Jimmy Giuffre (cl); Pee Wee Russell (cl); Danny
Barker (g); Jo Jones (d)*
CO59472 Blues   *Columbia CL1098*

1957
Dec 8   New York
Television show
Billie Holiday with the Mal Waldron All Stars
*Billie Holiday (v); Doc Cheatham (t); Roy Eldridge (t); Vic Dickenson
(tb); Lester Young (ts); Coleman Hawkins (ts); Ben Webster (ts); Gerry
Mulligan (bs); Mal Waldron (p); Danny Barker (g); Milt Hinton (db);
Osie Johnson (d)*
Fine and Mellow   Avenue (E)AVINT1019

The rehearsal for this session was recorded on December 5
(Matrix 59473, issued on *Columbia CL1098*); Hinton and
Johnson replaced Jim Atlas (db) and Jo Jones (d).

1958
Jan 27
*Lavern Baker (v), accompanied by Buck Clayton (t); Vic Dickenson
(tb); Paul Quinichette (ts); Sahib Shibab (bs); Nat Pierce (p); Danny
Barker (g); Wendell Marshall (db); Joe Marshall (d); Phil Moore (a)*
2936 Gimme a Pigfoot   *Atlantic LP1281*
2937 Baby Doll
2938 On Revival Day
2935 Nobody knows you when you're down and out

Jan 28
*Jimmy Cleveland replaces Dickenson (tb); Nat Pierce, Ernie Wilkins
(a)*
2939 Money Blues
2940 Empty Bed Blues
2941 I ain't gonna play no second fiddle
2942 There'll be a hot time in the old town tonight

Jan 29
*Urbie Green replaces Cleveland (tb); Jerome Richardson replaces
Shibab (bs)*
2943 Backwater Blues
2944 After you've gone
2945 Young Woman's Blues
2946 Preaching the Blues

1958
Feb 20   New York
*Jimmy Rushing (v), accompanied by Emmett Berry (t); Mel Davis (t);
Buck Clayton (t); Bernie Glow (t); Vic Dickenson (tb); Dickie Wells
(tb); Urbie Green (tb); Earl Warren (as); Rudy Powell (as); Buddy Tate
(ts); Coleman Hawkins (ts); Danny Bank (bs); Nat Pierce (p); Danny
Barker (g); Milt Hinton (db); Jo Jones (d)*
CO60472 I'm coming Virginia   *Columbia CS8060*
CO60473 Mister Five by Five
CO60474 June Night
CO60475 Rosalie

1958
Feb 26 New York
*Jimmy Rushing (v); accompanied by Emmett Berry (t); Mel Davis (t);
Buck Clayton (t); Doc Cheatham (t); Frank Rehak (tb); Dickie Wells
(tb); Urbie Green (tb); Earl Warren (as); Rudy Powell (as); Buddy Tate
(ts); Coleman Hawkins (ts); Danny Bank (bs); Nat Pierce (p, clavi-
cimbel); Danny Barker (g); Milt Hinton (db); Jo Jones (d)*
CO60476 Knock me a kiss   *Columbia CS8060*
CO60477 Jimmy's Blues
CO60478 Someday sweetheart
CO60479 Harvard Blues

1958
Feb 27 New York
Same personnel as session of Feb 26 1958
CO60480 It's a sin to tell a lie   *Columbia CS8060*
CO60481 Travelin' Light
CO60482 When you're smiling
CO60483 Somebody stole my gal

1958
Oct 28 New York
*Buck Clayton (t); Vic Dickenson (tb); Herbie Hall (cl); Hal Singer (ts);
Al Williams (p); Danny Barker (g); Gene Ramey (db); Marquis Foster
(d)*
3178 Has anyone seen Corinne?   Unissued
3179 The lamp is low   *Atlantic LP1303*
3180 Under Plunder Blues   Unissued
3181 Harlem Nocturne   Unissued
3182 Undecided   *Atlantic LP1303*

1958
Oct New York
*Wingy Manone (t, v); Sidney de Paris (t, tuba); King Curtis (ts);
Charlie Queener (p); Danny Barker (g, bj); Babe Pizzelli (g); Freddie
Moore (d)*
Hold on, baby, rock!   Pepper 866
Tuba Boogie   Pepper 866
Central Plaza Rock (WM:v)   unissued
All Day Long, All Night Long Rock   unissued

1958
New York
Danny Barker's Band
*Joe Muranyi (cl); Don Frye (p); Danny Barker (bj, v); Wellman Braud
(db); Walter Johnson (d)*
Bye Bye Blackbird   *Period SLP1205*
Lazy River
Sweet Sue
Bill Bailey
Careless Love
World is Waiting for the Sunrise
Tiger Rag
Tishomingo Blues
Chinatown
Charleston
Royal Garden Blues

1959
New York
*Tommy Flanagan (p, celeste); Mary Osborne (g); Danny Barker (g);
Tommy Potter (db); Jo Jones (d)*
I love Paris   *Warwick W2004*
I let a song go out of my heart
How high the moon
When your lover has gone
Mary's Goodbye Blues
I found a new baby
Sophisticated Lady
I'm beginning to see the light
Body and Soul
I surrender dear
These Foolish Things

1960
March 28–31, April 1 New York
*Wingy Manone (t, v); Harry de Vito (tb); Lou McGarity (tb); Peanuts
Hucko (cl); Charlie Queener (p); Danny Barker (g); Chubby Jackson
(db); Jimmy Manone (d)*
Rose Room   Roulette
Downhearted
How come you do me like you do?
'S Wonderful
I wish
Swingin' Music
You, after all these years
Fancy Woman Blues
Darktown Strutters Ball
Emaline
Orchichorniya
Count me in baby

1961
May 19 New York
Prestige Blues Swingers, also known as the Swingville All Stars
*Joe Thomas (t); Vic Dickenson (tb); Pee Wee Russell (cl); Al Sears (ts);
Buddy Tate (ts); Cliff Jackson (p); Danny Barker (g); Joe Benjamin
(db); J. C. Heard (d)*
3037 Things ain't what they used
       to be   *Swingville LP2024*
3038 So Glad   *Swingville LP2025*
3039 I want to be happy (1)   *Swingville LP2024*
3040 I may be wrong   *Swingville LP2024*
3041 Phoenix   *Swingville LP2025*
3042 Years Ago   *Swingville LP2025*
3043 Vic's Spot   *Swingville LP2024*

1966–7
New Orleans
*George Finola (c); Paul Crawford (tb); Raymond Burke (cl, ts);
Armand Hug (p); Danny Barker (g); Sherwood Mangiapane (db);
Louis Barbarin (d); Blue Lu Barker (v)*
Hot Lips   New Orleans Originals
Junk Man   *JM65-4*
Sugar Baby
Someday sweetheart
It's right here for you
Blue (and broken-hearted)
My Pet
Melancholy Baby
Walkin' the Dog
Daddy, won't you please come home
Sheila

1967
Feb 6 Southern Illinois University, Carbondale, Illinois
Journey into Jazz
Direct from New Orleans, vol.1
*Johnny Wiggs (c); Emile Christian (tb); Harry Shields (cl); Jeannette
Kimball (p); Danny Barker (g); Chester Zardis (db); Louis Barbarin
(d); Blue Lu Barker (v)*
At the Jazz Band Ball   *GHB 65*
Up a Lazy River
Save the bones for Henry Jones
Eh La-bas
Clarinet Marmalade
Big Butter and Egg Man
Gulf Coast Blues
Muskrat Ramble
Pretty Baby

Direct from New Orleans, vol.2
(same date, location, personnel)
Make me a pallet on the floor   *GHB 66*
Don't you feel my legs
I wish I could shimmy like my sister Kate
Farewell Blues
Milneberg Joys
Tin Roof Blues
Everybody loves my baby

1967
Dec 18–19   New Orleans
Alvin Alcorn's Band
*Alvin Alcorn (t); Jack Delaney (tb); Harry Shields (cl); Armand Hug
(p); Danny Barker (bj); Chester Zardis (db); Louis Barbarin (d); Dave
Oxley (v); Blue Lu Barker (v)*
When the saints go marching in (DO:v)
High Society
Tin Roof Blues
Way Down Yonder in New Orleans
Basin Street Blues (BLB:v)
Muskrat Ramble
Just a Closer Walk with Thee (DO:v)
Louisiana

Issued on *The Right to Profit State and All That Jazz* (no number)
     Goodtime Louisiana and New Orleans Jazz (no number)

1968
July 27   Meriden, Connecticut
Onward Brass Band
*Alvin Alcorn (t); Ernie Cagnolatti (t); Clement Tervalon (tb); Wendell
Eugene (tb); Louis Cottrell (cl); Jerry Green (tuba); Freddie Kohlman
(snare d); Paul Barbarin (bass d); Danny Barker (Grand Marshall, bj)*
Maryland My Maryland   *Connecticut Traditional Jazz Club*
Just a Closer Walk with Thee   *SLP-5*
Second Line
Original Dixieland One-step

1968
Dec 5   Memphis
Johnny Wiggs and his Bayou Stompers
*Johnny Wiggs (c); Raymond Burke (cl); Danny Barker (g); Chester
Zardis (db)*
Peggy O'Neil   *Jazztette 1002*
Yellow Dog Blues
Lillian Gaspergou (Mama's Baby Boy) (JW:v)
The One I Love Belongs to Somebody Else

1969
June 3   New Orleans
Danny Barker's Congo Square Marching Band
*Alvin Alcorn (t); Sam Alcorn (t); Wendell Brunious (t); John Brunious
(t); Wendell Eugene (tb); Clement Tervalon (tb); Edward "Noon"
Johnson (bazooka); John Brunious, Sr. (baritone horn); Wadleigh
Johnson (bass horn); Jerry Green, Jr (bass horn); Earthy
"Bibbs" Lazard (snare d); Calvin Spears (bass d); John Smith (bass d);
Alfred "Dutzey" Lazard (banner carrier); Danny Barker (Grand
Marshall)*
St. Louis Blues (lacks beginning)   unissued
Unknown title (incomplete)   unissued

1969
Dec   Manassas, Virginia
Zutty Singleton—Johnny Wiggs
*Probably Ernie Carson (t); Johnny Wiggs (c); George Brunies (tb);
Walter "Slide" Harris (tb); Bobby Gordon (cl); Walt Gower (cl); Bob
Greene (p); Danny Barker (g); Van Perry (db); Zutty Singleton (d)*
Just a little while to stay here   *Fat Cat's Jazz FCJ116*
Just a little while to stay here (alt take)
Make me a pallet on the floor
Girl of my dreams
The one I love belongs to someone else
Ole Miss
Gettysburg March
In the Morning Blues

1970
Oct 22–3   New Orleans
Alvin Alcorn's Jazz Band
*Alvin Alcorn (t); Wendell Eugene (tb); Harry Shields (cl); Armand
Hug (p); Danny Barker (g); Chester Zardis (db); Josiah Frazier (d);
Dave Oxley (v); Blanche Thomas (v)*
Bogalusa Strut
Sugar Blues (DO:v)

Piano Medley: In the Gloaming
            Pretty Baby (DO:v)
            King Porter Stomp
Chimes Blues
Up a Lazy River
Wang Wang Blues
Trouble in Mind (BT:v)
Mama's Gone Goodbye
Piano Medley: I'm Sorry I Made You Cry
            Tiger Rag
            Don't Leave Me Daddy
Wolverine Blues

Issued on *The Right to Profit State and All That Jazz Again* (no
number)

1970
Dec   Manassas Festival, Virginia
*Collective personnel: Maxine Sullivan (v), accompanied by Jack
Maheu (cl); Wally Garner (cl); Tom Gwaltney (cl); John Eaton (p);
Claude Hopkins (p); George "Butch" Hall (g); Danny Barker (g);
Steve Jordan (g); Van Perry (db); Billy Taylor, Jr. (db); Cliff Leeman
(d); Freddie Moore (d); Oliver Jackson (d); Bertill Knox (d)*
I'm coming Virginia   *Fat Cat's Jazz FCJ136*
One Hundred Years from Today
As long as I live
Georgia on my Mind
St. Louis Blues
I've got a right to sing the blues
I've got the world on a string
Every time I fall in love
Skylark
I thought about you
Loch Lomond

1971
Spring   New Orleans
Kid Ory at the New Orleans Jazz Festival
*Thomas Jefferson (t); Kid Ory (tb); Raymond Burke (cl); Don Ewell
(p); Emanuel Sayles (bj); Danny Barker (g); Ed Garland (db); Freddie
Kohlman (d)*
Big Butter and Egg Man   All unissued
Sister Kate
Bill Bailey (KO:v)
Yellow Dog Blues
Muskrat Ramble (KO:v)
Milneburg Joys
Muskrat Ramble (part only)
Aunt Hagar's Blues
That's a Plenty

Recorded at a rehearsal

1971
Memphis
Memphis Cotton Carnival
Highlights of the 1971 Jazz and Blues Festival
*Dan Havens (t, v); Raymond Burke (cl); Jean Kittrell (p, v); Danny
Barker (g, v); Chet Ely (v); Harry Goodwin (v)*
Ragged but Right (DH:v)   *Jazztette 1006*
Rosetta
My Memphis Baby (HG:v)
Nagasaki (DB:v)
A closer walk with Thee (JK:v)

plus Dawed "Fat Daddy" Thompson (g)
Shorty (JK:v)   *Jazztette 1006*
Some of these days (CE:v)
Alice Blue Gown (CE:v)

plus George Brunies (p, v)
Is there a change for me (GB:v)   *Jazztette 1006*

1972
May 1   New Orleans
George Probert's Fine Time Band
*George Probert (ss, ocarina, v); Jeannette Kimball (p); Danny Barker
(g, bj); Placide Adams (db); Frank Parker (d)*

Blues Prelude   Nobility: all unissued
Petite fleur
Dinah
Sweet Lorraine, pts. i–ii
I'm confessin'
Do you know what it means
Summertime
Black and Blue
Sleepy Time Down South
I can't give you anything but love
Never swat a fly (GP:v)
Swanee River (with ocarina chorus)

1972
Dec   Manassas Festival, Virginia
"Cornets Together"
Wild Bill Davison (c); Tommy Saunders (c); Danny Williams (tb);
Jack Maheu (cl); Art Hodes (p); Danny Barker (g); Frank Tate (db);
Ken Underwood (d)
Keeping out of mischief now   *Fat Cat's Jazz FCL134*
I never knew
Someday you'll be sorry
Struttin' with some Bar-B-Q
There'll be some changes made
Fidgety Feet
All of me
Undecided
Wolverine Blues

NB: Some tracks were recorded at the 1971 Manassas Festival

1972
Dec 2   Manassas Jazz Festival, Virginia
Tony Newstead (t); Danny Williams (tb); Country Thomas (cl); Art
Hodes (p); Danny Barker (g); Frank Tate (db); Freddie Moore (d)
Royal Garden Blues   *Fat Cat's Jazz FCJ127*

1972
Dec 3   Manassas Jazz Festival
Johnny Wiggs (c); Graham Stewart (tb); Raymond Burke (cl); Claude

Hopkins (p); Danny Barker (bj); Billy Goodall (db); Cliff Leeman (d);
Fat Cat McRae (v)
Postman's Lament   *Fatt Cat's Jazz FCJ129*
Oh! You beautiful doll
I cried for you (FCM:v)
2:19 Blues

1972
Dec   Manassas Jazz Festival
Johnny Wiggs (c); Graham Stewart (tb); Raymond Burke (cl); Bob
Greene (p); Danny Barker (g); Freddie Moore (d)
Old Stack O'Lee Blues   *Fat Cat's Jazz FCJ129*

c1974
Ernie Carson (c); Bobby Gordon (tb); Walter Harris (cl); Bob Greene
(p); Danny Barker (bj); Van Perry (db); Ellie Baker (d)
Somebody stole my gal   *Fat Cat's Jazz FCJ113*
Just the blues
Doctor Jazz
Nobody knows you when you're down and out
Angry

c1975
Manassas, Virginia
Ballin' the Jack
Collective personnel: Wallace Davenport (t); Doc Evans (t); Wild Bill
Davison (c); Tony Newstead (c); Herb Gardner (tb); Danny Williams
(tb); Al Winters (tb); Mason "Country" Thomas (cl); Tommy Gwalt-
ney (cl); Spencer Clark (bass s); Art Hodes (p); Steve Jordan (g); Danny
Barker (g); Van Perry (db); Bill Goodall (db); Freddie Moore (d); Skip
Tomlinson (d); Cliff Leeman (d); Frank Marshall (d)
Milneburg Joys   *Fat Cat's Jazz FCJ148*
Washboard Blues
'Way down yonder in New Orleans
Avalon
Blues yesterday, today and tomorrow
Do you know what it means to miss New Orleans
Bye and Bye

Index